Praise for *Unblocked*

You can't fix what you can't see. Alison McCauley presents a smart business case for the world's next digital transformation with *Unblocked*.

—*Keith Weed, CMO, Unilever*

It's essential to understand the disruptive potential of blockchains, the behind-the-scenes technology of cryptocurrency. Just as the internet transformed business models, blockchains are poised to do the same again. Alison McCauley deftly educates business leaders on the context and implications of this coming shift with *Unblocked*.

—*Eric Ly, Cofounder, LinkedIn*

With *Unblocked*, Alison McCauley gives a clear and compelling explanation of the six forces powering the massive, but yet to be fully realized potential of blockchain technology.

—*Bharath Kadaba, Chief Innovation Officer, Intuit*

A must-read book for any executive or investor who wants to know how to benefit from blockchain's potential.

—*Matthew Le Merle, Managing Partner, Keiretsu Capital and Author*, Corporate Innovation in the Fifth Era

Blockchains hold the potential to completely transform our digital lives. If you want your business to stay relevant in this future, you need to read *Unblocked*.

—*Troy B. Parkes, FedEx Institute of Technology*

Alison deftly breaks down the opportunity and the risk of blockchains in this engaging book that every business leader should read.

—*Mari Cross, Head of Customer Success, Adobe*

In her remarkably accessible *Unblocked*, Alison McCauley pulls back the curtain to demystify this new technology and how it is inspiring the next generation of visionaries and entrepreneurs.

—*Andy Cunningham, Founder, Cunningham Collective, Aspen Institute Trustee, Author,* Get to Aha!

Blockchain and related technologies are poised to create massive disruption and wealth creation over the next 10 years. If you want your business to thrive in this new world order, the first thing you need to do is read *Unblocked*.

—*Lou Kerner, Co-Founder, CryptoOracle*

Blockchains could shape a better future for consumers to engage with brands. An open framework that puts consumers in control of privacy is long overdue, and could drive new ways for brands to deliver value. But first you have to understand what's coming—start by reading *Unblocked*.

—*Carissa Ganelli, Chief Digital Officer, Subway*

Unblocked

How Blockchains Will Change Your Business (and What to Do About It)

Alison McCauley

Beijing · Boston · Farnham · Sebastopol · Tokyo

Unblocked

by Alison McCauley

Published by O'Reilly Media, Inc., 1005 Gravenstein Highway North, Sebastopol, CA 95472.

O'Reilly books may be purchased for educational, business, or sales promotional use. Online editions are also available for most titles (*http://oreilly.com*). For more information, contact our corporate/institutional sales department: 800-998-9938 or *corporate@oreilly.com*.

Acquisitions Editor: Alicia Young	**Interior Designer:** Monica Kamsvaag
Development Editor: Melissa Duffield	**Cover Image:** Stephen Swintek
Production Editor: Christopher Faucher	**Cover Designer:** Randy Comer
Proofreader: Rachel Monaghan	**Illustrator:** Rebecca Demarest
Indexer: Ellen Troutman-Zaig	

June 2019:   First Edition

Revision History for the First Edition
2019-06-17:   First Release

See *http://oreilly.com/catalog/errata.csp?isbn=9781492057970* for release details.

978-1-492-05797-0

[LSI]

To Wyatt and to Eleanor,

My dear children, my cheerleaders, my loves,

May the architects of your tomorrow make this world better.

Contents

Preface

THE ELEPHANT IN THE ROOM

Since you opened a book on blockchains and business, you probably already know this technology offers more than a new form of money called *cryptocurrency* —which is more than most people realize. In 2018, blockchains were caught in the crossfire of both cryptocurrency's swift peak and dramatic plunge. This is not surprising: cryptocurrency is the first and most visible application of blockchain technology, and many people think they are one and the same.

It would have cost you less than $1,000 to purchase a bitcoin (the most well-known cryptocurrency) in early January 2017, and a year later it would have been worth over $14,000. By the end of 2018, it would have plunged under $4,000. That's a pretty sensational journey. It's no wonder the headlines focused on it.

This obscures what's really happening in blockchains. The core blockchain functionality underlying bitcoin and other cryptocurrencies is being leveraged to do new things in just about every industry. Thousands of companies are hard at work to solve real problems and unlock meaningful opportunity with the technology. They seek to create, in many cases, an entirely new foundation for our digital world.

Cryptocurrency is, in a way, a fantastic first proof of concept: Can blockchains really be a way to safely transfer digital value from one person to another? (We'll talk more about what that means in Chapter 3.) Over the past few years, bad actors, scandals, and large-scale hacks of various companies filled headlines. But at the same time, millions of people around the world battle-tested the wherewithal of the core technology, safely holding or transferring billions of dollars of digital value in the form of blockchain-driven cryptocurrency. There is still much work to do, but overall, the technology fared well. This inspired entrepreneurs to explore not only how blockchains could solve business and social problems, but also how digital assets could evolve to become a new kind of tool that removes friction or enables new business models.

In November of 2000, CNN declared that an index of a few hundred internet stocks lost $1.7 trillion.[1] Yet what came out of that bust changed all our lives. There are many similarities to this moment, although arguably with even higher expectations. While the mortality rate may eclipse that of the dot-com bust, keep in mind that many of the most powerful companies in the world today rose out of that bust. Buried in blockchains and their related family of technologies are seeds of change that could be powerful enough to repeat this history.

This book will help you see around both the hype and decimation. It will help you tap into where the developers and executives working in this space have set their sights. It will help you see what they see.

Come, let's walk around that elephant blocking the view, and see what's unfolding just around the corner.

Introduction

DAWN, RISING

A mother and her two children hurry northward through the Eastern European countryside. They leave behind a region embroiled in civil war, its people devastated by mass genocide, crushing economic sanctions, political and religious persecution, and daily threats to their lives. Already 13-year-old Maja has been wounded in a mortar shell attack, while her father remains imprisoned in a concentration camp. The family has lost their jobs, their home, their possessions, any sense of security, and even their official identities: Yugoslavia is no more.

For now, mother, daughter, and son have only one intention—to escape alive. But first they must make it through this land of warring republics and political upheaval, where rape has become common and many women and girls looking to escape are instead taken into prostitution. A succession of drivers is paid to take them as far as each is willing to risk. For much of the journey Maja's mother hides her under a blanket.

At the southern border of the Czech Republic, a border patrol guard searches the vehicle and interrogates them. After a short, tense discussion, he nods to the driver. "Their country no longer exists," he says. "You can do with them what you like."

Formerly protected citizens of a sovereign nation, the family is now stateless, vulnerable to abuse from anyone in power. With no proof of their names, birth dates, educational or professional histories—with no official data at all—they have, for all intents and purposes, ceased to exist.

The driver speeds onward, and dumps them out in the middle of Prague with a warning: "I never saw you, I never drove you."

Years later, Maja Vujinovic, now an executive working in mobile technology in Uganda, opens a cryptic email from a friend. It contains only one line of text—

you must read this—followed by a link to a whitepaper with an inscrutable title: "Bitcoin: A Peer-to Peer Electronic Cash System."

"I'm just sitting there in my office, minding my own business and eating some papaya," Maja recalls, "when this thing comes across my desk. I called my friend and asked him to explain. He said, 'Imagine being your own bank. You can transfer money anywhere to anyone, with your phone and in an instant, with no one in between.' Working and living in Africa, I'd seen firsthand just how difficult and expensive transferring money could be. I got that this was important."

The whitepaper, which was written by a pseudonymous author called Satoshi Nakamoto and published in the wake of the 2008 financial crisis, described a technology that could allow a new kind of digital money to be transferred anywhere around the world as directly as handing someone you meet on the street paper currency. To the first cryptographers who picked up on the idea, it was a tantalizing way to circumvent financial institutions.

It took a few years, but soon, technologists realized that the underlying technology Satoshi described—which they called *blockchain* for the way data is recorded in files called blocks, and then chained together—could propel the decentralization of not just money, not just financial institutions, but every industry. That's because blockchains enable parties that don't have an existing trusted relationship to agree on any type of shared digital history, not just monetary transactions, without a middleman. This means anything of value could be securely recorded and transferred through the blockchain.

Meanwhile, Maja was carefully watching the space evolve from its early focus on money to something larger. The more she learned, the more she saw in blockchains a powerful catalyst, what she calls "a forcing mechanism for change" for large organizations, governments, and society to move to greater transparency and to create a more equitable world. She recognized that blockchains could be a solution to questions she'd long been exploring in her quest to develop business models that drove value for *both* business and society. With this inspiration, she took on the role of Chief Innovation Officer of emerging technology at GE Digital to lead initiatives in artificial intelligence, machine learning, and of course, blockchains.

It was here that she had what she calls "a massive aha moment." In one of the pilots she was leading, her team had been exploring how a blockchain could establish a reliable, trustworthy identity for the billions of connected devices used by industry. Suddenly, Maja realized those same technological attributes could be used to give anything an identity.

"Not just every piece of equipment and every machine," she says, "but every human." And everything—equipment, machines, humans—could, with block-chain technology, carry not just an immutable identity but the reputation uniquely associated with that identity. In a rush of insight she understood how a blockchain could have made a difference all those years ago. It could be possible to develop a portable, permanent, and universally accepted form of digital iden-tity—owned and controlled by the individual, and not subject to war, natural dis-aster, or theft. "If we had our identity digitally during the war, we would not have had to start over from the beginning. Imagine," she says, "if our *identity* could be currency."[2]

***

While Maja Vujinovic was learning about Satoshi's whitepaper, Sheila War-ren was across the globe in San Francisco. Over dinner one night Sheila's hus-band mentioned that he had come across an interesting whitepaper describing a new form of digital money called bitcoin. The couple discussed whether this new thing could function as a store of value, like a digital form of gold. "But it had a shady undertone," said Sheila, a lawyer, "and I didn't want to be associated with that." For a while she ignored the whole subject—"at least until the helicopters started circling my neighborhood," she said with a laugh. That afternoon in 2014, as the noise overhead grew louder, Sheila and her husband searched Twitter to figure out what was happening.

Moments before and just blocks away, a 26-year-old programmer named Blake Benthall was pulling out of his driveway when 20 FBI agents surrounded him, guns drawn. From the social media stream, the couple learned that their neighbor, going under the pseudonym Defcon, had been running an anonymous narcotics marketplace called Silk Road 2.0— fueled by a digital currency called bitcoin. With the chop of the helicopter blades still whirring above, Sheila's hus-band turned to her and raised an eyebrow. "It looks like bitcoin just went on sale," he said.

Now she was curious. Sheila sat down and read the whitepaper. She could see that bitcoin was an interesting alternative form of money, and how it could be used as a tool in a hyperinflationary economy, or for censorship-resistant spend-ing, whether illicit or not. "I thought, 'well, this thing has some legs, I can see where it would be used, but it looks like it's got a limited market,'" she said. "I didn't see anything particularly transformative about it."

But when a former colleague casually mentioned over lunch that the underlying technology that powered bitcoin was being explored across industries to drive transparency and accountability, something clicked. "In fact," Sheila told me, "I became obsessed." She dove into research, reading and talking to as many people as she could about how this technology could be used. On a long-planned trip with family friends, she spent hours sitting by the pool completely immersed in a book on the technology. While her family and friends relaxed and enjoyed the sunshine, she was furiously annotating charts, filling the margins with scribbled questions, and dog-earing pages.

At her job as the General Counsel of a data-driven nonprofit spanning 200 countries, she started to ask questions about whether this technology could help protect data privacy. And she began waking up in the middle of the night "with lightbulbs popping off." First, she saw philanthropic applications. The humanitarian disaster following the Haitian earthquake of 2010 was still fresh in her mind, "and I had seen money that was earmarked for reconstruction diverted or used for things that didn't really help," Sheila said. "I wondered, 'Could blockchain technology trace if money was going where it was intended? Could this make it possible to tie funding to the completion of discrete milestones?'"

Then, she saw "blockchains everywhere—travel, insurance, it felt like every industry. I could see so many places where the technology could be useful." Sheila would be walking down the sidewalk and suddenly stop short, overtaken by a new idea for how the technology could have impact. "When you really start to think about what it means to eliminate a central authority, there is a boundless list of areas that could be made more fair and more efficient," she explained. It was during this time that the media started recycling footage from the O.J. Simpson trial in recognition of the 10-year anniversary. "I even started to wonder if you could have put that bloody glove on a blockchain!" Sheila said. "Sure, you couldn't solve whether it had been planted, but at least if you had put a chip on that thing and registered it on the blockchain there could be no question if it was the same glove. Then this got me thinking about IoT plus blockchain, and supply chain, then human labor and trafficking, forced migration . . ." She paused and smiled at me. "You know what this is like—all of a sudden you see the possibility for a better future in everything."

Ultimately, Sheila thinks that "everyone is going to be interacting with a blockchain in some fashion, whether they know it or not, in some aspect of their civic or business life. But this technology will not change the psychological make-up that we've had from the dawn of humanity. It does give us an opportunity to build transparency, accountability, and fairness into the system, but this isn't necessarily the case that this is what we will build. If we are going to build systems for billions of people, we need to be intentional about how we do it."[3]

This is why, from her dramatic initial exposure to the technology, Sheila accepted a job in 2017 to become the first head of blockchain and distributed ledger technology for the World Economic Forum.

***

"I don't know anyone who is in the space that didn't get whiplash when they finally got what it could do," laughed investor Ken Seiff when I asked about "that moment" he understood what blockchains made possible. For Ken, it was when he sat down in March of 2014 with Gavin Wood, the CTO and cofounder of Ethereum, the second-largest blockchain project to date.

"He very patiently walked me through it," said Ken, a multi-time CEO who also launched retail pioneer Bluefly.com and consulted for Amazon. "And once I finally got it, I recognized that this could create disruption of the same magnitude as the internet. It's not clear what will ultimately be built with blockchains. But that feeling mirrors the early days of the internet—we couldn't envision Facebook or Amazon back then. From where we are standing now, we can't envision the big thing that will be built on the blockchain. It might come from a mashup of a blockchain plus something—artificial intelligence, virtual reality, augmented reality, or some other enabling technology. But what is clear now is that it is going to be big, and this technology is going to change all our lives with the same force that the internet did."[4]

Wall Street veterans have refocused their careers on the space. Long-time CEOs like Patrick Byrne of Overstock are making major moves in the technology. Sandy Pentland, who helped create the MIT Media Lab and is one of the most cited scientists in the world, cofounded a blockchain company. Founders from Web 2.0 standouts like LinkedIn and Wikipedia are building new blockchain-first companies. Even the creator of the World Wide Web, Sir Tim Berners-Lee, has left work at MIT and the World Wide Web Consortium to found a blockchain-first company that aims to "take the world to a new tipping point."[5]

A massive shift has begun, and it is steadily gathering force. What, exactly, is happening here?

PART I

A MOVEMENT BUILDS

KINDLING, MEET MATCH

Our world is now 30 years into its internet-driven, digital-centric life. This has changed us. It's reshaped how we do the business of life—running a household or working a job. It's dominated our leisure time. Altered our patterns of communication. Given us new ways to influence. Changed the architecture of our expectations—what we expect a friend, partner, colleague, or a business to be capable of.

It has also given us unprecedented capability. Inspired by the higher bar set by disruptive, digital-first players, we learned to demand more. We have a voice. And we can use it around the clock, through a spectrum of channels, to give rise to our collective influence. This power has shaped markets, as businesses clamored to respond to the new customer we have become. It has challenged established institutions, playing a role in evolving social norms, influencing geopolitical dialogue, and even toppling dictators. And it has moved us, since the dawn of the web, to a steadily escalating desire for more accountability, transparency, participation, inclusion, and openness.

But there is a dark underbelly to our digital transformation, and now, 30 years in, we are waking to a growing awareness of the implications of what we have created. Many people are realizing that the way the internet was built is costing us dearly. Power has become concentrated in the hands of a few internet giants, who now wield undue influence. Our digital lives generate heaps of data that propagate beyond our intent and control. It's poorly protected by the companies on whose servers it sits, and time and time again these organizations demonstrate they are poor stewards. Malicious actors have found they can leverage our inability to distinguish real from fake in the digital world, to doctor our perception of reality with ease.

This awakening is happening amid a backdrop of global discontent. We're witnessing a backlash over economic inequality, plummeting trust in institutions to protect citizens and consumers, widening political divides, escalating knowledge of discrimination and exploitation, and anger over the reach of state surveillance. Like dry kindling, this discontent holds enormous potential energy—energy that, with the right catalyst, could ignite fast and spark broad, disruptive change.

In this moment of amassing restlessness and discontent, we're entering the dawn of the blockchain era. One by one, this new technology has promised a solution to each concern of our digitally driven lives: lack of transparency, accountability, verifiable identity, control of data, and security. The technology's driving force, decentralization, has allowed its architects to envision an opportunity to topple institutional centers of power and address deep inequities—and to create a new era of entrepreneurism. They have envisioned moving *anything* of value securely and directly—as simply as handing a piece of paper currency to someone on the street—without a corporation or government sitting in the middle. And they can envision flexing it to attack unique challenges in every industry: energy, media, manufacturing, retail, telecommunications, agriculture, real estate, education, health care, transportation, and so on—even aspects of government.

This rising discontent is the kindling. In blockchains we've found the match.

Blockchains and the decentralization movement have now captured the hearts and minds and imaginations of an entire population of pioneers. They are many tens of thousands strong, hailing from well over 100 countries around the globe to join this movement. Among them you will find some of the best minds from lauded corporations, top academic institutions, think tanks, and government—not to mention plenty of burgeoning startups and scattered solo operators who've mastered the technology and are already building things we couldn't have dreamed of a mere decade ago. They seek no less than to remake the foundational systems that drive our world. They are forging an ethos to transform our digital lives with transparency, trust, and accountability that permeates walls, borders, and tribes.

The loudest battle cry may be to scatter and decentralize today's centers of power. But there is a twist that works symbiotically to foster blockchain investment from those very centers of power: it also holds the promise of making large organizations dramatically more efficient. From supply chain to finance, from marketing to operations, divisions across the corporation could find significant new efficiencies and cost savings from more mature blockchain solutions.

Bridget van Kralingen, IBM's Senior Vice President of Global Industries, Platforms and Blockchain, explains it this way: "Enterprises are not just experimenting with blockchains, but actually moving into production and scale with blockchains. It is early days of the technology in enterprises, but there are some very promising signs in terms of its uses and applications . . . We are seeing this move at a really fast pace toward industrial-strength."[6] International Data Corporation forecasts worldwide spending on blockchains to reach $11.7 billion in 2022.[7] Hundreds of the world's largest companies have joined consortia to collaborate on, learn, and experiment together. Deloitte's 2018 survey of more than 1,000 "blockchain-savvy" executives around the globe found that 74% of executive teams believe there is a compelling business case for use of blockchain technology and 84% believe it will eventually achieve mainstream adoption. Enterprises are clearly starting to realize that blockchains hold the potential to become an automated, secure backbone for payments and for contracts that could eradicate the paper and inefficiencies that still plague corporate ecosystems. The Deloitte survey concluded that "the only real mistake we believe organizations can make regarding blockchain right now is to do nothing."[8]

According to Deloitte, the only true mistake organizations can make regarding blockchains is to do nothing.

The early pioneers are working to take the movement to the next step—and they are actively recruiting an array of gifted minds from a variety of disciplines to join their ranks. While to date the movement has been driven by and focused primarily on technologists, Chris Dixon, a partner at venture capital firm Andreessen Horowitz, has said that we need "to grow the army. We need 10 million people—programmers and researchers and entrepreneurs and product designers and creative people."[9] With this next wave of diverse skill sets, the movement will gain even more power.

This growing army of brilliant minds is rapidly working through the many hurdles the still-raw technology presents. But even here in its early adolescence, and even if blockchain technology as we know it today is still a work in progress, the decentralization revolution has already begun. Our world has already forever changed.

European Parliament member and chair of the Science and Technology Options Assessment (STOA) panel Eva Kaili said, "Once I understood it, I saw the possibilities of the technology in basically everything. It removes friction and intermediation anywhere this is a problem. You cannot stop it. You have to understand it, and find a way to work with it."[10] Twenty-eight-year-old Steven McKie, a writer, developer, and founding partner at investment fund Amentum, says, "Some say blockchains are like a religion, others just an impassioned pursuit. But the younger crowd sees a platform for expanded freedoms they never imagined possible. Many projects will fail, but this won't be failure. The learnings will be reinvested in our ever-evolving education. We are learning how to build distributed, interoperable systems that change human incentives, and can increase global prosperity. Everything can be decentralized, and many of us believe the future of humanity depends on it. This is a battle for our future. And if you change the rules, change the tools, change the culture, you can change society."[11]

A decentralized future may just draw from technology that is yet to be developed. Interest in blockchains has unleashed a flood of exploration in other kinds of technology that also supports decentralization.And the movement will broaden to bring in other disruptive technologies to assist; artificial intelligence (AI), machine learning, and Internet of Things (IoT) are three key technologies that already play a big role. Blockchains have and will continue to stoke renewed interest and advancements in cryptography, which in turn could catalyze new innovation. But whatever the ultimate technical answer, we know already that blockchains are a social movement as much as they are a technology. They offer hope in a way our world is craving.

Vitalik Buterin, who proposed Ethereum—one of the top projects in blockchain history—before he was even 21 years old, speaks to how this movement goes far beyond technology. "What we are talking about here," Vitalik writes, "has more to do with reforming underlying patterns of behavior, and especially the incentives, monetary, social, and otherwise, that drive how we interact."[12]

This movement has stoked the passion of a growing contingent of blockchain enthusiasts—developers, policymakers, activists, investors—that, finally, can taste a better future, and can see a path in which they can contribute to building that future. They are motivated by the financial or societal returns of doing so, and often both. And they have gathered fuel in the form of staggering amounts of capital. "Now, whether right or wrong," says Diana Biggs, Head of Digital Innovation for HSBC Retail Banking and Wealth Management in the UK and Europe, "the financial incentives with blockchains have generated massive interest in the space, and that has brought more momentum to the movement and its focus on digital identity, financial inclusion, transparency, open source, and collaborative systems."[13]

Blockchain pioneers are aided by a technology that is inherently resistant to being constrained. Key ingredients are being baked into blockchains that serve to accelerate social change—decentralization and built-in incentive structures that, at the right moment, are poised to activate and engage communities en masse. Ready or not, like it or not, we are on the brink of a global conflagration that, once it catches fire, has the potential to proliferate at hyper-speed.

We can't put out the fire—nor, as you'll see, do we want to—but we do need to learn about it now, and actively feed and tend it in such a way that it lives up to its promise to make our world better.

"Nobody knows how this technology will be used," Maja Vujinovic observes. "We need to keep testing and learning, we need to keep rolling up our sleeves and pushing for pilots—and we need to be very conscious about what we want this technology to do when it reaches maturity." When people come together to use it for good, she points out, blockchain technology has the potential to propel us leagues forward. "We can't implement blockchains or any other technology and expect it to solve mass societal ills like poverty or expect it to save the world," she says. "It doesn't work that way. But *we* can do that. *We* can. If consciousness is present in the design, we can use the technology to advance our world."[14]

2

CATCHING FIRE

You probably don't smell the smoke, and most certainly aren't feeling the heat—but it's coming.

While the exact path it will take is unclear, blockchains and their related family of technologies hold the potential for significant change, with far-reaching implications, for every industry and every sector. They will not only alter our digital lives—there are early indications that they could influence the very shape of how we work, live, and play. They can change what business and government are capable of. They can change what a single individual is capable of. They will kill old business models and birth altogether new ones.

Make no mistake: we are at the dawn of a next great wave of disruption.

As in any time of change, there is a chance for smart thinkers, no matter where they come from, to end up on top when the dust settles. And with this technology, that is the case almost no matter what industry you're in, or the size or age of your business. Could we see internet incumbents topple? Heritage incumbents pull ahead? Still-young startups flip their business models and drive to dominance? It's possible. We may not yet even know the names of some of the companies that will be powerful a decade from now.

As the shift gathers momentum, it is conceivable that every business will need to adjust, whether they use blockchain technology or not. It's possible that tens or even hundreds of millions of people will be interfacing with a blockchain, whether they are aware of it or not, in a matter of years. Over time, decentralization will most certainly create massive shifts in what customers expect—and demand—from businesses of all types. Businesses that want to survive—and thrive—in this next era will need to be more transparent, more authentic, and more aligned with customers' needs and desires. This is the very early start of a culture shift, and indications are that it could bring sea change.

Even if your business never uses blockchain technology, your consumers will expect a relationship with you based on what they have been exposed to elsewhere.

As with the internet before it, the new things blockchain technology makes possible will, over time, and with broader adoption, influence new consumer behaviors and a new kind of standard expectation. Even if your business never uses blockchain technology, your customers will expect a relationship with you based on what they have been exposed to elsewhere. Businesses will need to re-envision the way they communicate and interact—and for some, even shift an entire business model.

Luminary John Henry Clippinger has held senior positions in government and large enterprises, founded four software companies, and started new programs and institutes at Harvard and MIT. But most recently he founded a non-profit foundation in Zug, Switzerland, in the blockchain space. "Blockchains unleash a whole new paradigm," John told me. "Ultimately, the question will become: are you about value extraction, or are you about value generation? This technology will accelerate the opportunity in value generation.

"For executives," John continued, "the reflex is to be defensive: 'How do we inoculate ourselves from this thing? How do we kill it?' But leaders will see this as the transformative shift it is. They will realign themselves to create value *with* customers, developing a whole new kind of customer relationship. This is a huge business opportunity, and there is a great business model for this—a model that looks like a virtuous cycle. It's no longer about a zero-sum game, about what you have I take from you. It's about jointly creating value *together*. And it makes economic sense—this is nonrival value. Eventually, everyone will need to compete against that standard. We could see banks go the way of newspapers. And across industries, we will see whole new categories of next generation companies emerge."[15]

Blockchains unleash a new paradigm—it's now
about jointly creating value together.

—JOHN HENRY CLIPPINGER

This transformation will take time. It may be early, but it is not too soon to prepare. In fact, because it fits closely with many prevailing needs, desires, and social shifts of our time, this next wave of disruption may hit us faster than any technology has before.

Bite While the Apple Is Raw

Much about "the blockchain space" is still raw. The underlying infrastructure is still being developed. Huge, fundamental challenges have not been addressed, such as scalability and user experience. The utility and adoption of blockchain-driven applications remains painfully low. Corporate pilots are fighting headwinds. There is a dearth of true experts. There are more questions than answers. More theory than use cases in market. Leaders are spending their time on projects that can look like an experiment.

As with any new technology, there will be sputters and missteps on the way to adoption. Expect many headlines over the next few years pointing out the disconnect between earlier hype and today's reality. Consultancy Gartner describes this predictable pattern as the "hype cycle," as shown in Figure 2-1. After inflated expectations (and for blockchains this peak was especially high), there is a "trough of disillusionment" as the technical and human challenges of adoption become more apparent. But over the long arc of time, expectations reflect the maturation of the technology and a productive equilibrium is reached.

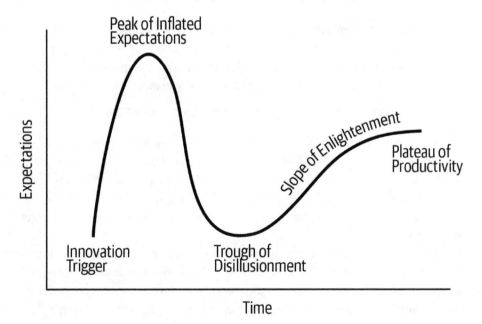

Figure 2-1. The Gartner hype cycle (source: Gartner)

Every time so much is in flux, it's tempting to just wait it out, to see what happens. For some, this restraint could be a crucial skill. But it could also be a death knell. The difference is knowledge.

Many companies missed the importance of the internet or mobile as they evolved from raw, clumsy technology to the key interface of much of our lives today, even just within the last few years. Take a look at a few memorable examples:

> *Neither Redbox nor Netflix are even on the radar screen in terms of competition.*[16]

—BLOCKBUSTER CEO JIM KEYES, 2008

> *The development of mobile phones will follow a similar path to that followed by PCs. Even with the Mac, Apple attracted a lot of attention at first, but they have remained a niche manufacturer. That will be their role in mobile phones as well.*[17]

—NOKIA'S CHIEF STRATEGY OFFICER ANSSI VANJOKI, 2009

> *We do not believe our vendors selling product directly on Amazon is an imminent threat. There is no indication that any of our vendors intend to sell premium athletic product, $100-plus sneakers that we offer, directly via that sort of distribution channel.*[18]

—FOOTLOCKER'S CEO AND CHAIRMAN RICHARD JOHNSON, 2017

Those who became today's dominant players were able to see—and effectively act on—what others missed. They did this by building knowledge early, while the technology was still bitter and raw. They invested in identifying what the tech made newly possible, understanding potential customers' needs and desires as they evolved, and timing their investment for the moment the market was ready.

Those who dig into gaining knowledge in blockchains and their related family of technologies now will be the ones who know when to make a move and when to hold back. They'll understand when to transition from study and experiment to betting the business. They're the ones who will be able to discern a shift in customer perceptions as it happens, identify which organizations would make good partners and which to steer clear from, and foresee when the market is ready to go mainstream for a particular use case. Knowledge can help you spot when blockchains are overkill, call out competitors' hype, or identify when an important aspect has not been properly thought through by whomever is leading a project. And perhaps most importantly, knowledge can help you identify areas in which to experiment. It is this—rolling up your sleeves and getting involved in the space—where the most learning will come from.

And in this space in particular, it is easy to be misled. Eager to make moves and capitalize on the hype, some companies—and even governments—appear to be leaping into blockchain-enabled initiatives without a deep awareness of their long-term implications or a robust understanding of the technology's capabilities.

No one knows when blockchain technology will become more widely adopted. Some leading thinkers project an ambitious two to five years; others say it will be decades. Certainly, the pace of innovation will vary significantly by category. But there is no doubt that the global inflow of financial and human capital into blockchain-backed initiatives is astounding.

CHANCE, UNCHAINED

My own entry into the world of blockchains was entirely accidental. Growing up in a Silicon Valley family of engineers, my nerdy style of teenage rebellion was deciding to become a social scientist rather than a technologist, training at Stanford in psychology, sociology, and organizational behavior. But when I finished graduate school I found myself at the dawn of the dot-com boom, and quite suddenly, all around us, hardware and software were working together to make noticeable changes in our lives. While at first these changes were small, it wasn't hard, even in those early days, to see where it could go. A glimpse at a new social construct was emerging, and it was clear we would need to learn how to manage a new, important relationship—our relationship with technology in an increasingly digital-centric age. I was captivated, and I suddenly found myself back in the world of tech, realizing that it was actually the *intersection* of social science and technology that was my calling.

Over the next two decades, I devoted my career to helping tech founders, entrepreneurs, and intrapreneurs drive behavior change and adoption in new markets, and in dynamic environments. I built a consulting business so I could spend my time embedded in a continual river of new innovations, traveling across industries and technologies, never willing to commit to just one.

All of that changed in a single hour.

One day, a client came to me with an idea to pivot to "the blockchain space." I knew very little, and remember crossing my arms in skepticism a few days later as I sat down to grill his lead engineer. I came out dazed: what I heard could change everything. Not just for my client, or his industry, but for my life, and my children's future, too.

That afternoon I caught the "brain virus"—an insider term describing how some find blockchains so engaging, such a rabbit hole, that they can't think about anything else. Overnight, I transformed from a mindful, eight-hours-of-sleep-a-night, family-dinner-insisting, devout meditator and devoted parent, to a woman who did nothing but research blockchains all day, and much of the night. I stopped meditating, barely slept, forgot to pick the kids up from school, and found myself telling them to eat cereal for dinner. While we attempted to find balance at a family camp in the mountains, my son even caught me placing a poster, right next to the rock-climbing signups, for an impromptu blockchain meetup. "Mom," he told me, "you've gone rogue."

OPPORTUNITY HIDDEN BY COMPLEXITY

The more involved I got in the space, the more I saw how the technology, and the movement behind it, held the seeds of the next shift in our digital culture. It also became clear that there was an extreme gap between what a community of "insiders"—predominantly technologists, investors, and financial services execs —understand about what's coming and what the rest of the world knows. And the more I learned, the more dangerous I recognized this dearth of knowledge to be. So dangerous, in fact, that I went on hiatus from my work with clients to write this book and help close the gap.

For the uninitiated, the risk of missing the telltale signs of the decentralization revolution—and both the risk and the opportunity it brings—is immense. But I also believe that what's coming is so important to get right that we need more minds involved in shaping it. We need more minds prepared to make smart choices about which solutions to support and which to ignore. (And possibly, which to condemn.) We need more minds thinking ahead about how decentralization could reshape organizations and communities. And we need more people lending their voices to influence how this all goes down. The more demographic and skill diversity in this space, the better chance our world has for this redo of foundational systems to be remade, *better*.

The first step, of course, is knowledge. At once, blockchains are stunningly elegant and staggeringly complicated. Today the space is dominated by technologists talking primarily to technologists, which is a key reason the learning curve can be arduous and steep. But it's not just the technology that is complex—it's the far-reaching implications of how it can change the way we operate, even down to foundational tenets we have long considered a given. This means many different disciplines are colliding to make that change happen, which also makes it hard to follow. As thought leader Jill Carlson has said, "This space is extremely multidisciplinary, cross-cutting math, economics, cryptography, game theory, computer science, financial markets, distributed systems, governance, programming language theory, law, and many other areas. There aren't many people who can be called subject matter experts in more than one of these areas—and each of these areas has its own jargon."[19]

The potential to miss the true significance of blockchains and the waves of disruption they will set off is further obscured by breathless, frantic coverage in the news about blockchains and digital currency (also called cryptocurrency), especially bitcoin, the cryptocurrency that was the first application of blockchain technology. There is plenty to report that is suspect, scammy, or distractingly sensational, and these headlines tend to consume editorial real estate more than the steady progression toward real change.

All of these factors pool together to create a formidable barrier for anyone who wants to get in—except those lucky enough to have someone who cared enough to pull them through, and who had the fortitude to navigate the morass. This barrier makes it easy to tune out the true power that blockchains and related technologies represent. It puts you in danger of not understanding the full extent of how they could change our world—and your life—until it is too late.

But there is massive opportunity in this moment. Right now, we have the chance to grab a front-and-center seat as the next digital foundation is forged. It's a chance to see the threats and to spot the opportunities—before they snap into focus for your competitors. To foresee the uptick of adoption that will occur just before this movement accelerates to broad acceptance. To lend a voice to how it should be shaped before new power structures take hold. And to bank the knowledge that will—when the time is right—enable you to make potentially trajectory-changing moves to build, join, acquire, or partner.

This moment offers a chance to grab a front-and-center seat as the next digital foundation is forged.

My hope is that this book will be a field guide to help you enter the world of blockchains. In these pages I work to lower the barrier, pull back the curtain, and welcome you inside. Instead of giving in to the conventional temptation in this space to throw every feature and piece of functionality at you at once, I cover basic driving forces that blockchains unleash, and give you a glimpse into how this could impact you and change our world. I give you a taste of the work that is already being done so you get a feel for the direction things are moving. And I give you some ideas for things you can do right now to prepare for what's coming.

This book will not only help you grasp the basics and give you the context to better understand developments in the space, but also help you think about if, when, and where to do the important work of experimenting with this new technology. It is written for executives and leaders and business owners in established enterprises as well as emerging companies that are not blockchain-first. It paints a story of a world that is being actively architected today, and is poised to grow quickly from awkward adolescent to a force strong enough to change what your customers expect from you. This book speaks to a future of indeterminate horizon, as that will vary greatly based on your particular business and the traction that early pioneers achieve. But regardless, *Unblocked* will help you accelerate your learning, increase your blockchain literacy, give you a framework with which to better understand new developments in the space as they evolve, and equip you to act on those developments more wisely. It will prepare you to see that dawning horizon as it clicks into focus.

THE SIX FORCES OF AN UNBLOCKED ERA

I've organized Part II by six basic key forces that will drive change in this next era, and will be important for every organization to grasp. Obviously, they don't cover all implications of blockchains and their related technologies, nor does this framework focus on the immense potential to drive efficiency in back office operations (although the same principles apply there as well). I am focusing on these six elements for their enormous potential to drive new customer expectations and evolve the relationship between customer and business as blockchain functionality is more broadly integrated and adopted.

The first three forces are cultural shifts: More Value, Deeper Transparency, and Fair Compensation. The final three are strategic shifts that blockchains make possible, and that businesses will need to understand and potentially leverage to be successful in this next era: Aligned Incentives, Bigger Data, and New Models. This matrix is illustrated in Figure 2-2.

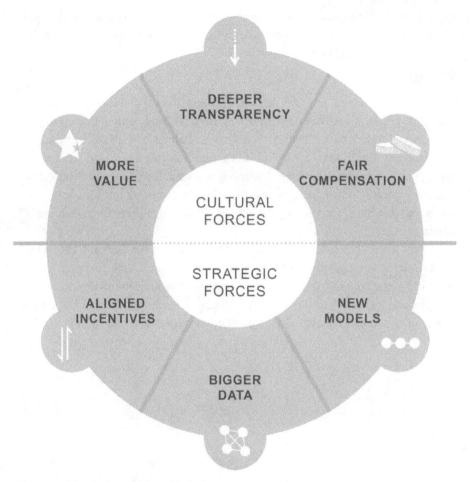

Figure 2-2. The six forces of the unblocked era

For each of the six forces I:

- give you context to understand why it matters,
- help you understand what new things the technology enables,
- outline implications,
- list some cautions and considerations to think about, and
- show you examples of the projects early pioneers are working on.

At the end of the book, I share some guidance on how to think about raising blockchain literacy in an organization, including case studies of several organizations who are doing this exceptionally well.

IT'S TIME

Some of what you read here will feel esoteric, and all of it ambitious, so consider a pause to pour a glass of wine or steep a cup of tea, and come sit down to geek out with me on this new world. As you do, think about how all of the unfolding developments you'll read about could change the rules of your business or infringe on your existing models. The more you read, the more you will discover your own questions and insights. Please ask, and please share. This is a space that needs dialogue from many voices and many perspectives to achieve its potential.

If you are inspired, check out my website at www.alisonmccauley.io, where you'll find links to more resources. At the very least, you'll have cool examples to throw out at the next cocktail party when someone mentions blockchains.

My hope is that I will not only help you gain knowledge, but also inspire you to learn more about this space. Just please, don't neglect to eat and sleep.

3

WHAT IS A BLOCKCHAIN?

So basically, this is just a safe, secure way to exchange pretty much anything of value on the internet with someone you don't know.

—BETH, MY YOGA INSTRUCTOR, AFTER I EXPLAINED BLOCKCHAINS

Beth Is Correct

Looking to understand the technology behind blockchains is a little like asking for an explanation of what makes the internet work. While I believe more technical knowledge is always better, this doesn't make your average executive better at using it to deliver business value. And blockchains are complex. In a recent *New York Times* article, journalist and author Nathaniel Popper wrote, "If you ask even the people who work with blockchains to define the technology, you are likely to get a stuttering response."[20] In his book *Radical Technologies*, the urban designer Adam Greenfield calls blockchains the first technology that's "just fundamentally difficult for otherwise intelligent and highly capable people to understand."[21]

But with press coverage of cryptocurrency's sensational ascent, blockchains have received more curiosity and engagement than most early technologies. There is a craving to understand—and explain to others—what this thing is. It serves, thus, to have some working knowledge. What follows on these next few pages is a basic explanation to ground you before we return to the main business at hand: to help you understand why blockchains matter.[i]

Before we dive in, a caveat: I must note that many components of blockchain technology aren't really new. The core idea behind blockchains—a database that is maintained by a network of users—was described in a 1991 paper by Dr. Scott Stornetta and Dr. Stuart Haber, while working at research center Bellcore.[22] However, some clever game theory and cryptography twists were added to this idea to make it possible to do some cool new stuff.[ii]

AT THE CENTER: DECENTRALIZATION

At its most rudimentary level, you can think of a blockchain as a very special database. What makes it special is that it can be used very flexibly to *directly transfer anything of value safely from one party to another without central institutions or middlemen getting involved.* This makes all sorts of new things possible, but if you were to simplify it down to one single attribute that makes the technology revolutionary, this would be it.

You can think of this database as a ledger, but not the kind you learned about in accounting class—this one has new superpowers. This ledger not only ensures the transfer is secure and records this transfer permanently for all of time, but also gives everyone in the world (who wants it) instant access to that record. In fact, in place of a single ledger maintained by a central party, blockchain technology maintains a multitude of exact copies (sometimes thousands), distributed all over the world—and every time there is a transaction it is recorded simultaneously in all of them.

Confused already? Let's unpack that. First, let's look at what we mean by "anything of value." That's anything that can be represented digitally—which is truly just about anything. You're no doubt familiar with certain assets that already are in digital form—for example, a photo, music, a medical record, or

---

i. Although the focus of this book is on blockchains, they are part of a larger category called *distributed ledger technology*, or DLT. There are many kinds of DLT, and some are betting that other forms of DLT will eventually eclipse blockchains. At a high level, different forms of DLT (whether blockchains or not) can contribute to the shifts described in this book. For simplicity's sake, I have chosen to use the word *blockchains* in this book, as this is being used frequently as an umbrella term today.

ii. A word of clarification: Since the first blockchain, the bitcoin blockchain, there has been a great deal of evolution, with different people tweaking specs, criteria, and underlying mechanisms to create new versions. To keep things simple, the focus of this chapter is on so-called "public" blockchains that use a methodology called *proof of work* to drive consensus (which is the approach the bitcoin blockchain uses). See "Consensus Mechanisms Are an Ongoing Battle" on page 219 for more on consensus mechanisms.

WHAT IS A BLOCKCHAIN? | 21

even a collectible in an online game. You've likely heard quite a bit about crypto-currency, or digital money. You may be aware that internet-enabled sensors (like a Nest thermostat) gather digital data—all of this has value too. Valuable certifications such as a college degree, land title, or even a vote are also commonly represented in digital form today. But it may surprise you that even physical assets like a house, a car, or a piece of fine art can be represented in code as well. The ownership of all these things could be securely transferred with a blockchain, and we'll look more closely at some of these examples and more in the rest of the book.

Next, let's examine that word "transfer." Digital things are easily copied. Traditionally, someone could copy a digital asset and use its value more than once. But blockchains track everything on a ledger, and because each transfer is confirmed against the ledger, it prevents "double-spend." Thus ownership is truly transferred.

Next, let's look at "from one party to another." To use the blockchain, each party is assigned a set of *keys*, which are unique numeric identifiers. These keys are linked to each other through cryptography.

One key is given out publicly and acts as a pseudonym, or proxy, for your identity. The other key is kept private—this is the secret code that gives the owner of that key control of anything associated with it. No one can make any changes, share information, or transfer things of value without this private key.

This pseudo-identity can be tied to anything—it could be a specific person, or even a thing (for example, you could establish an identity for your car or that Nest thermostat). However, if the owner of the key allows it, it is possible for the blockchain to verify that a particular pseudo-identity meets certain criteria or attributes, without visibility to that real identity. For example, the blockchain could validate that this is a real person (rather than a bot), or is someone who has earned a certain reputation (like size of social network or number of degrees). This unlocks the possibility of all sorts of interesting functionality, which we will cover later in the book.

The *transfer of value is direct*, and because the blockchain does the work of a middleman—ensuring that the parties involved have the item of value, that the transfer occurs, and that the result is recorded—there is no need for any other party to be involved, obviating the need for middlemen or intermediaries. Value could be transferred in just one direction, or in two (i.e., an exchange).

Finally, let's look at some of the attributes that make sure *the transfer is secure*. Blockchains are cleverly designed to render all the elements needed to create trust between two or more strangers into code. They:

- Verify identity (even while the actual identity may remain anonymous).

- Record the transaction permanently and immutably—no one can reverse it or change it.

- Send an exact copy of the transaction to distributed nodes around the world. (A *node* is an important point of connection within a network. In this case the nodes serve as the validators of every transaction on the blockchain record. For the first blockchain, the bitcoin blockchain, there are about 10,000 nodes globally, so far.) Every node compares the record to make sure it is the same. If a certain number of nodes don't agree (as set in the governance rules for that particular blockchain), the record is rejected.

- Are open to anyone. If you were technically inclined, you could download a copy to inspect right now. If you want to take just a glimpse, there are multiple websites, often called *block explorers*, that enable you to look at it without technical expertise.

Okay, so frankly, this isn't standing up to all the excitement yet, is it?

Well, consider this: because the record is distributed immediately, and because the parties are transferring value without a middleman, *the entire system is decentralized*. Which means it operates outside of the control of any organization or sovereign—there is no central point that can be hacked. Blockchains inherently resist attack, censorship, and control.[iii]

Blockchains are ownerless, stateless, value-transfer systems. This gives blockchain technology the potential to scatter and decentralize today's centers of power.

VALUE EXCHANGE MADE SMARTER THROUGH "SMART CONTRACTS"

Things get really interesting when you can put rules around the circumstances in which value is exchanged. This is done through something called a *smart contract* that sits on top of the blockchain and self-executes transactions based on pre-set

---

iii. This does not mean that attacks won't happen. In fact, hackers are becoming increasingly sophisticated, and this is an area of great discussion and research in the blockchain community.

instructions. Many times when people use the word "blockchain" they are actually talking about smart contracts.

An easy way to picture how this works is to pretend we have a bet on the highest temperature your nearest city will reach tomorrow, and the winner gets one bitcoin. We could code the terms into a smart contract, which would check the weather for us at the appointed time (using a source we have agreed upon), and automatically execute our agreement, sending the bitcoin to the winner of the bet—no third parties involved.

In a business, this opens up all sorts of new possibilities for efficiency, automation, or even new applications or services for customers. Smart contracts could release passwords, distribute funds, or allow the next step in a business process to take place. We are just starting to see the potential, and we have a long way to go before smart contracts can reliably enforce rules as intended.[iv] However, this will be a rich area of innovation. Smart contracts play a significant role in many shifts described in this book.

WHY IS IT CALLED A BLOCKCHAIN?

Each of those transactions we've been discussing is recorded (with a group of other transactions) onto a "block." These "blocks" serve as a container for this data, a sort of protective cocoon that is very difficult to hack.[v] Each block is linked to all previous blocks, from all of history, in a permanent and auditable chain— thus "block*chain*."

The link between each block is called a *hash* and serves a powerful role. The hash not only links two blocks together, but also functions as a unique ID generated by running the previous block's hash *and* the data stored in the current block through a cryptographic algorithm. This makes a sort of thumbprint that carries with it the history of the blockchain from all of time—if the data was altered in any block it would produce a different thumbprint for the current block. Said differently, no one can mess around with a single block without changing all the subsequent blocks.

---

iv. Smart contracts act as programs, and if there is a bug in the smart contract it could be exploited, just like a bug in any program. We also have a lot to learn about how smart contracts will be treated in the legal system. Over time, we will become much more experienced at developing and using smart contracts that function as intended—contracts in which code can truly stand in as a proxy for trust.

v. It appears no one has succeeded in hacking the bitcoin blockchain so far, although bugs have been found and resolved. Of note, however, is that hackers have discovered other ways to steal cryptocurrency—for example, many centrally controlled exchanges used for trading cryptoassets have been breached.

Different blockchains have different governing rules, but to add a new block to the bitcoin blockchain, for example, computers around the world, owned and maintained by "miners" (for more on mining see "WHO ARE THE MINERS?" on page 28), race to guess the hash. Once the winning computer solves this cryptographic puzzle, the block is added ("hashed") to the chain, and the owner of the computer that solved it receives cryptocurrency or tokens as a reward (in this case, bitcoin). While the winning miner's computer is responsible for hashing the new block to the chain, the miner can't alter any of the transactions in the block.

As soon as one puzzle is solved, computers around the world start racing to solve the next. The system self-regulates so that solving each puzzle takes about 10 minutes. All the transactions over that time period are included, up to the maximum capacity, and any transactions that exceed the maximum capacity are rolled into the next block.

It would take great effort to hack just one block. If you think of each block as an apartment, and the blockchain as an entire city, hackers would need to take down more than half the city to truly change the record of transactions. This is far less attractive to hackers than attacking centralized "honeypots" of data sitting on corporate servers—even before you consider that the change would be immediately caught by the other computers on the network and rejected.

BLOCKCHAIN OR BLOCKCHAINS?

Often people use the word "blockchain" on its own when they are referring to the entire space, which is actually composed of many, many blockchains. This has contributed to confusion about whether there are one or many.[vi] Developers are continually releasing new blockchains, each a different flavor, optimized for a specific set of use cases. There is a blockchain optimized for building applications and smart contracts. There are blockchains that are built to make it easier for illiquid assets like houses and art to become divisible, liquid assets. Some are used to build reputation around a unique identity, whether that is a person or an IoT device. Still others track the rights of music or photographs, or components as they move from partner to partner through a supply chain.

---

vi. In this case, use "the blockchain space" or "blockchain technology." Saying "I work in blockchain" is like saying "I work in robot" (you might say you work with "a robot" or "the robot" but not "in robot").

WHAT DOES BITCOIN HAVE TO DO WITH BLOCKCHAINS?

A common point of confusion arises from the association of cryptocurrency with blockchains. While they certainly are related, many people mistakenly assume that bitcoin and blockchains are the same thing. But blockchain is the technology that underlies and enables bitcoin (and other cryptoassets). In fact, the first blockchain was built specifically to make bitcoin possible (bitcoin was the first widely adopted cryptocurrency and the subject of Satoshi Nakamoto's whitepaper). You can think of bitcoin as the first application of the blockchain space. Its debut offered the world a decentralized currency, outside of any nation-state, that could be traded from one person to another without the assistance of any financial institution. The first block generated by a blockchain is shown in Figure 3-1.

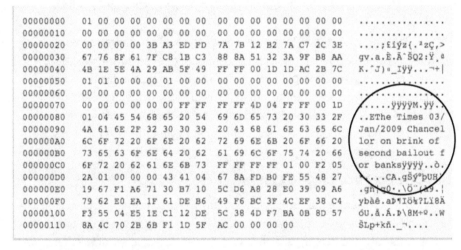

Figure 3-1. The "genesis block," the first block generated by the bitcoin blockchain on January 3rd, 2009, contained a single transaction. Embedded into this block was the text, "The Times 03/Jan/2009 Chancellor on brink of second bailout for banks," referring to a headline in The Times on that date. The act of mining this "genesis block" resulted in the creation of the first 50 bitcoin, which were awarded to the miner for solving the cryptographic puzzle. This first miner is believed to be Satoshi Nakamoto. At the time, bitcoin had no recognized value.

WHO IS SATOSHI NAKAMOTO?

In short: we don't know. We do know that in October of 2008 someone (an individual or a team) using the name Satoshi Nakamoto published a whitepaper on a cryptography mailing list describing bitcoin for the first time. In January 2009 Satoshi released the first bitcoin software, launched the network, and mined the "genesis block" of 50 bitcoins. In mid-2010, Satoshi handed over control of the code and transferred related domains to various members of the growing early bitcoin community—and then disappeared from public view. Except for test transactions, the estimated 980,000 bitcoin that Satoshi mined in those early days has never been spent (this is traceable on the public ledger). At bitcoin's December 2017 peak, Satoshi's bitcoin was worth over 19 billion dollars.

Satoshi's online footsteps have been endlessly scrutinized by amateur detectives all over the world. Timestamps for every forum post have been charted in an attempt to analyze Satoshi's time zone. Writing analysis experts have dissected the language used in the whitepaper and posts. A dozen or so suspects have been identified, but to this day, it is still a mystery who launched this new technology on the world.

THE MANY ROLES OF CRYPTOASSETS

Cryptoassets is an umbrella term used for any asset (currency, financial instruments, physical assets, digital goods, etc.) whose existence and ownership are cryptographically secured by a distributed ledger. Cryptocurrency, tokens, and digital coins are types of cryptoassets.

Cryptoassets are at once one of the most ingenious, important, and confusing elements of the blockchain space, primarily because a single cryptoasset can play many roles. They may be known most commonly today as a *speculative investment* or even called a *new asset class*.[vii] But you can also consider them a resource used to send value or a tool used to pay for transactions on a blockchain. Let's break down some of the *active* functions cryptoassets can play in the system:

---

vii. They can be used to digitize the value of an asset. For more on this, see "Atomize—and liquify—assets" on page 188.

Aligns incentives of participants:

- Incents maintenance of the network: miners who contribute to network security by running nodes and producing blocks of transactions may be rewarded automatically, via the network's rules and typically through newly "minted" cryptocurrency or token. This helps the network run smoothly without central control.

- Incents protection of the network: if miners are rewarded in cryptocurrency or tokens, they (and any other holders of that asset) theoretically have a disincentive to hack it, and are incentivized to protect it from being hacked. The value of the asset would immediately plummet in a successful hack (if widely discovered), and the hack would be self-defeating. Its existence gives everyone skin in the game.

- Incents user actions: Cryptocurrency or tokens can be leveraged in many ways to reward a wide range of individual and community behaviors and actions. Ideally, the value of these assets should loosely represent the value of a network (although in these early days, this is yet to be proven). The more of a particular asset a person holds, conceptually, the more incented they are to invest time and attention in growing the network, and thus increase the value of their holdings. And various incentives and rewards can be creatively designed into the token "economy" to shape actions and behaviors. When thoughtfully designed, this may be a powerful tool in creating ecosystems with the potential to be sustainable and successful long term.

Facilitates exchange of value

Cryptoassets can be exchanged for things of value on the network, or for other cryptoassets.

Pays for compute cost

Cryptoassets can be used to pay for the compute cost of a transaction, again helping the network run smoothly without central control.

WHO ARE THE MINERS?

Anyone, theoretically, could become a miner, and I run across old mining rigs occasionally while visiting the offices of a wide range of technology enthusiasts. (A rig looks like specialized computer equipment, typically lined up on a rack, with wires everywhere.) It has become increasingly difficult to mine profitably, however, as professional operators have moved in, making large investments in high performance equipment, and locating their facilities near inexpensive sources of power around the world (a lot of energy is needed to run all those computers). The faster their computers, the more they have, the greater their chances of winning the race to solve each cryptographic puzzle (and thus getting the cryptocurrency or token reward from adding a new block)—and miners have made billions of dollars this way. Smaller, hobby miners have thus given way to *mining farms*, which are essentially huge warehouses filled with tall rows of computer-filled racks. The cryptocurrency mining industry (it is now an industry) spans over 100 countries.

RETAINING PRIVACY WHEN THE LEDGER IS OPEN TO EVERYONE

Clearly, for blockchains to have broad applicability, there needs to be a way to retain more privacy than a publicly inspectable ledger would suggest, even if it is pseudonymous. And in certain industries—such as financial services or health care—this can be a regulatory imperative. There are various technologies and cryptographic approaches that are under development to address the privacy imperative, and much experimentation is being done with securing sensitive data "off chain," while linking it to an "on chain" record. There is a raging debate in the community over "public" versus "private" or "permissioned" blockchains, with the latter restricting access—and thus not truly eliminating the middleman, but keeping sensitive information from public view.

SO WHAT?

How will blockchains be so much better than what we have today? The answer: it depends.

Blockchain technology is *only* useful where trust is truly a problem—and nowhere else. If parties know and trust each other already, a blockchain is not necessary. If a middleman does not cause friction, a blockchain is not necessary. In fact, this kind of shared ledger technology can be expensive and inefficient for many applications. Especially while the technology is still clunky, it is always better to look everywhere else first to find a solution to your business problem before you look to blockchains. That hasn't stopped some businesses from experimenting with blockchains when an old-school database would suffice. While these businesses may gain experience, they will not gain a sustainable solution.

That said, there are many places in which blockchains do deliver great promise: where a lack of trust has created a big problem, or using code as a proxy for trust unlocks a huge opportunity. There are many flavors of potential impact to a business, from streamlining internal processes to introducing new blockchain-based consumer services to facilitating collaboration among complex ecosystems.

Blockchains Across Industries

It's the financial services examples that tend to dominate the media, but here are just a few compelling examples of how blockchain applications are being tested across industries:

Agriculture

- Track provenance of food, from origin to store, preventing food fraud and false labeling.
- Ensure safe handling practices from farm to market, and more quickly pinpoint source when food safety has been compromised.

Energy

- Standardize clean energy tracking, incentive structures, and production around the world.
- Enable distributed energy producers (such as via rooftop solar panels) to efficiently trade energy directly with consumers.

Manufacturing

- Ensure the authenticity of components and goods as they flow through the supply chain to prevent, for example, counterfeit drugs from entering the market.
- Deliver more transparency to suppliers' practices and compliance.

Media

- Register copyrighted works, and enable owners to more easily protect and track usage of those works.
- Make it possible for brands to see if digital media dollars are spent as intended, reducing fraud.

Government

- Reduce costs of distributing government services, such as welfare.
- Cut fraud and increase the efficiency of public record keeping, from birth records to property ownership.

Retail

- Prevent counterfeit goods from entering the system and more easily identify stolen merchandise.
- Make warranties easily transferable and keep them current without administrative work.

Real estate

- Automate the process of buying real estate, enabling transactions, title transfers, and recording to occur without human intervention.
- Enable owners to gain liquidity by selling fractional shares of real estate.

Health care

- Reduce friction and increase the security, privacy, interoperability, and regulatory compliance of electronic health records.

- Make it possible to contribute data to a study without compromising the identity or privacy of the individual patient.

Education

- Fight education credential fraud and enable employers to cut administrative costs of verifying degrees.

- Create a universal, trusted, lifelong record of learning that recognizes education outside of a formal degree program, such as online courses.

Transportation

- Achieve hyper-visibility to goods as they move through the supply chain when combined with sensors or tracking devices.

- Increase the efficiency of managing a global ecosystem of carriers, and accelerate the movement of goods across borders.

Telecommunications

- Unlock the promise of ubiquitous 5G access by enabling dynamic, automatic contracts across an ecosystem of access nodes.

- Advance IoT connectivity with more secure, reliable, and cost-efficient self-managed peer-to-peer networks.

Now that you have some grounding in what blockchains are, and a glimpse of how they are being used across industries, let's explore the setting in which they were birthed. Why is this technology capturing the attention—and even the hearts and minds—of so many people? What is it about *this* moment that makes this technology so important?

4

THE GENESIS OF THE UNBLOCKED CUSTOMER

The Consumer Technology Created

Today's consumers have more power than ever, and they know it. They type, swipe, and click their way to nearly anything they desire. They put a few words in a search bar to comparison shop across thousands of sources. They summon groceries and gas, dinner and dates—all with a few taps and the help of accurate geolocation services. They expect free shipping. They assume you can anticipate their needs. They expect you to know them, whether they are using their tablet, smartphone, or even a watch. They want to reach you whenever, however, be it via voice, web, chat, email, video, or social media. And if they're under 40, you can bet they'll abandon you the moment there's friction.

> *Today's consumers type, swipe, and click their way to nearly anything they desire.*

How Did We Get Here?

The industrial revolution marked a shift to factories and mass production, and with this new industrial capacity came a surplus of goods. The answer to this surplus? Using advertising to create markets—which launched a new relationship between a business and its customer. Money flooded into the advertising industry, and spots in newspapers, magazines, direct mail, radio, and television sprang up like dandelions. This relationship was relatively "light touch"—hear about my product, buy it, use it, and buy it again—and these behaviors were encouraged by consistent advertising and the emerging practice of brand marketing.

Maintaining this basic cornerstone of "being heard" became a lot more difficult in the internet era, as shown in Figure 4-1. Channels and information exploded, and all of a sudden it became staggeringly difficult to stand out among all the digital noise. But it got even more complicated: consumers expected you to hear *them* as they shouted out their gripes and delights about your products on dozens of social channels, review sites, and blogs. Now, the relationship meant not only being heard, but listening—and responding.

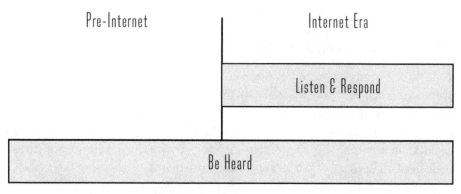

Figure 4-1. How the internet triggered new challenges for brands

Whether a young startup or an established brand, companies that have a good relationship with their customers today have recognized the shift in power, and have found a way to deliver to it.

But they are not done.

In his outgoing speech, John Chambers, Cisco's CEO of 20 years, warned 25,000 listeners that "Forty percent of businesses in this room will not exist in a meaningful way in 10 years . . . companies cannot miss a market transition or a business model or underestimate your competitor of the future."[23]

> *Companies cannot miss a market transition or a business model or underestimate your competitor of the future.*
>
> **—JOHN CHAMBERS, FORMER CISCO CEO**

Whether you have a good relationship with today's customer or not, be warned: the world is about to shift again.

THE INTERNET: BUILT TO FAIL

In the 1980s, scientists at European physics lab CERN were struggling to share, track, and collaborate on their research. Tim Berners-Lee, a contractor with the lab, provided an answer: he created the World Wide Web. Tim designed this new platform to be permission-less and free, an open space for creativity, innovation, and free expression that transcended geographic and cultural boundaries. And in many ways, it still is. But something else happened: "free" services that made revenue by harvesting the attention and data of millions of users became the prevailing force on the internet.

They were staggeringly successful: the average American now spends 24 hours a week online.[24] Affluent millennials spend over 50 hours.[25] The internet has become the dominant global platform for social interaction, commerce, media, and entertainment. And with it, a new dynamic has emerged: power has become concentrated in the hands of a few giants like Google, Facebook, and Amazon. They wield undue influence as a result. Everything you post, click, or search for online is recorded, and it is used to influence your behavior and make money for a broad range of companies—but not for you. Entire industries have sprung up to perfect the harvesting of your attention so that someone else can monetize it. Meanwhile, all this data that is being collected is often poorly protected by the companies who have taken it. Even those organizations that are serious about security are under a constant barrage of cyberattacks, with quite a few suffering breaches.

Because nation-states can censor, media outlets can prioritize the content you see, and finely tuned AI and bots can create and distribute content that appears legitimate, our view of reality can also be easily manipulated. And, with great irony, many of today's hyper-connected and broadly social-networked people report feeling more disconnected than ever. Tim Berners-Lee himself has sounded the alarm. "Over the last 12 months, I've become increasingly worried about three new trends," he has asserted—namely, how we have lost control of personal data, how easy it is to spread misinformation on the web, and a lack of transparency.[26] "The web has evolved into an engine of inequity and division, swayed by powerful forces who use it for their own agendas."[27]

There was nothing in the original specs of the internet to code trust between two participants.

How did this happen? A key driver: there was nothing in the original specs for the internet to code direct trust between two participants.

ENTER BLOCKCHAINS

Staggeringly complex, disarmingly raw, and complicated by a seemingly distracting (yet crucial) tie to cryptoassets, blockchains can be intimidating to even seasoned technical executives. Yet they hold the seeds of deep transformation that could equal—or perhaps even eclipse—what we have seen in the last decade.

> *Blockchains offer a wealth of new functionality that can address the shortcomings of the internet's original design.*

Blockchains offer a wealth of new functionality that can address the shortcomings of the internet's original design, and are poised to shift the way we interact with each other, with brands, and with businesses. At the center? An ability to replace subjective trust with code. The dominant feature? They do so through *decentralization*—removing power from a centralized body and instead giving it to the crowd. This feature has become one of the core tenets of the blockchain movement, the ethos of which is being coded into protocols (the standards dictating access and exchange of data on a network), being written into governing standards, and stoking social movements targeted at bringing change to a range of industries across the globe.

In the 1440s, Johannes Gutenberg launched a technology onto the world that would permanently alter the very structure of society: the printing press. Books, once painstakingly copied by hand and available to few outside of the church, broke loose into the population. Rather than deferring to the clergy, laypeople could access a book, and the ideas within it, directly. Likewise, ideas could spread from a single individual to an entire population quickly through the authorship of a book. This technology fractured the church's hold on renaissance Europe and paved the way for social and scientific revolutions. Information and revolutionary ideas could now transcend borders and social classes. Centers of power and authority were threatened and monopolies of the literate elite were broken.

Blockchain technology releases a modern, but analogous, shift in society.

Launched in the wake of the financial crisis, Satoshi's infamous whitepaper described a striking solution to widespread discontent with centralized financial institutions. It showed how to circumvent centers of power by coding trust that could, through decentralization, function even between strangers. This was the first blockchain, and its first application was a digital currency designed to work without any bank, central government, or organization. Like the printing press, the technology it described would loosen the hold of centralized bodies and give new powers to the people.

THE ERA OF THE UNBLOCKED CUSTOMER

At this very moment, as you read these words, there are tens of thousands of pioneers and provocateurs around the globe coding a new foundation for our digital future. At its core is the concept of decentralization, and all the benefits this brings to an individual or a business. Behind many of the new protocols being developed is a social movement. Some of these protocols will never turn into much, but others will cluster and build, channeling great human and financial capital into educating people about this new alternative. In some areas, change will come in a matter of years. In others, it will move slowly, in small gradients that eventually, over decades, change the underlying hue. But the movement—and it *is* a movement—will gather force and gradually, over time, bring about a new, more powerful customer.

This new customer will be able to cut you out. To go direct. To see if you are really standing by the values you claim. To know if what you sell is what you say it is. To barter or sell their own attention, data, posts, reviews, writing, and photos. To make money doing what you used to do. This is the customer of the blockchain-era world: *the unblocked customer.*

There is an important place for businesses and brands in this world, but for many it will likely look very different from today. Competitors—both new and old—who "get it" first will debut new products, packaging, pricing, services, and value that deeply resonates with the unblocked customer. And in doing so, they will train this consumer of the future to have these same expectations of you.

> The unblocked customer has a lot to give, but she expects a great deal more in return.

By what it makes possible, this technology has the potential to forever change the relationship between a customer and a brand. The unblocked customer has a lot to give, but she will expect a great deal more in return. Unblocked customers will know the value of what they're contributing to your business because someone—perhaps a competitor—is willing to pay them for it. They will be skeptical of you if you sit in between them and what they want. They may be willing to give you more—more data, more content, more exposure to their inner workings—but only if you demonstrate you are worthy.

A WHOLE NEW LAYER OF EXPECTATIONS

Many companies have become quite adept at listening and responding to meet internet-era customer demands. But this new customer will demand a new kind of relationship. They will change the power dynamic, and the businesses that understand this will see that this requires a relationship that looks a lot more like a partnership.

This means companies will need to dive much deeper into understanding their customers and what they really value. And they will need to more actively engage across the entire organization to discover and deliver on this. They will need to learn how to communicate differently, so customers understand and respect all that a business brings to the relationship. And they will need to recognize—even reward—the value customers themselves contribute to the business. This is a new ethos, and it is based on collaboration.

BLOCKCHAIN-ERA EXPECTATIONS WILL PUT MORE PRESSURE ON BUSINESSES

The businesses that pull ahead in the era of the unblocked customer will be those that regard their relationship with customers as a form of collaboration. This means that customer and brand find and exchange value in ways that drive great benefit to them both, as shown in Figure 4-2. In many areas this is a natural progression from where we were already headed. Customers have been demanding increased transparency—they want to know where products are from, and how data is used —and some companies have worked hard to provide this. Platform players such as Airbnb and Uber have created significant markets out of people selling a night in their house or a ride in their car, to great benefit for buyers, sellers, and the platform. For years, loyalty programs have compensated consumers for behaviors and buying decisions that benefited a business. In these examples, blockchain technology could simply make it possible to do these things better—sometimes much, much better. In other areas, it makes entirely new business models and incentive structures possible.

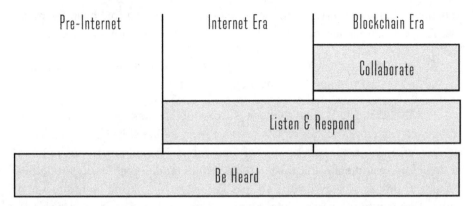

Figure 4-2. How the blockchain era will evolve customer relationships

This shift may start in a few seemingly disconnected areas where block-chains solve a pressing pain—international remittances or title insurance, for example. But it will spread, slowly yet steadily, to influence many customer relationships—from B2B to B2C to B2B2C and any other configuration. The technology naturally favors businesses that understand the importance of partnerships, consortiums, and collaborative ecosystems. At their very core, blockchains are a team sport, making it possible for multiple organizations to work together to do more than they could do on their own. Ultimately, this could very well rewrite what drives competitive advantage, with collaboration championing over purist competition.

> *The businesses that pull ahead in the era of the unblocked customer will be those that regard their relationship with customers as a form of collaboration.*

For some organizations, blockchain capabilities may become the next add-on to digital transformation initiatives. Others may, more dramatically, disinter-mediate digital transformation and create their own next-generation blockchain-first competitors. But regardless of approach, smart organizations will also focus on transforming their relationships to meet new blockchain-era expectations as the technology is more broadly adopted. They will focus on delivering real, authentic value to customers, and demonstrate their alignment with customer needs and values. They will proactively work on shifting internal mindsets and developing a new way of interacting with customers and partners. They will change how they think about marketing, branding, customer experience, digital experience, customer service, product development, and even core business models. They will learn a new paradigm that is, essentially, the business of trust.

Smart organizations will also focus on transforming their relationship with customers to meet new blockchain-era expectations.

It will be much harder to be a successful business in the era of the unblocked customer. But those who are able to make the shift have a chance to get in exchange a more holistic view of their customers, an opportunity to build stronger, more authentic and trusted relationships, and deeper loyalty. And, ultimately, as the technology matures, it has the potential to bring both direct and indirect impact to the bottom line. Many established brands will not be able to make the transition. Many startups will fail to capture this new paradigm. But the companies that pull ahead will be those that understand these new dynamics and proactively work to shift their relationship with customers even before they've mainstreamed blockchains as part of their business. It is quite possible that this next era will be remembered for its great shift toward more equitable power between organizations and individuals, and the amplified influence of the crowd.

WHY NOW?

When you're finished changing, you're finished.

—BEN FRANKLIN

It was just three decades ago that Tim Berners-Lee first sketched out the idea of the World Wide Web. Today, the internet has become so pervasive in our lives that people need to go to great lengths to avoid it.

As a society we have shown a pattern of adopting new technologies at an ever more rapid pace, as shown in Figure 4-3. It took 35 years for the telephone to be adopted by one-quarter of the American population. The web took only seven years to reach this milestone.[28]

Years until used by one-quarter of American population

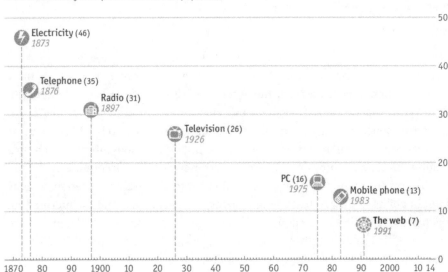

Figure 4-3. Society is adopting technology at an increasingly fast pace

This accelerated pace is one of the key reasons businesses have struggled to respond quickly to new technologies as they become mainstream. The web, mobile phone, and even personal computers required adjustments to business as usual—and with each new wave, companies have had less time to react to these new, fast-approaching realities and the threats and opportunities that come with them.

We can expect blockchain applications to blindside even more businesses than previous waves of technology change did.

If the adoption of blockchain applications follow this well-worn pattern, we can expect it to blindside even more businesses than previous waves. And the adoption curve could be further fueled by characteristics of the technology itself. It contains, as social media did, attributes that encourage network effects to build quickly, seemingly out of nowhere. However, in many ways, one could argue that the blockchain version is supercharged, because additional incentives are built in. Participants—whether individuals or organizations—can *directly* benefit from the growth and success of the network.

Yet there is an argument for an even stronger catalyst for adoption: it is hitting at a particularly ripe moment.

A HUGE AND DISILLUSIONED GENERATION

New York Times writer David Brooks traveled to college campuses to understand how students see the world. In a story he wrote after the experience, starkly titled "A Generation Emerging from the Wreckage," Brooks describes a cohort with diminished expectations. Their lived experience includes the Iraq war, the financial crisis, police brutality, political fragmentation, and the advent of fake news as a social force. In short, an entire series of important moments in which "big institutions failed to provide basic security, competence and accountability."[29]

To this cohort in particular, blockchains' promise of decentralization, with its built-in ability to ensure trust, is tantalizing. To circumvent and disintermediate institutions that have failed them is a ray of hope—as is establishing trust, accountability, and veracity through technology, or even the potential to forge new connections across fragmented societies.

Jeremy Gardner cofounded Augur, a blockchain project that, for a time, reached a market cap of over $1 billion when he was in his early 20s. He also founded a hedge fund, a blockchain publication, and Blockchain Education Network (BEN)—a nonprofit that seeds education at college campuses around the globe (and counts members from nearly 100 countries). Jeremy coined the hashtag #GenerationBlockchain to describe the students who, once they have glimpsed what blockchain technology makes possible, cannot go back. After meeting at an event for BEN, Jeremy and I caught up by phone as he traveled around the world for his work.

"We have the potential to create a generation of youth who think about blockchains as intuitively as we approach email or social media," Jeremy said. "It's bigger than money—this is about values. The internet has been this incredibly powerful, revolutionary tool for the uploading and dissemination of information. But if you want to exchange value, you rely on the same centralized intermediaries that have existed for decades, or even centuries—banks, governments, clearing houses—or central repositories such as Facebook, iTunes, and Netflix. Our digital lives are owned by these oligopolies. But in the age of blockchain technology, the individual can have sovereignty of their digital life. It is such a powerful notion. And it's a reason young people are the ones at the ground level of this network-driven software movement, they are the ones evangelizing this, and they are the ones that will drive adoption."[30]

The youth are not alone in their discontent. Diverse adult populations across the globe have escalating skepticism of institutions, with moves on Wall Street triggering financial crisis, corporations proving poor stewards of data in an age of continuous cyberattack, governments failing to protect citizens, and economies collapsing. A widening gap between the rich and the poor, and deliberate manipulation of the news, has contributed to deeper fragmentation.

On the cusp of surpassing baby boomers as the nation's largest living adult generation, millennials are a massive force. In the United States, they are also becoming the wealthiest: over the next 30 years and as they are entering their prime earning years, millennials will inherit $30 trillion from their baby boomer parents and grandparents. Receptive and quick to adopt new technologies, millennials, through their influence and demands, have already played a huge role in shaping the way we shop, work, and live. They may very well be one of the first —and highly influential—major segments to adopt blockchain-fueled development. A recent Pew Research Center study found that just 19% of millennials (those born from 1981 to 1996, according to Pew Research) feel that "most people can be trusted."[31]

Blockchains' capabilities match up in seemingly ideal alignment to this perfect storm of discontent. It comes at a particularly potent time. Entire populations are activated, and ready for change.

I recently sat down with European Parliament member Eva Kaili, who also chairs the Science and Technology Options Assessment (STOA) panel aimed at assessing AI, fintech (technology used to support financial and banking services), and blockchains, to hear her perspective on adoption. "Young people discovered this technology that makes it unnecessary to have intermediaries," she said. "I first heard about blockchains from 20-year-olds—they're very comfortable explaining it and working with it. For them, it's natural for everything to happen on an iPhone, and they very easily understood the potential of digitizing value. They don't have traditional ideas that value can be restricted by borders."

"When ATMs first came out," Eva went on, "everyone thought it would be difficult for customers. There were some people who needed an explanation, of course, but now we have so many people that never go into a bank, because they can do everything online. Now I see this next generation who will be able to do anything on their phones—sell a house, buy something, without intermediation."[32]

THE FIRST TECHNOLOGY WITH DEMOCRATIZATION BAKED IN?

Columbia Law School professor Tim Wu has found that throughout history, information technologies, from the telegraph to radio to movies and the internet, behave in a similar, recurring cycle. From a utopian, democratic birth, they end up centralized and hegemonic.

"History shows a typical progression of information technologies: from somebody's hobby to somebody's industry," Wu says in his book, *The Master Switch: The Rise and Fall of Information Empires*. "From jury-rigged contraption to slick production marvel; from a freely accessible channel to one strictly controlled by a single corporation or cartel—from open to closed system. It is a progression so common as to seem inevitable." When radio operators began stringing up towers in the early 1920s, he goes on to explain, it was so people could talk to each other and share ideas over an open broadcast medium. The assumption was that disconnected communities and houses would be united through radio as they were never united by the telegraph and telephone. But that's not what ended up happening. By the mid 1920s AT&T and RCA had created the National Broadcasting Corporation, NBC, which controlled access to bandwidth via what has become a massive multinational company. Wu believes there is no question more important than who owns the platform by which people access and share information. "Before any question of free speech," he writes, "comes the question of who controls the master switch."[33]

But decentralization of that switch can be baked into blockchains, which, if done well, makes them less susceptible to co-opting. Could this be the first technology that successfully resists centralized control? In its original design, the first blockchain intended just that. It is important to note, however, that an authoritarian regime could require use of a restricted, private blockchain to gain access to government services and participate in the economy. In this case, that regime would control the master switch—and could thus use it to exert dystopian, near-complete control and monitoring of all its citizens' data, including their economic activity, crime records, education history, military service, and health records.

Amber Baldet is the former blockchains lead at J.P. Morgan and now the cofounder and CEO of blockchain startup Clovyr. She recently wrote about how several nations are experimenting "with creating tokenized versions of their sovereign currency on ledgers they control, which gives them much more granular access to individual transactions of its citizens and anyone else using the new currency. Combined across supply chains that span people, businesses, and government entities, these projects may end up giving governments, banks, and businesses alike more direct access to all our day-to-day financial activity than ever before."[34]

Like any technology, this one can be used in a way it was never intended. But with their promise to create opportunity that sits outside of centralized control, blockchain capabilities conceptually match up in seemingly ideal alignment to a brewing "perfect storm" of discontent. They come at a particularly potent time. Entire populations are activated and ready for change. In many ways, blockchains represent not just a technical revolution, but a political, social, and economic movement all rolled up into one.

5

TORTOISE OR HARE?

Everything changes and nothing stands still.

—GREEK PHILOSOPHER HERACLITUS (535 BC–475 BC)

How Far Along Are We?

It's still achingly early.

Satoshi Nakamoto's 2008 whitepaper was ignored by all but a fringe group of cypherpunks for a handful of years. They were joined by a group of particularly visionary entrepreneurs a few years later. Then, the idea catapulted into broader public awareness in 2017 with blustery media attention to bitcoin's stratospheric ascent. Fast-forward to today: this single whitepaper spawned a massive global computer network with over 10,000 nodes and a vast ecosystem of developers, users, and companies around the globe in a few short years. Now, thousands of companies (both new and established players) are looking to build businesses or experimenting with blockchains in parts of their business.

But what they are building today is often clunky, ugly, and frustrating, and it doesn't scale well. In a recent *New York Times* article, journalist Nathaniel Popper warned, "Few blockchains have been used and battle-tested in the real world for any amount of time, which leaves significant questions about how they will perform once they make it into use."[35] Right now, blockchains are also painfully slow. Of course, this was how the web looked back in 1994—and a YouTube launched back then would have failed. As with anything so new, we first need brave pioneers to build infrastructure, increase speed, battle-test innovations, experiment with business models, and improve user experience.

But the pressure on these pioneers is extremely high, with new technology bumping up against the expectations of a particularly active hype cycle. Compared to a Web 2.0 timescale, "it's like we're dealing with 1991 technology, but

1999 economic enthusiasm and 2018 customer expectations—all colliding at once," says Gina Bianchini, the founder and CEO of Mighty Networks, who also cofounded social platform Ning with Marc Andreessen in 2004.[36]

The speed of innovation and adoption will vary widely—some initiatives will take off in a matter of years, while others will take decades to mature and encounter major setbacks along the way. But one thing is clear: for new players who eventually get it right, it is a chance to threaten incumbents. And for incumbents, internal forces provide sufficient motivation to explore moves in advance of market demands: those that are more visionary see an opportunity to cut costs and build platforms that deliver more flexibility, efficiency, and capabilities for future growth. Many are immersing themselves in blockchain-driven experiments, collaborations, or formal consortiums. In certain segments, like financial services and supply chain, having a blockchain strategy is already an expectation. Juniper Research found that nearly 60% of large corporations are either actively considering, or in the process of, deploying blockchain technology.[37] According to research firm CB Insights, 119 corporations (or their venture arms) invested in blockchain companies in 2017.[38] The EU has invested more than €80 million in projects supporting the use of blockchains, and the European Commission has said around €300 million more will be allocated by 2020.[39]

Within a few years, average consumers may be interacting with blockchain-driven applications, cryptoassets, and smart contracts without even knowing it.

While the impact of true blockchain-led transformation will be enormous, it will most likely take decades to fully seep into the foundations of our economic and social institutions.

While the impact of true blockchain-led transformation will be enormous, it will most likely take decades to fully seep into the foundations of our economic and social institutions. Even the core idea of decentralization is still taking shape. Meltem Demirors is an advocate for thoughtful development in the space. She is also Chief Strategy Officer at CoinShares, is cocreator of the Oxford Blockchain Strategy Programme and Future Commerce at the MIT Media Lab, and manages her own investment and advisory firm, Shiny Pony Ventures. She warns, "There are so many people mindlessly using words like 'decentralization' in a very esoteric and poorly defined manner."[40]

A battle rages in the blockchain community over what decentralization really means, with tension between those who consider blockchains that aren't purely decentralized to be flawed, and others who feel there can be many degrees of decentralization. Extreme decentralization can be inefficient and conflicts with a natural tendency for both synthetic systems and biological networks to become hierarchical. Hierarchy can improve both performance and speed adaptation to new environments—but only to a point.[41] Extreme hierarchies also breed inefficiency, and it is likely that this is where the shift will begin. Meltem explains, "Decentralization exists on a spectrum, not as an absolute."[42] Instead of an abrupt transformation to "decentralized everything," it's possible we'll see more of a gentle progression toward more equitable distribution, less hierarchy, and all the benefits that come from that—and this will take time to do well. Sheila Warren explains, "Centralization is as natural to human beings as entropy is to systems. We have an inherent bias towards centralization because we don't have time to research every decision. As we push against centralization mechanisms, we need to be careful which we choose, when, and how. This is going to be hard to get right."[43]

Nick Soman, the CEO of a health care company that leverages blockchain technology, explains, "We think about responsibly decentralizing over time, and I think the projects that will be taken seriously, that touch the real world, will take this approach. Decentralization is not our core value—our core value is to deliver more affordable health care to our customer, and we see decentralization as a way for an inefficient and misaligned system to become far more efficient."[44]

There are other challenges. Few applications can boast a consumer-ready user experience, and key scalability challenges have yet to be solved. But there is another battle to fight before the space can go mainstream: the money flooding into blockchain startups has also attracted scams—making headlines, creating negative perceptions of the space, and making it harder to see the signal within the noise even from the inside.

"Blockchain technology is early, but it should not be written off," warns Diana Biggs, of HSBC. "It is important to experiment and test—and especially to learn. Certainly right now there are people, given the energy and excitement around the space, that are playing off the fact that many people don't have the technical literacy to be able to gauge what is real and what isn't. And it's early—saying something isn't scalable right now doesn't mean it will not be useful in the near future."[45]

"I think most of us got into crypto because we believed it would change existing power structures in our world," Meltem Demirors tells me. "I have seen a lot of problems over the last few years—so many scammers, so many people in it to make money. People mismanaging or abandoning projects. People signing contracts without reading them. Trying to be first and rushing to market. It's innovation theater. And there will be political and social consequences. But I am here for the next 20 years to make sure this is built the right way." Meltem started investing in crypto companies while at Digital Currency Group, and built Shiny Pony Ventures to support projects that she believes could make a difference in the world. Together with the entrepreneurs she advises and works with, Meltem told me, "We are going to break some #@$%."[46]

She cautions that that won't happen if teams remain stuck in their current technology-centric mode. "Really great projects are about winning hearts and minds," she said. "I don't know how my iPhone works, nor do I care. There needs to be more thoughtful communication and more education on why blockchains matter."[47]

In *Crossing the Chasm*, organizational theorist Geoffrey Moore gives a framework for how new breakthroughs happen. At first, only those people willing to tolerate the risk and uncertainty of a novel technology get on board, a trade they make for the benefits of being early adopters. This is followed by a gap, which Moore calls the "chasm." Any idea has to cross the chasm to access a larger audience, the early majority. According to Moore, this ability is the true mark of successful innovation.[48]

When I sat down with Eric Ly, the cofounder of LinkedIn who is now the CEO of blockchain startup Hub (known as Human Trust Protocol), our conversation quickly moved to this challenge of consumer adoption. Eric offered a historical perspective. "I remember in the late '90s when the web was new, people didn't seem to understand what a URL was, or a link, and it took them a while to see that they could type an address into a web browser and see something interesting," he said. "It's that kind of education process that the mainstream audience will need to go through with blockchains as well. Hopefully there are not too many things they will have to learn."[49]

In 2005, Lou Kerner was running the largest user-generated content streaming service, Yashi, when someone uploaded the SNL skit *Lazy Sunday* to tiny competitor YouTube. That day, YouTube became the fastest-growing website in the history of the internet and the rest was, well, history. "It was lightning in a bottle," Lou, now the cofounder of consulting firm and advisory CryptoOracle, told me over coffee. "And now, we have some of the smartest people in the world going into crypto. They're leaving McKinsey and Goldman and MIT. With all this incredible brainpower, we are going to get that lightning in a bottle that takes crypto mainstream sooner rather than later."[50]

Analyst firm Kaleido Insights founding partner Jessica Groopman shares her perspective on adoption at the corporate level, and the challenges it faces. "Right now, there is a lot of activity in certain industry sectors—partnerships, announcements, pilots, proof of concepts, alliances, and industry consortia. With scalability issues and the magnitude of what these companies are trying to overcome, they're running into brick walls, hindered by core physics. Yet," she continues, "at the same time, there are a lot of technical levers to pull to drive evolution, and we're seeing innovation in every single one. There are new designs, new consensus mechanisms, new predictive capability in chips, lower compute costs—and more advancements continually coming down the pipe. I am optimistic."[51]

Change does take time. Broad adoption that stretches across industries will be gradual, not sudden. Initial versions may be hybrid models: semi-centralized, partly "on-chain" and partly "off-chain." But over time, maturity will begin to catch up to vision. And the maturation cycle will be propelled by a totally new age of innovation.

THE AGE OF OPEN INNOVATION

Chris Anderson, the curator of TED, tells a story about a filmmaker named John Chu. One day, John came across a YouTube video of Anjelo Baligad, a six-year-old-boy from Hawaii, performing dance moves that even professional adult dancers would find difficult. John realized that dancers around the world were using online video to learn and evolve dance at a speed never seen before. What had started with challenge videos posted by rival groups of street dancers had exploded into a kind of global laboratory for dance innovation. "Kids in Japan are taking moves from a YouTube video created in Detroit, building on it within days and releasing a new video, while teenagers in California are taking the Japanese video and remixing it to create a whole new dance style in itself. This is happening every day. And from these bedrooms and living rooms and garages with cheap webcams come the world's great dancers of tomorrow," Chris quoted John in an article he wrote for Wired.[52]

Open innovation propels hyperspeed evolution. This idea and its importance have been around for a while and are well documented. Henry Chesbrough, Director of UC Berkeley's Center for Corporate Innovation, talks about using both external and internal ideas to advance an organization's technology.[53] MIT professor Erick von Hippel speaks to the impact of distributed and open innovation in the evolution of everything from surfboards to software security.[54] Chris Anderson calls it "crowd accelerated innovation." And open source software became a force that changed the course of technology, releasing an explosion of software development that has influenced nearly every industry.

But what has happened in the last five years of blockchain development is unlike any kind of open innovation we've ever seen. The technology was born to be open. The culture that galvanized around the technology is markedly open. But there was also a brief, year-long moment in which billions flowed into the community in an unprecedented open funding mechanism. Even as the frenzy receded, it left in its wake the beginnings of an all new *Age* of Open Innovation.

UNLOCKING THE NEW TOOLS OF OPEN INNOVATION

In 2013, J.R. Willet, a software engineer living in Seattle, published a paper describing a new protocol layer he wanted to build on top of the bitcoin block-chain. He included an address that anyone could use to send him bitcoin in exchange for a piece of that new protocol. He raised $500,000, and the concept of the *initial coin offering* (ICO) was launched.[55]

Since then, well over 1,000 teams have raised over $20 billion through ICOs, and in so doing have forever changed the magnitude of open innovation.

These ICOs (sometimes called *token sales*) raise money by issuing their coin, also known as a *token* (which is a cryptoasset). In exchange for the investment, investors receive these digital coins, which will also be used as a medium of transaction when (and if) the product is built. As Matt Levine of Bloomberg News has said, it's like "the Wright Brothers sold air miles to finance inventing the airplane."[56]

It took some time, but regulatory agencies eventually clamped down on this fundraising method, and ICO activity dramatically plunged from a high of 114 ICOs in December 2017 (and for a four-month period, over $2 billion each month) to just 6 ICOs a year later, in December 2018.[57]

However, as ICOs became, in the words of one executive, "unfashionable," new approaches sprung up in their place. *Security token offerings*, or STOs, became a popular way to issue tokens designed as securities. *Initial exchange offerings* (IEOs) are now offered through several exchanges. IEOs mirror ICOs, but are hosted by the exchange, on their platform—and currently ban US investors. While the models (and names) are still evolving and the regulatory environment still shifting, it has become clear that the initial ICO rush roused desire for low-friction, open forms of fundraising. We most certainly have not seen the last of this phenomenon.

Fundraising via token sale exploded in late 2017, as shown in Figure 5-1.

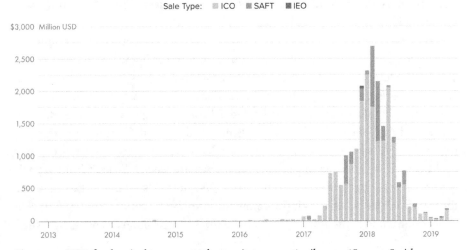

Figure 5-1. USD funds raised to support token projects, 2012–April 2019. (Source: Smith + Crown (https://www.smithandcrown.com).)

But the ICO heyday also jump-started global interest more quickly than possibly any other nascent technology. While early technologies often struggle to break out of the small communities that can understand them, the excitement of this unique moment in history triggered curiosity from a broad range of people. In the early days, all you needed to open a path to capital was to name a team, publish a whitepaper describing what you would build, and provide a cryptocurrency address. Suddenly, people were moving into the space from a range of backgrounds. Others were simply curious enough to read an article, attend a meetup, or make an investment. For a painfully early technology, blockchains had succeeded, in a very short period of time, in becoming the talk of the town. Even as the market turned, many of the minds that became involved in the ICO boom days stuck around to continue to work in the space. They had a lot to inspire them.

This new phenomenon had broken out into the open what used to take place behind closed doors, locked away from all but those with special pedigrees, access, and networks.

This new phenomenon had broken out into the open what used to take place behind closed doors, locked away from all but those with special pedigrees, access, and networks. For the first time, via a token sale, smart teams could connect to capital, no matter who they were, what they looked like, or where they came from. As long as they had great brains and a decent internet connection, they were in the pool of candidates.

Whereas startups traditionally guarded their strategy, many were typing up their vision and even technical detail of how they are going to get there in neatly organized whitepapers, which were widely circulated or even published online. Where once teams would pitch venture capitalist after venture capitalist, aspiring to get into the offices of the most lauded Silicon Valley players, they could now get tens of millions of dollars from anyone—and without diluting equity or giving up a board seat. And, since most blockchain protocols are open source, they could copy anyone's code to get a running start: no need to make it from scratch if someone else has already made progress. Just "fork it" and make it work better for you. Even the inner workings of how these young teams code the governance of a protocol and sometimes even manage their organizations may be published to the world.

BREAKING AWAY FROM SILICON VALLEY

This Age of Open Innovation also disperses innovation from a Silicon Valley–centric hub. We are at the beginning of the most globally dispersed digital transformation of all time. Countries in Asia and Europe see the opportunity in creating friendly environments for cryptoassets, attracting both investment and entrepreneurs. Leading blockchain development is coming out of countries such as Switzerland, Estonia, and Israel. And we can expect many compelling early-use cases to come out of emerging regions, where arguably blockchain functionality is most urgently needed. Entrepreneurs in less developed regions are also free from the obstacles presented by legacy institutions, systems, and processes that teams in more developed countries face. As parts of Sub-Saharan Africa completely skipped the "landline phase" of development, adopting mobile phones (and all the rich functionality they enabled) faster than consumers in the United States, it's conceivable that consumers in developing regions could become sophisticated users of blockchain-enabled technology in advance of more developed countries.

> *We are at the beginning of the most globally dispersed digital transformation of all time.*

Jalak Jobanputra founded venture firm Future Perfect Ventures, and has worked and traveled in nearly 40 countries throughout her career. "Crypto and blockchains are capturing the imagination of young people everywhere," she explains. "In traditionally underserved and underrepresented regions—Africa, India, Indonesia, and the Philippines, for example—people see that it can give them a voice. Anyone, anywhere, has access to the tools to build on top of this open source technology. They don't need formal education or much capital to start innovating, to find a solution to problems in their market, or tap into new opportunities. And this is happening for thousands upon thousands of people around the world. They are building for their communities, their cities, their countries."

But, Jalak believes, this innovation could jump borders with the right mentorship and capital. "One of the reasons I started Future Perfect Ventures was for the investment opportunity in cross-border learning," she says. "I saw that solutions developed in Mexico were also relevant to India, that innovation could move from India to China, Africa to Latin America. The next three billion people that are coming online will be in these markets, and they're going to do it through a smartphone. They are likely to be crypto-native from the beginning in a way we don't understand, sitting here in New York, or in Silicon Valley. It is from these emerging markets that the business model of the future may very well emerge."[58]

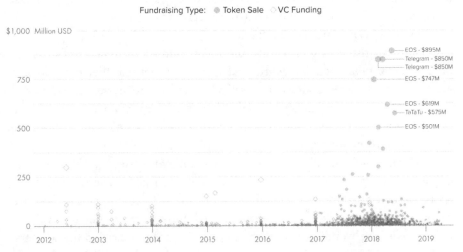

Figure 5-2. Blockchain-focused venture capital and token project fundraising events, 2012–April 2019. (Source: Smith + Crown (https://www.smithandcrown.com) and Crunchbase Data.)

In late 2017, fundraising via token sale eclipsed blockchain-focused venture fundraising (see Figure 5-2). Even though ICO activity slowed in late 2018, token sales were still the primary method of funding.

THE DECENTRALIZATION OF ENTREPRENEURSHIP

In short, we are seeing potential for the decentralization of funded entrepreneurship. More people, and different kinds of people, will be working to solve the world's problems and seize the world's opportunities. They are more distributed than ever, bringing a broader range of diverse perspectives to the solutions they propose. They will use blockchain technology to fight critical global challenges, such as food insecurity, social and financial inequality, and climate change—problems that urgently require the minds and energies of the global brain trust. They will use blockchain technology to come up with attractive alternatives to every internet giant today. The next Uber? Airbnb? Facebook? Amazon? Dozens of teams around the world are already working on new versions of all of these (although they can look dramatically different from what is in place today). They will also attack totally fresh ground with innovations made possible only through a blockchain business model. And indeed teams—some composed of just a few college-age kids—are discovering new mind-expanding applications of the technology every month. Since the technology is so new, even the most experienced are typically just a few years in, which not only levels the playing field (and makes it much easier for a newcomer to catch up and add value) but also suggests that we could see another acceleration cycle once there is a large body of thinkers with 5 or 10 years of experience behind them.

There are many factors driving the great number of developers devoting themselves to this space. Many are guided by the belief that they can offer the world something better than what is available today. But many also are motivated by the potential of great financial reward. There was no money made in the development of the underlying suite of protocols that drive the internet. Instead, the money came from applications built on top of the protocols. Blockchains appear to reverse this—if you build a successful protocol that is used widely by a range of players, you potentially stand to do very well financially. Whereas just a few teams were involved in the development of the internet's core protocols, this next cohort of protocols is being developed, iterated, improved, and iterated again by thousands of the world's smartest developers in a race to develop the winners, across the globe. The winning protocols—the ones that grow to dominance years out—are well positioned to be incredibly sophisticated. And lucrative.

The sheer volume of teams simultaneously attacking the same challenges; the new, diverse thinking that comes from the many more able and willing minds contributing; the open ethos of the community; the reams of code contributed to a protocol laid open to inspection or duplication by anyone—they all build to one fundamental truth: we are entering a totally new age of open innovation.

There is a long way to go, but it is going to move very, very fast.

THERE WILL BE BLOOD

As you can see, we're looking at an insanely accelerated innovation cycle. We'll have more creative solutions—but also more competition than ever. And, as we will see, higher rates of failure.

Conventional wisdom in the hallways of venture hub Sand Hill Road is that 9 out of 10 startups fail. While the actual data is hard to find (there is no startup "death certificate"), research firm CB Insights recently did an analysis of 1,000 startups from the moment they raised seed investment, and found that just over 70% of startups stall at some point in the process and fail to exit or raise follow-on funding.[59] While venture funding arguably filters with bias, it also filters for some tell-tale markers of success: a capable team, a working product, traction with customers, and an attractive market. These same filters are not applied consistently in ICO, IEO, or STO fundraising. Products are often not yet built. Teams can be technology-centric with varying levels of knowledge about their actual market and the pain they are solving for prospective customers. Some projects feel more like science experiments than the beginnings of a viable company. Sadly, during the ICO rush, more than a few were outright scams. And because success in the blockchain world depends on large-scale adoption, all face the uphill battle to attract others to their particular movement and develop thriving ecosystems. Vitalik Butarin, the co-creator of Ethereum, one of the most widely adopted blockchain protocols to date, has asserted that 90% of ICO projects or tokens launched on top of the protocol will likely fail long-term, a metric oft-repeated from the stages and in the hallways of blockchain industry events.[60]

Regardless of what actual failure rate transpires in coming years, it is not a stretch to believe that it will eclipse that of venture-funded startups—significantly. However, while in the world of blockchains 2017 had the feel of an untamed wild west, 2018 and 2019 signaled more experienced entrepreneurs moving in the space and the birth of many thoughtful projects.

On a rare sunny day in Portland, Oregon, I visited the offices of Smith + Crown, one of the world's leading cryptofinance research organizations. Over lunch, the unassuming and deeply intelligent head of research, Matt Chwierut, and I discussed the new field of cryptoeconomics and what characterizes a successful token.

"Network effects are so important," Matt emphasized. "Tokens need to achieve network effects at the market level through liquidity, and at the user adoption level through utility. This will weed out a huge portion—at some point there will be a dramatic reduction in the number of viable projects."[61] Basically, not only are blockchain entrepreneurs wrangling a new technology and creating new companies, but they also need to develop an entire mini-economy in order to achieve success. This is staggeringly difficult.

The blockchain battlefields will be littered with the carcasses of ideas that never connected to users, missed a key piece of business design, or were built with the wrong protocol.

It also means that one day, the blockchain battlefields will be littered with the carcasses of ideas that never connected to users. That missed a key piece of business design. That never built traction in a confusing and fragmented landscape of competing ideas. That blundered a good idea by building on the wrong protocol. Or that were unable to build the complete ecosystem upon which so many of these business models depend.

BUILDING ON THE BACKS OF FAILURE

I prefer to profit by others' mistakes and avoid the price of my own.

—PRINCE OTTO VON BISMARCK

The Age of Open Innovation has a corollary: an abundance of second mover plays. A "second mover advantage" is the edge a company gets from following others in a market or mimicking an existing product. Facebook wasn't the first social platform and Google did not pioneer the search engine. These players leveraged others' innovations, coupling what they learned with astute business and marketing strategies to climb to the top. Creating a product is costly, in terms of both hard dollars and mistakes made on the journey. When pioneers pay a steep price to create a product category, a later entrant can use the knowledge of what worked and what didn't to win at the game the pioneer created.

With the rawness of blockchain technology, blockchain business models, and today's gap in addressing the basics of good user experience, there will be a lot of skeletons for second movers to choose from. And many will be well documented in great detail, with the code still beating and available for the taking. Some of these failures will be technical; some may have been sound if better executed, or stewarded by a team with stronger business acumen. And still others may find their stride only when wrapped with a new business model or mashed up with other emerging technologies. In the Age of Open Innovation, the second wave of players will be at a great advantage to learn from the mistakes and sweat of those who failed before them.

Spotting the spoils among these skeletons requires a deep understanding of what you are looking for. It takes knowledge of how blockchain technology could create new opportunity or solve key obstacles in your business. It demands acumen in the technology, and cross-functional teams that are able to identify the points of failure and grasp how your business could succeed where others failed.

The first place to start is understanding the potential—and the threats—that all businesses will face as we curve toward new kinds of decentralization.

PART II

THE SIX FORCES OF AN UNBLOCKED FUTURE

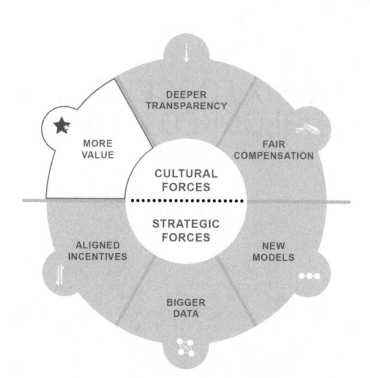

6

MORE VALUE

Whatever you are, be a good one.

—ABRAHAM LINCOLN

Summary

Businesses will no longer be able to passively extract value for the privilege of sitting in the middle of a transaction. Instead, they will need to work harder to actively contribute value to all parties—and authentically market that value.

The days of passively extracting value for the privilege of sitting in the middle of an exchange between two parties are numbered. Today, the real cost of using a middleman is often hidden. But blockchain entrepreneurs, lured by the prospect of disintermediating incumbents, will launch attractive alternatives that open customers' eyes to those costs. These new offerings will use blockchain features to reduce friction and cost.

Customers will grow skeptical of middlemen, and more carefully scrutinize what value they actually provide in exchange for the cost of working with them. Middlemen—and most businesses have at least some middleman role—will have to more actively provide value versus passively extracting it. They'll also need to work harder at making sure their customers see the magnitude of the value they provide, and this will become an important focus at every customer touchpoint. Incumbents will need to continually increase the value they provide in lockstep with an increasingly competitive landscape as the technology matures.

 **The Setting**

WIRED FOR MIDDLEMEN

Since the dawn of trade, middlemen have played a valued role in getting buyers what they wanted, when they wanted it. In ancient Indus Valley cities, traders brought minerals from Iran, copper from India, and jade from China. City workers turned these materials into finished goods, and traders then sold these finished products. Vikings established trading centers; goods were brought in via merchant ships and sold to merchants, who would then resell to the public. Across early civilizations, "if you or someone in your town didn't grow it, herd it, or make it,"[62] you needed a middleman to get it. These middlemen often took on great risk—traveling slowly over long distances, fronting the cost of goods, and facing the difficulty of finding interested buyers. These services were of high value to the parties on either side of the transaction, and the middlemen were rewarded with lucrative margins.

As commerce became more globally interconnected and products more complex, additional layers of middlemen were introduced. Many of these middlemen helped to transform raw materials into finished goods. But many more were recruited to serve as an intermediary in place of trust, protecting one party from the potentially bad actions or outcomes of another.

> *Middlemen serve as an intermediary in place of trust, protecting one party from the potentially bad actions or outcomes of another.*

If two parties trust the intermediary, they do not have to trust each other. Middlemen such as escrow services, insurance providers, dispute resolution services, credit reporting agencies, and payment processors all serve in place of trust.

The rise of the internet has made it possible for many more people and organizations to collaborate and transact, but it has also increased the physical and cultural differences between parties. This has created more risk because we end up dealing with parties with whom we have little shared history or knowledge. It's made it even more vital to have systems and intermediaries in place to facilitate those interactions.

THE RISING COST—AND POWER—OF THE MIDDLEMAN

Each middleman plays a role that parties on either side of the transaction value, or they would be disintermediated. But with each added layer of complexity comes a layer of fees. This compensates the middleman for their role, but compounds expense for the customer. A 1% transaction fee may seem nominal, but if applied a dozen times as a good moves through a supply chain, it adds up.

Driven by economies of scale, sophisticated management practices, and modern technology, many of the companies in the middle have grown very large. And many have become very powerful. For example, a few huge companies dominate digital access to sellers and their products, and exert massive control over the goods consumers can discover, what they pay for them, and the data they give up in exchange.

These middleman can add value, or they can detract from it. They can provide an important role of curation and connection—or they can make it hard to discern real from fake products, or hide better-fit listings below pages of search results. They can provide valuable recommendations based on the data we provide, or they can turn around and sell it to someone who blasts us with ads.

With so many layers between origin and final product, customers have lost touch with the real costs of middlemen.

With so many layers between origin and final product, we have lost touch with the real costs of middlemen. These can include hard costs (the fees baked into each layer), or soft costs (such as how much extra time it takes a product or transaction to move through the system). Even for businesses, it is very difficult to know the true cost and value of an entire ecosystem of middlemen lined up between them and the products, services, and materials they use.

Until someone presents an alternative.

WHEN COST IS UNCOVERED

Recently, new models—such as modern direct-to-consumer and the "sharing economy"—have squashed these layers.

Disruptive direct-to-consumer retailers maintain end-to-end control over the making, marketing, and distribution of products, circumventing middlemen. For example, Warby Parker brought stylish prescription glasses to the consumer for a fraction of the price. Startups attacked the notoriously heavy-toll mattress industry with a dozen venture-funded players fighting for consumer mindset and even an early standout, Casper, raising almost a quarter billion in funding since inception. All of a sudden, consumers understood that they were overpaying middlemen for their glasses and mattresses. These companies cut hard costs; their products could be accessed at a fraction of the price. And they delivered additional value, as each company threw in new services that were important to the customer. Warby Parker made it easy to try on glasses at home. Casper provided 100-day no-questions-asked returns. Both provided careful curation of their product, and diligently crafted their brands to connect with their markets and communicate quality.

In under a decade, sharing economy players like Uber and Airbnb have changed the entire shape of industries. These modern middlemen serve as a platform to connect people with extra capacity in their cars or homes with people seeking rides or rooms. They provide value with a robust two-sided network of buyers and sellers, facilitating rapid, high-quality connections between them, handling payments, and providing controls (like insurance and ratings) that protect both sides of the network. But they have also unlocked new kinds of value by making it possible to do things that were difficult previously, such as finding a safe ride home from a dinner party in a sleepy suburb, or spending the night in a lovingly built, one-of-a-kind treehouse.

In exchange, they take fees that, while significant, can bring the cost lower than traditional alternatives. And customers have responded: the sharing economy is estimated to grow to $355 billion by 2025.[63] It has become a phenomenon, shifting social norms and creating an entirely new precedent for our capacity to trust a stranger. When I was a child, it was clear I was never to enter a car of someone I didn't know. The concept of sleeping in the bed of a stranger was so foreign it was never even discussed. I now hop into the cars of people I have never met, and sleep in strangers' beds thousands of miles from home without hesitation—accompanied by my own beloved children.

These new models are opening our eyes, industry by industry—giving us a glimpse of the new kinds of value that can be released when the middlemen are compressed, and setting a new precedent for peer-to-peer commerce.

But what comes next could be even more profound.

What Blockchains Make Possible

PURE PEER-TO-PEER

"Peer-to-peer" typically appears in the first five words of blockchain definitions. And indeed, the blockchain was born from the desire for extreme peer-to-peer. It was architected to make high-risk transactions between strangers safe. And it captured the hearts and imaginations of its devoted early developers for this feature possibly more than any other.

In Chapter 3, you learned that blockchains make it possible to directly transfer anything of value safely from one party to another without any kind of middleman. The linchpin is trust. The blockchain was cleverly designed to render all the elements needed to create trust between two strangers into code. Innovators are continually releasing new blockchains optimized for a specific set of use cases. But many of these blockchains focus on enriching the ability of two parties to safely exchange something of value that can be described in code, and just about anything can.

> The blockchain was cleverly designed to render all the elements needed to create trust between two strangers into code.

In Code We Trust

Blockchains, in essence, make it possible to replace a middleman—and all the activities a middleman would perform—with code. That means that participants —whether consumers or businesses or both—can safely exchange valuable goods or services with someone on their street or across the world. They can do this without a company or any other organization sitting in the middle, siphoning off fees or "charging rent." And if that person or business doesn't come through on their commitment, they're protected too.

The code can verify participants' identity and reputation, register the transaction in a permanent record, and execute an escrow-like transaction when the goods or services are actually exchanged. The code can execute recourse, automatically, if one of the participants defaults on the arrangement. And that can become part of the permanent record (and reputation of that participant) as well.

Of course, evolving the way we make payments is one obvious use case, and there are many organizations—both new and incumbent—that are working hard on this.

But this is only the beginning.

A BROAD RANGE OF INDUSTRIES ARE VULNERABLE

Any industry in which middlemen cause friction in a transaction—creating inefficiencies or skimming off significant fees—is a target for disruption. Not all businesses will be impacted the same way, as there are many different kinds of middlemen. But regardless, the pressure is on.

As we sat down over drinks one summer evening in San Francisco, Arianna Simpson, the Managing Partner of Autonomous Partners, shared her perspective with me. "I was in Zimbabwe, and saw firsthand that the institutions, the systems, weren't serving people—there was a huge gap. I saw an answer in block-chains." She continued, "The technology allows people to work outside of a system. If your financial system isn't serving you, for example, well, you can just be your own bank. While I don't think traditional infrastructures will completely go away, innovation will force existing players—players who have rigged the system to work in their favor—to become more transparent, to lower fees, and to pass more down to the end users instead of hoarding." Arianna noted how in Zimbabwe's recent political turmoil, the local price of bitcoin surged as citizens turned to the currency for its comparative stability.[64]

Use cases go far beyond the financial system. Here are three examples of middlemen that will experience different kinds of disruption as the technology matures and gains traction:

Traditional intermediaries

These companies can be in industries as diverse as banking, insurance, music, real estate, energy, and advertising. These entrenched players, with business models dependent on capturing high fees from the flow of value from providers to customers, are likely to experience significant new pressures and competitive threats. In each area, blockchain entrepreneurs are working on alternatives that offer direct exchange of value between parties. However, it will take some time for the technology to mature and for new competitors to unseat them. A more imminent threat may come from established players who acquire or partner with a blockchain-native team, combining their strengths and knowledge to move more aggressively in the market.

Sharing economy players

This category includes companies such as Airbnb, Uber, and Lyft. It seems almost every region has a team building the blockchain version of " " (insert your favorite sharing economy company here). They are using blockchain functionality to lower costs and introduce stronger protections, such as verifying identity and reputation or providing micro insurance. However, these businesses live or die on the power of their two-sided networks. While some startups have certainly achieved explosive network growth (Instagram grew from 80 users to one million in just two months), any new sharing economy competitors will be significantly hampered by the challenges of creating both sides of a two-sided platform from the starting gate.

We can expect that new, blockchain-native startups will open up surprising sharing economy plays using creative approaches, and in unexpected industries. They will be able to leverage what they've learned from the giants, as well as the best of the new functionality made available to them via blockchains.

Other modern platform players

This category includes companies like Craigslist, Facebook, LinkedIn, Medium, NextDoor, Upwork, eBay, and Getty Images. Established platforms could use blockchain features to add new value to their existing business, leveraging their positions in the market and the strength of their communities to solidify their dominance and move into new areas that only blockchains make possible.

However, they will also get pressure from new competitors. Threats could come from companies that use blockchains to solve a key pain point or provide a significant upgrade in value for a large and highly networked community. They could conceivably leverage a rapid early foothold to springboard into related communities and gain network effects. Additional pressure could come from scandals that motivate consumers to move en masse to relatively young alternatives (if they have sufficiently evolved), jump-starting network effects.

 Implications: A New Balance of Power

DEATH BY BLOCKCHAINS?

As blockchain development gathers steam, both insiders and casual observers have declared the death of the middleman. Purists even project a death knell for entire systems of government and finance. Venture capitalist and billionaire Tim Draper asserts "Blockchain is much bigger than the internet. It has the potential to transform industries that have historically been government regulated because they are so big. For example, banking, real estate, insurance, venture capital, health care, and government itself can all be completely transformed by blockchain."[65]

It's provocative thinking, and pushes our understanding of what's possible. And it is answered by blockchain entrepreneurs who are developing true peer-to-peer, govern-by-crowd technology that can facilitate connection and exchange through a network without a middleman at all. From music to financial exchanges to advertising, there are dozens of industries that will be pushed by these extreme peer-to-peer models.

THE MIDDLEMAN IS DEAD. LONG LIVE THE MIDDLEMAN!

But this picture is likely to reflect the spirit rather than the actuality of our world, at least for quite a while. Certain industries and types of customers will flow more easily into these new models. But others will move very, very slowly—and the total abolishment of the middleman goes contrary to behavior we've exhibited for centuries.

The value of a good or service is not intrinsic. It's driven by whether it's available when needed, where needed, and how difficult it is to attain—and if something goes wrong, how easy it is to fix. This is the role of the middleman: to create value by getting goods and services from low-value settings to high-value settings. They save us time. They save us effort. They provide essential services to make our experience of the product or service easier, start to finish. In 1995, at the dawn of the internet, Bill Gates wrote *The Road Ahead,* envisioning a friction-free economy, cleared of middlemen.[66] And certainly, the internet unleashed a tsunami of disintermediation. But something else also happened.

WE'VE WELCOMED NEW MIDDLEMEN INTO OUR LIVES

Entire new services have sprung up to curate products or save us time. Stitch Fix, with a market cap of over $2 billion, selects clothes for us and delivers them to our home. DoorDash and Instacart pick up takeout from restaurants or food from the grocery store, and bring it to our doorstep. Plated delivers recipes from top chefs with just the right ingredients so our family can try a new home-cooked meal without any research.

Now, more than ever, we want to get more out of our limited time. Many consumers have demonstrated that they are willing to pay extra to have others navigate through a complex and noisy world on our behalf.

THE HINGE IS VALUE

These new categories of middlemen each offer a fresh value proposition, finely tuned to the mindset and desires of today's customers. These next-gen middlemen are laser-focused on getting inside the head of their customer so their service can command a (sometimes quite high) premium.

These new categories of middlemen each offer a fresh value proposition, finely tuned to the mindset and desires of today's customers.

Blockchains' capability to replace many traditional middleman functions with code means that many of these models may eventually be under attack (and most businesses play at least some middleman role). These businesses will need to focus relentlessly on creating perceived value for customers. Your particular flavor of disruption will depend on what kind of middleman you are. But regardless, the magnitude will be measured by the gap between what your customers understand your cost to be, and their perception of the value you provide. It is in these margins that the battles for the unblocked customer will rage.

CUSTOMERS DON'T UNDERSTAND WHAT THEY CAN'T SEE

Today, customers may not understand the full hard tolls and soft costs hidden away among layers of middlemen. Today, customers may not have a way to truly gauge your value. But as disruptors provide alternatives that cut cost and demonstrate more value, the gap will be revealed. Just like we saw as the internet matured, incumbents will fall that we didn't think possible. Buy a house without title insurance? Send money to a stranger without a financial institution in between? These may be some of the first. By their very nature, blockchains were designed to shake the foundations of the most concentrated centers of power in our world today. This is where the gap tends to be largest, and this is where it will begin, but not where it will stop.

The disruption of your business will be in proportion to the gap between what your customers understand your cost to be, and their perception of the value you provide.

At Some Point, the Unblocked Customer Will Question Your Worth

There are different kinds of middlemen serving different kinds of customers, and so this must be interpreted in different ways depending on your particular business. But as blasts of disruption pock the B2B and B2C landscape, it will trigger a shift in customer mindset. As they are trained to expect a new way of business, customers will exert pressure, over time, that will metamorphose the role of a middleman.

We have seen the pervasiveness of this kind of pressure before in a movement coined the "consumerization of IT." Trained by the slick and easy-to-use interfaces they were using in their personal lives, businesspeople started to expect the same standards in the workplace. While we are still midway through this transition, business software interfaces have gradually started to look more like consumer interfaces. And as millennials (who have been exposed since birth to excellent digital design) have increasingly dominated in the workforce, it has amplified this pressure. A client, the CIO of a midsize technology company, laughed as he told me a story about a recent hire. After a day of onboarding, in which the new employee got her first glance at the HR and business software she would use in her work, she knocked on my client's door. "With all due respect, sir," she began, "WTF?" Imagine what a baby born today, who may very well never use a bank, will demand of her middlemen when she enters the workforce in 20 years.

> At some point in the coming years, your customers may start to question whether they really need you. For anyone that has dated, you know that moment can be the beginning of the end.

Businesses will no longer be able to passively extract value for the privilege of sitting in the middle of a transaction. Instead, they will need to work harder to actively contribute value to all parties—and proactively market that value.

VALUE IS NOT ONE-SIZE-FITS-ALL

Customers who have the resources to spend for curation and convenience may someday see an explosion of middlemen offering to eradicate every inconvenience, every undesirable task from their lives—for a premium. Blockchains may help these middlemen harvest savings from the system, but instead of passing them on to consumers, they could invest it in adding blockchain-driven services and protections that remove friction, enrich their offer, and help grow their markets. For example, imagine a TaskRabbit-like service that comes packaged with identity and reputation verification of your service provider, as well as micro-insurance for all parties. Or a large retailer that could give you both one-click ordering and assurance that your products are not counterfeit.

For customers with fewer resources, the value of saving money may be paramount. We will see a full-frontal attack on models that have layers of tolls levied simply to pass a transaction through. One of the most extreme examples of this is the international money transfer. To send a payment cross-border, a customer must find and hire a transmitter to handle the transfer, which would have contacts with financial institutions in both the transmitting and recipient countries. Further complicating the process, these banks often have their own intermediaries. There are typically at least four banks involved, and potentially others just confirming the transfer. They communicate with each other through a service called SWIFT. The process can take a week and each of the institutions involved charges its own fees. The World Bank tracks a global average of these fees—and it's over 7%.[67]

In some regions it's even higher. An immigrant sending money to family in Africa will work over nine days out of every hundred, just to pay these fees. Meanwhile, the financial institutions that are digitally moving this transaction do so at a compute cost that is roughly equivalent to sending an email. In contrast, the blockchain can send bitcoin across the world within minutes and for nominal cost. But the user experience of buying, sending, and safeguarding bitcoin is still poor. Many users, even those without great resources, are likely to pay a little more for services that facilitate this in a way they value.

THE SHARING ECONOMY, EVERYWHERE

We've seen the creation of new value almost out of thin air with the advent of the sharing economy. And now, blockchains have the capability to overcome obstacles that have held back the sharing economy from achieving wholesale transformation of the way we purchase goods and services. What we saw with rides and rooms could jump to drones and drills, art and umbrellas.

To safely share a hard good between strangers, it would need to be documented, proven authentic, valued, located, and even insured. With blockchains, an item, say a power drill (of which there are some 80 million sitting in garages and sheds), could theoretically be registered upon purchase from the manufacturer, and with microchips, tracked through its entire lifecycle. Sensors could assess its condition and need for maintenance, and a value could be assigned to it that reflects the shape it's in. The person who bought it could rent it out to others, with a micro-insurance policy protecting both parties involved. This model could be applied to most of our physical goods. And blockchain entrepreneurs like Australian ShareRing, German Fainin, and United States–based Origin, among others, are all working to enable this future.

What happens to Black & Decker when a single drill can be used by everyone on your block, and what should Black & Decker do about it?

We can get some pre-blockchain inspiration from the auto manufacturing industry. There is a great crisis afoot for these companies: people aren't buying cars like they used to. Millennials, especially, value access over ownership. A single car, when shared through a service like Zipcar or divided into single-ride portions like Uber, can serve a dozen people a day, and many urban areas offer shared scooters and bikes. Automotive brands, facing a threat to their core business model, have been racing to offer subscription services of their own or wrap value-added services into a purchase. You can now subscribe monthly from brands ranging from Ford to BMW. You get a complete hassle-free bundle: a car, insurance, maintenance, and even swaps so you can have an SUV for a family road trip, or a convertible for a day at the beach. This addition of new services—services that are well tuned to customer needs—can completely change a consumer's perception of value.

WE MAY END UP SOMEWHERE IN THE MIDDLE

The models that become sustainable long term—those that strike the unblocked customer as just the right balance of value and cost—may be those that land somewhere in the middle. At one extreme, you can buy a car via a traditional model, with layers of baked-in costs from every party who sourced the materials, created the components, assembled them, got the finished car to the dealer, or was involved in selling and financing it. At another, you could participate in a completely decentralized car ride service in which drivers and riders deal directly with each other (without Uber or Lyft extracting fees for sitting in the middle) and payments are made without a financial intermediary of any kind. Especially over the next decade as user experience moves through its current awkward adolescence, many customers will value the handholding and services offered by a middleman, and willingly pay a price for it—just less than before.

Ethereum cofounder and blockchain luminary Vitalik Buterin has emphasized that it's not that the intermediary will be removed, but that the role will change. "I recommend crypto discourse changes emphasis from 'eliminating the middlemen' to some combination of 'shackling the middlemen' and 'making the market for middlemen more competitive,'" he said.[68]

The question then becomes: how can you become a middleman with a *sustainable* competitive advantage, even as the world shifts around you?

THE NEXT-GEN MIDDLEMAN

Models for more evolved middlemen are connected by the same principle: a shift to a more collaborative relationship between business and customer. Shared economy analysts and entrepreneurs have called this idea "platform cooperativism"; that is, all users qualify as both contributors and shareholders of the platforms to which they contribute. In the extreme case—and blockchains can facilitate this—there is no intermediary operator and the value produced is distributed equally among all who have contributed. But across many industries and regions, and until truly decentralized models have matured, we will see the emergence of an evolved, next gen-middleman—one who is more dialed into what their customer needs and desires, and proactively provides greatly treasured value to these customers.

Evolved middlemen models are connected by the same principle: a shift to a more collaborative relationship between business and customer.

The Importance of Clear Value

As this blockchain-driven shift begins to destabilize markets, businesses must not only find new forms of value, but also put more focus on educating customers on the value they provide, whether it is blockchain-driven or not. Across the business, from marketing to customer service to digital experience, professionals will need to be more attuned to how they are communicating their company's value to customers.

Businesses must not only find new forms of value, but also put more focus on educating customers on the value they provide.

This impact could be felt no matter the business or customer type. Internet retailers may need to prove they can prevent counterfeit items from entering their ecosystem. Social media players may need to show they can protect your data. Advertising networks may need to demonstrate they can prevent fraud. Travel intermediaries may need to prove they are more effective distribution channels than hotels and airlines could be on their own.

THE VALUE OF AN ECOSYSTEM

Business in the blockchain future is made more valuable through partnership. The blockchain facilitates businesses working together and creating or exchanging value among them. Value can be found in understanding not only how your business can deliver to the needs and desires of a customer, but also how you can nurture an ecosystem that together can provide more value to these customers. As in the non-blockchain automotive example described earlier, a bundling of services, for example, can provide a differentiated and highly valued offering.

Visionary and engaging, Jessica Groopman is an industry analyst and founding partner at research firm Kaleido Insights. With a perspective informed by an earlier career in academic anthropological fieldwork, she specializes at the intersection of consumer-side IoT, AI, and blockchains, and has been named one of the most influential thought leaders in IoT. We recently sat down together to compare perspectives on the evolution of the space.

"I've been thinking a lot about how blockchains could change the shape of the entire customer journey," Jessica said. "It's no longer linear—they could impact the whole experience of selecting, buying, and owning a product. Ecosystem-based business models are hard to do today, because there aren't shared ways of processing an entire experience. But with a blockchain and IoT technology, a washing machine, for example, could send out the notification that it has broken, triggering smart contracts that automatically arrange for services like support, repair, insurance, and even the reconciliation of payments. There could even be decentralized ways of rating product experiences, and activating loyalty and rewards." But, she said, in a decentralized world, "someone will still need to be responsible if something goes wrong."

PUT A SPOTLIGHT ON HIDDEN VALUE

There are many forms of value that businesses have not traditionally emphasized in their communication to customers. As decentralized alternatives enter the market, incumbents (at least those that aren't ready to change their model) will need to work harder to articulate the uniquely differentiated value they provide. Helping a customer understand how they benefit from the investments a business has made, when messaged appropriately, can help the unblocked customer assign more value to a middleman.

One key is to look for those forms of value that are, at least in the early stages of this revolution, best delivered by a centralized organization versus a decentralized network of users. Decentralized systems use rule-based governance and often voting to make decisions. There is a lot of work to be done in developing decentralized governance, and we will learn a lot about what is most effective in the years to come. But until there are great advancements in this practice, some initiatives will continue to be challenging to fund and manage by crowd. These could include:

User experience
> Good digital products require exceptional design and user experience, which is expensive and difficult to do right, at least at the level required to encourage mass adoption.

Regulatory compliance

Lawyers and lobbies are expensive and often require centralized effort that will likely be difficult for most decentralized entities, at least until they become collectively more powerful.

Customer service

Some forms of crowd customer service work (like answering support questions), while some are much better when centralized (handling administrative-level issues).

Customer journey

We are a long way from governance models that can effectively manage end-to-end customer experience without a clear line of responsibility.

The value of these services can feel esoteric to customers. Marketing needs to find a way to communicate differently to help customers understand the value they are getting from centralized investments like these. But marketing can only bring visibility to value that exists within; delivering to the unblocked customer's expectations will require the coordinated effort of an entire organization.

 Cautions and Considerations

As customers become more sophisticated at scrutinizing value, new threats and opportunities arise. While some of these cautions and considerations are very future-focused, they are meant to provoke your thinking about what could come. This is by no means an exhaustive list, but simply additional food for thought as you prepare for this new paradigm. We can expect that these will change as the space evolves.

CAUTIONS

Sharing economy chokes your business model

Understand your risk by carefully evaluating what kind of models, once widely adopted, could impact your business. Study not only these models and the players who are launching companies that embody them, but also how customers like yours are responding. Evaluate what it would be like if you were to get in front of potential competitors by introducing your own service, and run the analysis to understand how it would impact your business.

Competitors give middlemen the boot before you do

If a competitor were to aggressively adopt new models in their partner and supplier ecosystem, it could significantly reduce their friction and cost structure. They may pass these savings on to customers, undercutting your prices, or invest them in new services that differentiate their offering. Map your ecosystem to identify the middlemen whose elimination would most impact your business (these are the ones with high costs + high potential for blockchain-driven replacement). Use this exercise to focus your study of the market. As viable options emerge, be proactive about studying the cost and benefit of moving to a new model, and experiment with pilots for applied learning.

Executives don't think they have responsibility for the customer

In the best organizations, every executive knows they have a role in how customers measure your value. But most organizations have varying levels of alignment around this customer-centric idea. In a blockchain world, divisions such as product, engineering, supply chain, service, and marketing will need to work together more than ever to find ways to bring customers more value. And the drumbeat needs to begin from the top.

CONSIDERATIONS

Get closer to what customers value

It's hard to imagine a book that offers advice about customers that doesn't advise you to get closer to them. The twist here is to get a better understanding of what customers truly, deeply value and what they don't. And this applies not only to what you provide, but also what happens upstream and downstream of your interaction with them. Why are they coming to you today? What alternatives are they passing up? What do they do with your product once they get home? How does it fail, and when does it work? What services do they use that could be complementary to what you provide? What skill sets do they develop by using your product or service that they could monetize if they had a platform? Exploring questions like these can help trigger ideas to bring your customers more value—or to remove the cost associated with something they don't.

Start marketing the value of what you are already providing

Start now to more clearly demonstrate the value of what you are already providing to your customers. Use research to better understand how they perceive value that you may not be fully aware of, and how they speak to it. Find appropriate ways to market this, and work harder across all customer touchpoints to prove the value of the relationship you already have, and develop feedback loops to tap into any shifts as they happen.

Line up a network of like-minded partners

Value can be found outside the walls of your organization. Well-managed collaborations can return more than the sum of their parts. Start by finding potential partners whose customers intersect with yours—those who share the belief that collaboration could pave a better path in a business process. Figure out which are aligned with you in a mission to bring more value to customers. Focus on key questions that you both face, and work together to research the blockchain landscape.

Seek a lower-friction place to learn

If you map your ecosystem of middlemen as described in the "Cautions" section, you'll have a sense of where to start cutting costs. Find one area, even if it is small, to start and use that as a launchpad for gaining knowledge, while building a case for impact. For example, one area that could offer a strong business case for change is your advertising budget. Blockchains offer intriguing potential to fight ad fraud, from click farms to bots (projected to reach $19 billion in 2018).[69] Start by quantifying your costs today so you can assess if it makes sense to focus resources on getting involved early with consortiums and the teams building startups in this space, and exploring pilots.

Examples

Talented and well-funded teams are attacking intermediaries across every industry. I could fill a whole book with stories of teams that are building alternatives to today's middlemen, but here's a glimpse of just some of the entrepreneurs and pioneers that are working to bring this dimension of the decentralized future to the world. Time will tell if they will work out in the long run, but right now, here are a few projects chosen to whet your appetite for what's to come.

DECENT: AFFORDABLE HEALTH INSURANCE FOR ALL

I first met Nick Soman at a health care blockchain event in early 2018. He told me, with clear enthusiasm, that he was working on something stealth—and important. We stayed connected, and a few months later I learned just how important it was. Nick is taking on the mission to do nothing short of making health care affordable, for all.

Nick sat down with me to explain the core problem his company, Decent (a clever play on words), seeks to fix. Today, health insurance companies can keep up to 20 cents out of every dollar earned from premiums for administrative costs and profit. "This means," said Nick, "as long as they can pass costs on to members, these companies actually make more money when costs go up. Hospitals are paid to do things *to* patients, not *for* them." Nick grew up in a home in which this topic was frequent dinner table conversation. His father, who became the Chief Medical Executive of an award-winning, 600,000-member health cooperative after decades as a practicing doctor, would say, "If future anthropologists study the US health care system, they'll conclude that its purpose was to create reimbursable events."

Nick and his team believe that middlemen with misaligned incentives are at the heart of the problem, and see in blockchains a path to fix this and deliver more value to patients. "Decent will align our incentives around quality affordable care," he said. "Businesses supporting a patient's care will only be healthy when patients are. The system will reward choices that lead to better health. We'll all have a financial stake in our own health, and perhaps in the system itself."

Nick's vision goes far beyond his company. While Decent will build what is essentially a modern health care co-op, they also want to make the protocol open and decentralized, so others can more easily build health care co-ops that also remove unnecessary middlemen, boost transparency, and reduce waste.

This is a big vision, but the team is thoughtful about how to drive transformation in this complicated industry. They will use a phased approach to build increasing patient value over time. They plan to start by serving focused populations in a specific region, and using blockchains on the backend. Once they have proven the long-term cost savings and better value that can come from focusing the technology on the task of cutting waste and fraud, they'll layer on more functionality and regional reach. "Blockchains are uniquely suited to make things better, faster, and cheaper," said Nick. "But, we are a health care company that happens to use blockchain, and it is not the only tool in our arsenal. We are fixated on anything and everything that delivers more value to patients."[70]

OPEN GARDEN: DISINTERMEDIATING THE INTERNET SERVICE PROVIDER

The team at Open Garden is building a product that could make it possible for anybody with a mobile phone to become their own internet service provider (ISP). Cellular and data plans charge one rate, regardless of usage—and in the US, an average of 70-80% of that goes unused. Open Garden is part of a broader movement for "peer-to-peer mesh networking," using connected devices to deliver service instead of a centralized provider like AT&T or Verizon.

Users who sign up on Open Garden will be able to buy or sell service from each other. They decide when they want to share capacity, how much, and with whom. The more participants, the higher the availability and the lower the cost—and this cost is potentially much, much lower than what customers pay today. Transactions happen between participants using Open Garden's OG token. Sellers earn OG, and buyers pay OG. The company is focused on building a service strong enough to connect the "next five billion mobile devices" through this people-powered internet.

Backed by investors that include Verizon's own venture arm, the company has gained significant experience with peer-to-peer mesh networking through a free, non-blockchain messaging service that debuted in 2014, called FireChat. This service, used in pro-democracy protests in Taiwan and Hong Kong, the Bersih anti-corruption movement in Malaysia, and historical elections in Venezuela and the Republic of the Congo, works by connecting devices stepping-stone–style into a rich fabric that enables broad coverage. And, unlike mobile and internet networks that break down with more users, the more people in a mesh network, the better it works. Micha Benoliel, the creator of FireChat and founder of Open Garden, explains, "a swarm of smartphones can build a real networking infrastructure—decentralized, resilient, and local."

LANTMÄTERIET: STREAMLINING LAND REGISTRY

The Swedish land registry authority, Lantmäteriet, has, with a diverse team of partners, been testing land registry on a private blockchain. Around the world, land titling systems are susceptible not only to forgery and clerical error, but also to large fees levied by middlemen such as title insurers, who have little competition in many markets (in the US the industry has attracted much criticism for high prices and scams). In many emerging economies, land titles aren't even possible. At Lantmäteriet, which is relatively advanced—the process is already paperless and highly digitized—it can take months from the signing of a contract to register the sale.

In June of 2018, Lantmäteriet completed the third phase of its experiment. With a group of participating banks, businesses, and startups, they were able to demonstrate the creation of smart contracts that automated transactions on a blockchain, enabling buyers and sellers to digitally sign a bill of sale, with signatures verified automatically instead of at an agent's office. When a land title changes hands, it would be verified via the blockchain, and recorded again. It's still a long way until a blockchain-driven registry is widely available in Sweden, but estimates put taxpayers' potential savings at over $100 million a year.[71]

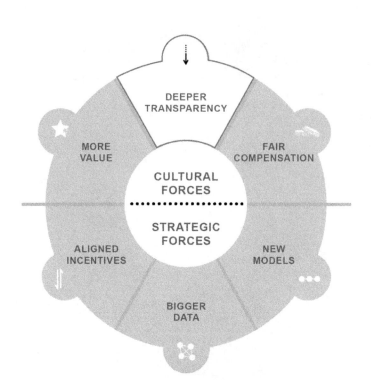

7

DEEPER TRANSPARENCY

The currency of the new economy is trust.

—RACHEL BOTSMAN

Summary

Leaders will actively leverage blockchain-driven transparency to demonstrate adherence to corporate values and as a marketing tool. This will set new standards for transparency—and ultimately an expectation for it.

Blockchain technology has the potential to immutably track and make transparent many parts of a business. Leaders will actively leverage this functionality to demonstrate that they stand by their values and that their products are verifiable and compliant.

This will set new standards for transparency—and ultimately an expectation for it, creating pressure for other businesses to follow along. Customers' definition of quality will expand beyond the immediate characteristics of the good consumed or the service rendered to include a judgment on its creator, provenance, and journey into their hands.

Leaders will carefully craft and actively market their transparency story. While not all consumers will choose to inform their brand and buying decisions with this new information, others will increasingly demand it. Over time it could build to become a force, and businesses that don't offer transparency would ultimately be punished in the market.

 **The Setting**

SEEKING ASSURANCE IN A COMPLEX WORLD

We are asking tough questions of our brands. We want to know where our goods come from, what they are made of, and who made them. We increasingly expect the companies we buy from to have clarity and control of everything from ingredients to production practices. We are increasingly vigilant about choosing the "best" products: researching, comparing, and considering relentlessly, whether for a new car or a bottle of shampoo. More than anything, we are demanding transparency.

> *Customers are asking tough questions of their brands: more than anything, they are demanding transparency.*

Historically, a company could control brand image with marketing. Customers had limited access to information, and to each other, beyond school, work, religious community, and friend and family networks. Businesses invested in spin over the difficult work of transparency. But that all changed with the internet. Access to online information mushroomed. Social networks multiplied. Customers got smarter, and more connected. Suddenly, the discovery of child labor or a waste management disaster tucked deep within a supply chain could plunge stock and trigger consumer revolt—overnight.

CONSUMERS EXPECT MORE

Research firm Hartman Group has been tracking consumer attitudes and behaviors surrounding sustainability and transparency in the US since the 1990s. In a recent study, they found that consumers view sustainability more holistically than ever before, and that openness and honesty are becoming the currency of trust. More consumers seek out information about sustainability than in the past, and labor issues and environmental contamination have become more salient issues. Consumers also want to see corporate responsibility efforts that indicate an authentic commitment to ethical action.

> *Openness and honesty are becoming the currency of trust.*

The study found that sustainability-related concerns impacted the values, attitudes, and actions of nearly 90% of adult consumers. At the shelf level, transparency increases a product's chances of being selected over an otherwise identical product.[72] Research firm Nielsen found that 66% of consumers (and 73% of millennials) say they will pay more for sustainable brands.[73] Consumers are demanding more traceability from the food industry in particular. Fifty-four percent want as much information as possible on the label, and nearly 40% want country of origin, allergen alerts, and GMOs all identified on the label.[74]

This all points to the idea of "quality" evolving to be more expansive than just the immediate characteristics of the good consumed or the service rendered. Customers want to know what's "inside" in every sense of the word—not just the product ingredients and packaging, but the supply chain ethics and sustainability and corporate responsibility agenda of the company that made it.

SUSTAINABILITY AND RESPONSIBILITY: THE NEW CORPORATE NORM

The corporation is responding. They are addressing these heightened expectations by bringing *corporate social responsibility* (CSR) initiatives into the C-suite. Research from the Boston College Center for Corporate Citizenship showed that the number of companies directing corporate citizenship from the C-Suite has increased nearly 75% compared to five years ago.[75]

Corporate responsibility (CR) reporting has also become standard practice for large and mid-cap companies around the world. The KPMG Survey of Corporate Responsibility found that three quarters of companies issue CR reports. And this is true across industries—60% of industry sectors showed a healthy rate of reporting. The vast majority (78%) of the world's top companies are also including CR information in their annual financial reports, while 67% are conducting third-party assurance and audits of their CR data.[76]

EVERYONE IS A STAKEHOLDER

The underlying theme of all this attention is that companies are starting to understand that nearly everyone they come in contact with considers themselves a stakeholder. Not only does each customer get a vote with their wallet every time they choose one brand over another, but also the actions of a company can impact a population—and the population is starting to understand this.

Investors, employees, partners, NGO activist organizations, and even governments are asking for more information about what is really happening to source, make, and distribute products.

Investors, employees, partners, NGO activist organizations, and even govern-ments are asking for more information about what is really happening to source, make, and distribute products. A survey conducted by Ernst & Young and Green-Biz Group found that while customers were the stakeholder group driving most companies' sustainability efforts (37%), employees (22%), shareholders (15%), policymakers, and NGOs (each at 7%) were also key influencers.[77]

Many experts believe that more regulation is imminent. KPMG reported it as a clear and recurrent theme in their research as governments and stock exchanges around the world—from Latin America to Japan, the US and the EU, to India and Taiwan—are bringing in new layers of regulation for environmental, social, and governance disclosure. Voluntary guidelines are transitioning into mandatory reporting requirements in many parts of the world.

THE FOCUS ON SUSTAINABILITY IS HERE TO STAY

The Global Reporting Initiative published a forward-looking paper forecasting the environment in 2025. It spoke of a future in which companies will be held more accountable than ever before, and business decision makers will take sus-tainability issues into account more profoundly.It also predicted that stakeholders will have more access to data, which will require organizations to report and respond more in real time instead of annually, aiding in better sustainability-supporting business decisions.[78]

A BUSINESS CASE FOR URGENCY

But the case for transparency goes far beyond external pressure. Understanding what is really happening in the supply chain is simply smart business. In today's increasingly dispersed, diverse, and global supply chains, it is much easier for things to go wrong. Even small problems deep in the supply chain—an incorrect material used by a supplier's supplier—can become massive after that material has been molded, welded, and rolled down the assembly line as a finished prod-uct. As discussed earlier, human rights and environmental issues across a com-pany's vast ecosystems of thousands of suppliers and partners can be immensely costly when discovered.

Understanding what is really happening in the supply chain is simply smart business.

We saw how consumer demands have contributed to companies becoming more purpose-driven and sustainable. Now companies are realizing they need to demand the same high standards of their suppliers. They will be using their power to increase demands for transparency and hold suppliers accountable more than ever in the coming years.

Additional danger comes from the infiltration of fraudulent or contaminated ingredients in the supply chain. A recent study by Robert Scharff, a scientist with the Ohio Agricultural Research and Development Center, estimates the annual cost of foodborne illness in the United States to exceed $93 billion.[79] Former associate commissioner for foods at the US Food and Drug Administration David Acheson explains, "Thirty years ago if you had a little problem, you were not going to get discovered. Now the chances of getting caught are significant, and it can be the end of your company."[80] Scandals have involved everything from melamine in milk to horse meat in hamburgers. The direct costs of a food recall average $10 million,[81] and an estimated 60% of companies in the industry have been affected by recalls.[82]

Within the health sector, pharmaceuticals stand out as particularly prone to corruption, in every region of the world. The World Health Organization estimates that 1 in 10 medical products in low- and middle-income countries is substandard or falsified. From cancer treatment to contraception, fakes extend well beyond high-value meds or well-known brands.[83] The impact is vast, and hard to quantify. But studies often reveal chilling examples, such as the over 100,000 annual malaria deaths that are estimated to have resulted from falsified antimalarials in sub-Saharan Africa alone.[84]

TRANSPARENCY AFFECTS HOW OUR BRAIN PERCEIVES A BRAND

True transparency can transform a relationship tarnished by suspicion. It reduces fear of the unknown, and creates a platform for building trust. In one study in which all organizations used the same transparent messaging in response to a crisis, participants judged the companies that had a reputation for transparency as more trustworthy than those that seemed less transparent.[85] Charlie Arnot, the CEO of The Center for Food Integrity, talks about the results of the nonprofit's recent research: "Transparency in an organization's practices count most toward building trust. That's because practices are a demonstration of values in action, and our research shows shared values are the foundation for building trust."[86]

As businesses increase transparency, they will also increase customer trust.

Transparency in an organization's practices count most toward building trust.

—CHARLIE ARNOT, CEO, THE CENTER FOR FOOD INTEGRITY

Trust in Crisis

Customers are increasingly wary of the ambiguity of certifications like organic, fair trade, and local. They are taking time to do their research; they are thinking hard about these purchase decisions; they're spending more of their hard-earned income on these "higher quality" products. But they are not sure the claims are always real. They may feel better, but is all this extra work really keeping pesticides off their child's dinner plate? They've seen companies greenwash marketing, and it's increased their skepticism. The customer has become wiser: they want tangible transparency, for companies to prove they are doing what they claim they are, and improvement in areas that have real impact.

Even nonprofits are plagued by concerns over transparency. Donors are concerned that their dollars will be misappropriated, and these fears are stoked by more and more scandalous headlines each year. Executives for the Wounded Warrior Project were found to be holding lavish parties and staying in $500-a-night hotels (CBS News found that only 60% of the organization's funding went to serving vets, while organizations with comparable missions were over 90%).[87] The now-defunct Cancer Fund of America was found to have misused their $187 million in donations on items such as luxury cars, Caribbean cruises, and trips to Disneyland.

For 18 years, marketing firm Edelman has published an annual "Trust Barometer" study. The 2018 study, covering over 30,000 respondents across 28 markets, shows global trust in crisis. Twenty of the 28 markets surveyed demonstrated "deep distrust." The trust decline in the US was the steepest ever measured, with Edelman calling it a "trust crash."[88]

FAKE NEWS FUELS SKEPTICISM

Fake news is being used as a weapon. It was used to influence the 2016 US presidential race. It has disrupted elections in South Africa. Singapore is working on laws designed to fight fake news. And Germany has already passed a law that fines social media companies for failing to delete fake news. The Edelman Trust Barometer found that nearly 60% globally felt they "are not sure what is true and what is not" in the news.[89]

MIT researchers recently published the most comprehensive study of fake news ever conducted. The team analyzed data on every major contested news story since Twitter's launch—126,000 stories, tweeted by 3 million users, over more than 10 years—and found that the spread of truth simply cannot compete with the spread of hoax. By every metric, falsehoods dominate truth on Twitter. A false story reaches 1,500 people six times quicker than a true story does. And false stories outperform on every subject—including business, science, technology, and entertainment.[90] The study immediately prompted alarm in the social science community, with a group of 16 political scientists and legal scholars calling for a "redesign of our information ecosystem" in an essay published in *Science*.[91]

Cybersecurity firm Trend Micro did a pricing analysis of fake news campaigns. They learned it would cost only about $55,000 to conduct a trolling campaign to discredit a journalist, or $200,000 to whip up enough frenzy to draw a crowd into the streets to protest against a made-up offense.[92] This digitally driven erosion of information quality, and the ease with which malicious actors can hijack citizens' perspectives, will only further stoke the battle cry for transparency.

Paradoxically, we can expect the "quality" of the deceit to increase as AI and machine learning create even more convincing fakes. Researchers at the University of Washington recently took an audio track of a speech by former President Obama and created a chilling fake video of him giving the speech "on camera."[93] Realistic audiovisual fakes will be even more powerfully deceptive than the static form of fake news deployed today.

THE ELUSIVE NATURE OF TRUE TRANSPARENCY

Clearly, stakeholders—from businesses to governments to entire populations—desire transparency. But it is elusive. What's really happening in a supply chain is hidden in an ungainly maze of siloed systems and cross-border handoffs. We don't know what part of our news is real, and what is fake. We can't be sure if the food in our pantry is genuine.

No one can fix what they can't see. But what if we could finally, truly, see?

What Blockchains Make Possible

ALL-SEEING MEETS THE EVER-KNOWING

At times, the vision for this raw, unpolished technology can look almost beauti-ful, even elegant. This is one of those times, especially when IoT and blockchain technology are working together. It becomes possible to "see" hundreds of thou-sands of things pulsing through a tangled supply-chain maze. But this "seeing" surpasses human capability. Aided by the many smart sensors available today, we could understand so much nuance about what a thing has gone through to get to us. And with blockchains we can trust that what has been recorded has not been altered, even if many different parties have touched it on its way. In this vision of the future, we could even go back and see the details of a journey that happened many years ago.

This starts by giving each piece, component, or thing that we care about (whether tangible or intangible) a unique identifier. This identity can be tracked through its entire lifetime, like a bright star can be, night after night. The block-chain can "watch" and record all the conditions and interactions this thing goes through. This results in one view of truth, shared across an entire business network.

If the thing is a tangible asset, it may move from a mine through factories and ultimately to a store, jumping borders, traveling over buildings, and under bridges—all along the way changing form and function. Strategically placed sen-sors, recording their data to the blockchain, can ensure we have a record of so many dimensions of each step of the journey: temperature, humidity, time, speed, velocity, altitude, tilt, proximity, pressure, leaks, sound, light, vibration, air quality, and electricity use, to name a few. Or it could be an intangible thing: a watt of energy captured by a solar panel, fed into a network and then sent to where it is most needed, or an image perfected by its creator and then launched into the digital world, always retaining a clear trail of ownership.

CODING FOR TRUST

Regardless, the record is secure. Permanent, tamper-proof, it is shared by a com-munity and owned by no one. From origin to ultimate destination (and even beyond) it is traceable. Anyone in the community can monitor the activities and be sure the data on a blockchain has not been forged. Because it is based on mathematics and cryptography, we don't have to trust in another party, or rely on central institutions to supervise or direct our relationships. Instead, the trust is coded in—and inviolable.

This could ensure sensitive pharmaceuticals are kept at the right temperature. Verify the provenance of intellectual property. Identify whether fish came from a sustainable source. Find the point at which components "disappeared." Verify the historical storage of wine.

TRACKING THE INTANGIBLES: CAN BLOCKCHAINS KILL FAKE NEWS?

The same features used to track assets are the focus of startups looking to combat fake news. Many of their approaches center on proven validation. There are two sides of validation: the contributor's identity, and the content's authenticity.

Let's first look at contributor identity. There are many emerging companies that are seeking to become a trusted third-party verifier and protector of identity. The user shares enough with the third party so that they can verify who they say they are. This verified identity is safely stored (in anonymous, encrypted form) using a blockchain. Users could then approve specific applications, such as a social media platform, to access the stored identity and verify their credentials (again, staying anonymous to the social media platform). In this way, only "real" people with verified identities could get on the platform. Users could have confidence that they were not interacting with fake accounts (in 2017, Facebook revealed that they have up to 270 million fake and duplicate accounts).

Other companies are tackling the content challenge first. Approaches include encrypting stories on the blockchain so they are more difficult to modify, verifying the authenticity of user-generated content, or developing economic incentives and a transparent, auditable network to hold curators and the community accountable for the integrity of content.

Both can use lifetime reputation of an identity or a source to further improve their filters. Blockchain entrepreneurs also tie rewards to measures of quality.

This may be just the beginning of an arms race against fake news. There is a vast network of resources focused on generating and profiting from fake news today—and the rest of us haven't had much of an arsenal to use in the battle. Blockchains could make fake news more difficult to perpetuate, and less profitable. However, as AI, machine learning, and bots become more sophisticated, this will likely prove to be a long-term war.

ONE FEATURE SET DRIVES VALUE FOR ALL

Like a clever, multifunction multitool, the same blockchain could serve the needs of many stakeholders. One day, a supply chain executive could use a blockchain to optimize shipping routes and cut costs . . . which also cuts carbon emissions, pleasing environmental groups. Another application built on the same blockchain could give a consumer confidence that their dinner table was really built from sustainably harvested wood. And another could assure investors that the factory that built it does not employ children. Looked at from another perspective, the same underlying technology investment could drive savings for operations, assist compliance and legal departments in doing their job, and give marketing something real to talk about to drive consumer preference.

A STEP TOWARD A BETTER WORLD

Throughout human history, we've seen that people can be very talented at exploiting whatever system is in use. There is no doubt that bad actors will find ways to exploit these new systems as they carry more commerce than the experiments and pilots that are in place today, and become attractive targets. While blockchains may continue to be difficult to hack profitably, someone will find ways to work around their impenetrability—slipping minerals mined by a child among those "cleanly" mined, or tampering with sensors, for example. Sheila Warren of the World Economic Forum brings up another challenge: "In traditional tech we talk about 'garbage in, garbage out.' On the blockchain, it's 'garbage in, garbage forever.' And there are people who will try to game the system and put in garbage information. That's just a reality."[94] But blockchains are positioned to make it more difficult, and more costly, to cheat—especially at scale.

A thoughtful adoption of blockchains could fight fraud and corruption, reinforce a company's image, and enable open, reliable, and indelible reporting on sustainability and human rights commitments. While the work in this area is challenging and it will take a great evolution to get to prime time, there are pilots already happening around the globe. Blockchains may one day become the perfect tool for a company that seeks to generate financial, social, and environmental value—at scale.

Implications: When Authenticity Becomes More Than a Buzzword

*There have never been more opportunities for CEOs to demonstrate
leadership in addressing inequities and living up to social purpose.
Both consumers and their own employees are continuing to
push companies to respond.*

—JACK LESLIE, WEBER SHANDWICK CHAIRMAN,
2018 WORLD ECONOMIC FORUM MEETING

Blockchains for the Bold and the Brave

As our world becomes more digital, the urgency of trust moves to center stage. Renee James, the former president of Intel, has said, "The ability to know what's safe and good is going to become even more important to people in a world that's less physical."[95] But even for a single sliver of a business, end-to-end transparency will present technical and social challenges that are not for the faint of heart. This is because true transparency crosses organizational and national borders, often many times over. There are a lot of people involved, start to finish, and this is a great deal of change to broker. Even transparency of a digital asset, such as a piece of content on a social network, requires the correct placement of many pieces of the puzzle. A trusted third party may need to verify the identity of a contributor, sophisticated third-party AI engines may be used to analyze content veracity, and users need to be educated on their role in contributing to the quality of the network.

The Appeal of a Killer Combination

But industry after industry, persistent leaders are working to leverage blockchains to achieve breakthrough-caliber transparency. Irrespective of executives' personal belief in the importance of transparency, there are two business reasons for it: transparency can help optimize operations, and it can increase customer preference. The tantalizing promise of both cutting costs and generating new revenue is a killer proposition. It's already spurring blockchain interest, resourcing, experiments, and pilots among today's top brands, and will ultimately drive the ambitious level of innovation required to get real solutions into market.

The kind of transparency a consumer wants and that a purely numbers-driven supply chain executive needs has historically required investment in different processes and technologies. With blockchains, it is possible that many of these needs and desires could be met with the same investment (at least at the foundational level), much in the way a single investment of an email server and application is used for many diverse business purposes. For example, blockchain and IoT investments could both track the time it takes for a bag of minerals to get to a factory, and verify the point of origin as a mine with humane labor practices. While applications built on top of a blockchain may be tailored to specific users and needs, the core investment could be leveraged in flexible and creative ways. This means that businesses may find they can more easily gather support for coldly quantitative business cases, with investment that could later be extended to support sustainability, for example.

BUSINESS-FIRST VIEW: YET ANOTHER DIGITAL TRANSFORMATION MUST-HAVE?

As the technology matures and companies start to demonstrate ROI through pilots, blockchains may become an add-on to the existing digital transformation agenda. It fits right into the eternal quest to make operations more efficient and allow workers to accomplish more in a day's work. Those companies who are able to perform the extraordinary gymnastics required to adopt a blockchain across an ecosystem of suppliers and partners could introduce new speed and purity of execution to their operations.

No doubt, this requires massive investment, and it will be interesting to see who can act at the scale it will take to drive dominance. We may see less ambitious projects from smaller companies as well. These companies could leverage third-party services from blockchain-native companies, traditional technology vendors doubling down on blockchains, or blockchain development from existing partners (like UPS and FedEx). Regardless, with more and more companies making headlines each week with their blockchain pilots, it is only a matter of time before someone makes a breakthrough that drives real operational results.

SOCIETY-FIRST VIEW: WILL PIONEERS PUSH PROGRESS?

We've seen that businesses have strong incentives for proving products are made in an ethical manner, without exploiting workers or destroying the environment. And now true transparency—actual proof that sustainable, ethical, and responsible practices are being used in the production of goods—feels tantalizingly possible.

We will see a few pioneers in hypertransparency using blockchains to set a
new bar for what openness looks like.

We will see a few pioneers in hypertransparency using blockchains to set a new bar for what openness looks like. For years, marketing teams have made claims about social responsibility and product integrity, often with weak support. Whether or not the company delivered on the promises was really anyone's guess. As pioneers show that facts can be immutably tracked, and perhaps even made open to the public for verification, the unblocked customer could see that they can verify their coffee is indeed organic and fair trade. That a diamond was mined ethically. Or that their favorite social network is bot-free.

We can be sure that these leaders will do their part to educate customers on their unique value proposition and use their new level of openness as a marketing tool. While it's likely that customers won't know that a technology called blockchains made this possible, over time they will see the results of it and start to expect it from others. They not only may be able to click down on a claim to see it's true, but also could be exposed to new breadth of transparency. As more companies track and market different metrics, the average customer will become better educated on what, for example, sustainable harvesting or ethical labor practices actually mean. A customer who had thought only about "buying organic" might expand their perspective of quality to include other factors like these.

It's very, very early, but many well-known corporations are already experimenting. Starbucks is piloting "bean to cup" traceability, and Coca-Cola is working with the US State Department to evaluate using a blockchain to fight forced labor. Nestle SA, Unilever, and Tyson Foods are just some of the companies working with IBM on a project to explore how blockchains can improve food safety.

REFINING CUSTOMERS' TASTE FOR TRANSPARENCY

When leaders start marketing results, both flavors of transparency will shift what customers expect from a business. A more optimized supply chain can give customers lower prices and more consistently high quality. When a brand demonstrates verifiable labor practices, customers will start to question why others can't. Eventually, a new standard for transparency will emerge. In the same way consumers now expect to be able to place an order for just about anything from their phone, the unblocked customer of the future could expect to check up on a company's track record with ease.

This could put a huge, difficult burden of proof on brands not only to develop the capabilities for this kind of reporting, but also to continually prove their worth in a range of metrics. It may also embolden activists and NGOs to put pressure on businesses and governments to create new legislation or regulation. How many incumbent deaths in the next few decades will be driven by a lack of ability or willingness to open key metrics to the public?

A NEW SPIN ON SPIN?

It's possible that we may see a new marketing tone take hold. Already, we've seen that corporate responsibility initiatives without adequate transparency can be perceived as self-serving. In this future, companies may be even more sharply judged. It will be more difficult to selectively promote just the facts that support a brand's story when the ugly or missing facts are just a few clicks away. The marketer's penchant for spin may never go away, but marketing will need to move beyond blanket statements to speak more to veritable truth. Marketers could develop a style that authentically and appropriately frames "problem spots," and shows that their company is mobilizing to work on any problems that they have discovered.

This hard work opens up new potential in the relationship between a customer and a business. The openness and the difficult labor of recognizing and addressing problems (and reporting on that progress) could forge a new level of trust. Whereas the internet broke down many of the foundations of loyalty, a blockchain may be the critical element to build it back stronger than before.

> Whereas the internet broke down many of the foundations of loyalty, a blockchain may be the critical element to build it back stronger than before.

This Is a Natural Next Step in Our Journey

In many ways, blockchain-level openness builds on a foundation set in motion years ago. Open source software, which emerged out of the Free Software Movement of the 1980s, demonstrated the positive impact of releasing code to the public. This bold idea of "open" has bled into other areas. The "Open Movement" has become an umbrella term to describe multiple movements supporting the idea of a free and open society across government, health care, arts, education, technology, and more.

And we see more openness day to day in our digital lives. Khan Academy offers free online courses, retailers routinely encourage customers to post reviews, tech companies are increasingly making diversity stats public, and the public has grown accustomed to sharing intimate details about their personal life on social networks.

Blockchains, by their very nature, are public (although there are private blockchains, which are open just to members of a particular community). The code is typically open source, the data recorded on the blockchain is open, and the rules of governance of the protocol itself are open. Some blockchain companies are even working on models to open their day-to-day management and investment decisions to the community.

But perhaps the biggest contribution blockchains will make to this groundswell for a more transparent world is what they could enable our world's biggest and most influential corporations to do. Some could emerge as leaders that use blockchains to develop a new kind of collaboration between a customer's and a corporation's values, eventually pushing more businesses to strive toward a new standard.

 Cautions and Considerations

An expectation for blockchain-level transparency presents both threats and opportunities. While some of these cautions and considerations are very future-focused, they are meant to provoke your thinking about what could come. This is by no means an exhaustive list; it provides additional food for thought on how to prepare for this new paradigm.

CAUTIONS

The weak get weaker

Blockchains will not hide blemishes—they will expose them. This can be frightening for internal divisions that know there are problems in the system and don't feel equipped to address them. While there may be clear business benefit in finding and addressing problems, you may find well-fortified points of resistance. As the business landscape turns toward a culture of transparency, those companies that can't keep up could be further weakened. If you haven't yet felt any urgency to understand where competitors are making progress in transparency and focus on getting your own house in order, you should now. Face the problems you already know you have (or have a hunch you have), and get practice with working through them.

You pick the wrong thing

Transparency won't always translate into improved customer trust—customers are already overloaded with information, and often not invested in learning more. Pick carefully what to focus on and, through the development of business cases and pilots, validate that it will drive enough value (in all interpretations of the word) for the business to garner long-term support from executives and investors alike.

Blockchains are overkill

Some transparency can be achieved with a distributed database that is not driven by blockchain technology. In some cases, these databases could be managed by a trusted third party that could enforce trust more effectively and cost-efficiently than blockchains can achieve, at least until the technology significantly matures. Be critical in evaluating whether blockchains are truly the right solution to increase transparency for your specific use case. Make sure you start first by honing your understanding of the problem you need to solve, and evaluate only from that vantage point whether blockchains are the right answer.

CONSIDERATIONS

Get your priorities down now

Take this knowledge of what's coming and get deep with your customers to identify what transparency they care about most and how you stack up. Break down the data by segment to understand differences. You may be able to develop a stronger business case for investment in the areas that get the focus of your most profitable or highest-volume customers. What kind of transparency do they care about most? What makes them most skeptical? How do you fare compared to others, and what is driving any deficits in your credibility?

Practice a culture of openness

Take a look at what kind of transparency customers seek against what you could start to provide now, even without the support of blockchains. What could you start sharing? How can you start to authentically educate your market on your values, and how they are aligned to your actions and the metrics you can access now? How do your customers react to your attempts, and how can you involve your customers in improving your operations or your processes?

Identify a pilot with impact

From Coca-Cola to Starbucks to Walmart, top brands are far down the route of piloting blockchain-driven transparency. Yet in this early stage, pilots that are poorly thought through can easily look disingenuous to customers, the press, and the blockchain community, who may feel that your company is simply slapping the word *blockchain* onto a vanilla database project. With a solid understanding of what customers desire and what will drive value to your business, you can work to identify a pilot that will give you important practice in applying blockchain functionality to your business. You can experiment with finding the right tone with which to speak about your work, and deepen your understanding of how your customers react.

Examples

Talented and well-funded teams are focused on bringing transparency to a broad range of industries. While supply chains are an obvious and fascinating area of development, we'll see a wide range of projects launching in this area. Time will tell if they will work out in the long run, but right now, here are a few projects chosen to whet your appetite for what's to come.

PROVENANCE: MEANINGFUL CHANGE THROUGH SUPPLY CHAIN TRANSPARENCY

Technologist and designer Jessi Baker founded UK-based Provenance to bring what she calls "radical transparency" to materials in the supply chain. "There is an alarming lack of information around the things we buy," Jessi told me. "We may live in an age of hyperconnectivity, but we're disconnected from the origin of our products."

Provenance seeks to start a revolution in consumer understanding by making it possible for users to know more about where their products are coming from. Her team has been working on this complex challenge since 2014, and has been recognized as a pioneer in connecting physical "things" to a blockchain. Along the way, they've tackled challenges ranging from how to tag items (ever think about how a coconut could be tagged? This team has done studies), how to develop interactive smart labels, and how to make it easy for consumers to check on the item as they stand in front of it at a store.

Provenance has worked with over 200 businesses so far, with pilots from fishing (to ensure fish is coming from sustainable sources, and from those without human rights abuses) to tracking produce from "origin to supermarket" for a consumer cooperative. While scale is still elusive and the team is using hybrid "on-chain" and "off-chain" solutions for the time being, they have made notable progress. With their focus on helping producers and retailers to distinguish their brands and products and encouraging shopper engagement with the careful crafting of customer experiences, Jessi's design mindset shows through. "Getting buy-in from the entire supply chain, integrating into existing systems—these are big challenges," she explained. "But it's just a matter of time until more pioneers take the leap, and pressure the market to shape up or get left behind. We are already seeing the beginnings of this shift."[96]

BLOCKCERTS: TRUSTWORTHY DIGITAL RECORDS

Blockcerts, incubated by MIT Media Lab, is a protocol that makes digital credentials and official records trustworthy. Not only does using Blockcerts ensure the record is tamper-proof, but it verifies the identities of both issuer and receiver. A company called Learning Machine was founded to bring the technology to market. While the initial focus is on educational credentials, the free, open source, and blockchain-agnostic software could be used, according to Natalie Smolenski, a Vice President at Learning Machine, "for any kind of high-value, high-stakes credentials that need to have extraordinary longevity and remain verifiable across space and time—15 or 30 years from now, in any geographic context, anywhere I end up in the world. This could be diplomas or transcripts, drivers' licenses, passports, birth certificates—anything."[97]

There are many facets to the potential impact. Obviously, when records and credentials can be quickly verified, without question, it cuts time and increases quality in hiring. For example, in the US, over half the PhDs awarded in a given year are purchased from degree mills that exist only to issue fraudulent certifications.[98]

But Learning Machine has a bigger vision. "We need systems of record that can withstand war, economic collapse, and climate catastrophes," Natalie said. "They need to be internationally portable, universally interoperable, and fully verifiable without dependence on vendors or issuers. We need academic institutions, governments, and corporations to invest in the infrastructure to put this system of record in place before the war, before someone becomes a refugee, before the natural disaster. Look at the conflict in Syria. There are five million people who have been displaced, and this is one of the most highly educated refugee populations in human history. Without proof of their credentials, they can't practice medicine, or law, or teach at universities, as they were doing before. It's a massive loss of human capital."[99]

The same idea of universally trusted official records can be leveraged to enable more people—and assets—to actively participate in the global economy. The World Bank estimates that 20% of the world's population cannot legally prove their identity, restricting their access to employment and financial capital. [100] Prize-winning Peruvian economist Hernando DeSoto estimates that $20 trillion worth of assets have no titles—which means they are, essentially, dead capital. With no legal proof of ownership, it's hard for an individual or an organization to lend or borrow against them. [101]

GIVETRACK: HOLDING CHARITIES ACCOUNTABLE FOR USE OF DONATIONS

Blockchain pioneer Connie Gallippi created BitGive in 2013 after recognizing the tremendous opportunities for social impact in bitcoin. With many entrepreneurs making fortunes in cryptocurrency, Connie wanted to find a way for them to share their wealth and give back to society responsibly. The foundation's flagship project is GiveTrack, which uses the bitcoin blockchain to track contributions and engage donors in project results on the ground.

Charities are held accountable for the donations they receive—the blockchain publicly records every transaction, so donors can see exactly where money is spent. BitGive has worked with well-known nonprofits including Save the Children, The Water Project, TECHO, and Medic Mobile.

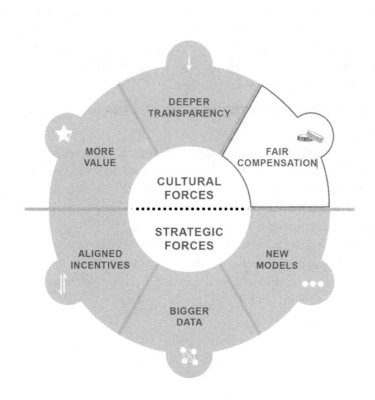

8

FAIR COMPENSATION

You are what you do, not what you say you'll do.

—CARL JUNG

Summary

Blockchains can enable the more equitable sharing of value creation between a contributor and the business that benefits from the contribution. Compensating fairly for the value contributed to a network could be the next step in a natural progression toward a more sustainable digitally driven world.

Consumers are accustomed to contributing great volumes of data and content to companies with little direct compensation. This has created an imbalance, of which consumers are increasingly aware.

Blockchains can provide plumbing to facilitate more equitable sharing of value. And they offer a new benefit of the digital experience: feature-rich compensation for consumer contribution.

As the space evolves, innovators will launch viable alternatives that embody this paradigm. As consumers are exposed to these alternatives, this will change the equation of what a consumer is willing to give up versus what they get. Over time, consumers will be trained to recognize the true value of their contribution and will be influenced by which brands or businesses compensate them most fairly for the value they help create.

 **The Setting**

IMBALANCE IS BAKED INTO OUR DIGITAL NORMS

Over the years we've become reliant on the internet. For many of us, internet applications are an essential tool for staying connected to the people in our networks. They are becoming the primary tools we use to learn, schedule, shop, research, manage finances, and entertain ourselves. And over these years, we've been trained to donate our search terms, our clicks, and our attention to those companies that provide these tools. We've even donated our thoughts in the form of posts, our opinions in the form of reviews, and our perspective in the form of videos or blogs.

Often we didn't even pause to think about this. Or, perhaps we hovered for a moment before clicking yet another "yes, I accept the terms" box wondering if we should, this time, read the reams of legalese—and then clicked, impatient that something was standing between us and whatever we were in the middle of doing. Reading privacy policies can come at a great cost of time. Researchers from Carnegie Mellon estimated that it would take 76 work days to read all the privacy policies that the average American encounters in a year.[102]

Our tendency to ignore all this legalese has proven very profitable to the companies behind these internet tools. We have granted them great flexibility to use our contributions for a host of self-serving ends. They've used our content to drive traffic and revenue. They use our search terms to serve us personalized ads that compel us to spend more. They sell our data to brokers, who sell it to other brands, and so on. Very infrequently are we offered specific compensation for what we contributed, whether data or content.

You are not the customer, you are the product.

In 1999, the author Claire Wolfe wrote in an article, "You're not the customer any more. You're simply a 'resource' to be managed for profit. The customer is someone else now—and usually someone without your best interests at heart . . . The customer is everyone who wishes to own a piece of your life."[103]

Feeding this trend are new smart, connected products that gather and transmit detailed information. The consultancy Gartner estimates that over 20 billion connected "things" will be in use in 2020.[104] We are increasingly surrounded by sensors and devices that gather information about us—sending it to the companies that sold us the product, who can then use it in any way they've specified in their user agreements.

WE'VE BEEN WILLINGLY LOOKING AWAY

These internet companies have set armies of researchers and engineers on a mission to harvest our attention in ways that, some say, render us defenseless. Former Google strategist James Williams, who cofounded an advocacy group to build public awareness of the impact of technology design, has said, "The dynamics of the attention economy are structurally set up to undermine the human."[105] But in addition to the intent behind technology giants' design, there are other forces at play.

Broader social forces make us feel like we don't have an alternative. We often perceive that we don't "have a choice"—and, indeed, opting out of using a tool like Google, Instagram, LinkedIn, Yelp, Facebook, or Amazon is seen as an extreme move. Tools like these not only help us run our lives more efficiently, but also have become a primary mechanism for commerce, connections, and communities.

We also see more value in what we get than what we give. Decades into internet application development, these products have become very finely tuned to give us utility, and so we tend to be very willing to make the tradeoff. When we do, we get to participate more fully in our modern, digital society, and access the cool things this new technology can do for us. We are rewarded with immediate benefit, in contrast to how we perceive the somewhat esoteric and far-off harm of giving up our data. We often even appreciate that donating data and content can lead to products and services that make our lives easier and more entertaining, educate us, and save us money. Our content, combined with that of others, drives value for platforms like Twitter, Facebook, Medium, or even the cultish spin bike Peloton, but in turn, gives us a more valuable product too.

The pull to give, and give more, is strong even for those that understand intimately how it is used. I've had the honor of working with top data scientists since the days the term was first coined in 2008. I am very well aware how my data can be cleaned, mashed, and leveraged to deliver a rich profile of who I am and what makes me tick—perhaps even richer and more accurate than my own understanding of myself. Yet, as I write this book, Gmail has access to my inner thoughts as I run them by friends and colleagues. Nest is tracking my movements from room to room, and knows when I am pacing back and forth to the fridge. Waze follows me as I escape to a quiet mountain retreat to work, keeping track of where I stop to eat, and how often I break the speed limit. I am giving

Google (who owns Gmail, Nest, and Waze) quite an arsenal of influence over me. And I've done it willingly in exchange for the assistance each has given me in my work.

BUT NOW, WE ARE POISED FOR A SHIFT

Consumers don't want to turn back the clock on these tools. But there is an increasing awareness that every like, share, search, or purchase is making these internet giants rich, giving them a highly effective tool for shaping our behavior, and influencing our thoughts. Consumers are more frequently asking, "Why should someone else profit off what I've given them?"

> *Consumers are more frequently asking, "Why should someone else profit off what I've given them?"*

When the news got out that a small research firm named Cambridge Analytica had used the data from 87 million Facebook accounts to influence an election, it triggered a highly public unpacking of what Facebook gathers, how they sell it, and how they obscure it in the tome of legalese that is their user agreement. There were grassroots campaigns to delete Facebook accounts. The regulators pounced. The advantages and disadvantages of opting out became the topic of dinner party conversation. The question was jettisoned into the mainstream: "Should we be just giving this away?"

PRIMED FOR A BETTER ALTERNATIVE

Crises like these jolt us from blissful ignorance to sudden awareness of the actual cost of this dependence. We may be disillusioned, but without attractive alternatives, and deterred by high switching costs, we continue our use (sometimes reluctantly). However, these moments lay the groundwork for change should a day arrive when new competitors arrive with a better offer for consumers. Once primed in this way, consumers may see alternatives that not only protect, but also *provide*, as very attractive—and this may neutralize any perceived cost of switching.

This progression—from ignorance to awareness to receptivity of alternatives —is a maturation that could move us as a society to a more sustainable digital future. It is a future characterized by more balance between business and individual contributor. It lays a foundation for longer-term relationships and mutual value. It could be an essential part of our digital "growing up," and a big part of how we consumers and companies learn how to navigate this digital future together, as shown in Figure 8-1.

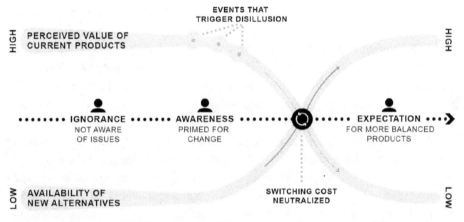

Figure 8-1. The path to digital sustainability. When consumers become aware of the true price they pay to participate in a platform, they may consider that platform less valuable. As alternatives come to market, a disillusioned customer may be more willing to try something new. Over time, and with more awareness of true costs, consumers will come to expect products that are more balanced.

When Web 2.0 products first came on the market we were enamored. We freely gave, were quickly hooked, and were easily harvested. For some, it may take a single dramatic awakening (like the Facebook scandal) to trigger disillusion. But for others, it may take a series of smaller events. But these are just precursors to change. These products are deeply entrenched in our daily lives. It will take more to incent a true shift. It will take the launch of more attractive alternatives.

 ## What Blockchains Make Possible

BLOCKCHAINS AS A FOUNDATION FOR A MORE SUSTAINABLE DIGITAL FUTURE

Blockchains, along with the use of tokens, offer several unique, core elements that can be designed to support the more equitable sharing of value between contributor and business. As innovators work to develop and launch products that embody these elements, they will trigger a next step in the progression toward a more sustainable, more balanced, digitally driven world.

Smith + Crown head of research Matt Chwierut explains how this could work: "One of the areas that excites me most is how tokens create an economic model for user-generated content and actions. Web 2.0 business models are often based on advertising and harvesting data, but blockchains open up a world in which micro-actions and micro-contributions can be compensated. They create ways to substantiate and reward value. Users can even build their own business models around their contribution of content or services. And blockchains provide a very efficient payment rail for everyone involved."

Certainly, some digital players today give a form of compensation for contribution. One could argue that YouTube's placement of video ads before content represents a kind of compensation for an action taken: watch part of an ad, and get rewarded with the video content they've hosted and served for you. Perhaps more directly, YouTube gives "creators" who meet certain criteria access to resources, events, and even a share of revenue made when viewers take action on the ads shown with their content.

But this is still a very lopsided arrangement. The percent of revenue that the contributor gets is small. The investment a creator needs to make in meeting the criteria and understanding the program is high, shutting out many who are not willing to make a dedicated effort, or aren't sure their content is strong enough to make the effort worthwhile.

BLOCKCHAINS PROMISE DIRECT AND FEATURE-RICH COMPENSATION

Compared to what is possible with blockchains and tokens, today's efforts to compensate consumers looks simplistic, almost crude. Multiple features of this new functionality converge to enable a way to finally, and potentially even elegantly, compensate customers for the value they contribute to a network:

- The flexibility to compensate a broad range of contributions, including data, content, or even attention or engagement. These could be micro-behaviors such as engaging with an ad, or something more involved, such as rewarding the impact of a piece of content measured by number of shares or high reviews. (See more on the potential for rewarding micro-behaviors in Chapter 9.)

- The capability to tie contribution to a unique identity, even as that contribution, whether data or content, moves from one application to another.

- The capability for the contributor to control how their contribution is used, and track that usage, no matter where or when it happens.

- A mechanism—in the form of cryptoassets or tokens—to compensate a user immediately and directly for this broad range of contributions (they can be used to incentivize behavior as well, as we will see in Chapter 9.)

- The ability for compensation to come from many kinds of participants, even directly from one consumer to the other, such as in the form of tipping or voting with tokens.

VALUE WILL SOLIDIFY (ONE WAY OR ANOTHER) WITH MARKET MATURATION

Today, the liquidity of cryptoassets varies greatly, and liquidity is a key driver of how value is perceived. Yet, as the space evolves, a wider range of merchants, service providers, and even other consumers will accept cryptocurrency or other cryptoassets as a form of payment. The exchanges that enable one cryptoasset to be exchanged for another, or for US dollars or other traditional government-issued money, will mature and be more accessible to the average consumer (today many are difficult to use). We have already seen companies like Expedia, Overstock, Dish Network, and Microsoft accept the first cryptocurrency, bitcoin. Japan passed a law accepting bitcoin as legal tender. While the number of US households holding cryptocurrency is still low, several analysts estimate that over a third of households in South Korea hold cryptocurrency. As the market matures, and these assets also become less volatile, the perceived value of cryptoasset-based compensation could very well rise.

Note, however, that compensation may be perceived as valuable even if it is not used as a traditional currency. In fact, as the space evolves and adoption rises, we can expect that consumers will have a choice to exchange "earnings" directly for products or services that are valuable to them, similar to the way that airline loyalty points might be used. (I discuss loyalty programs in more detail in Chapter 9.)

Implications: What Happens When Your Customer Knows Their Worth

THE BIRTH OF THE ALTERNATIVE

Innovators will leverage this new functionality to develop alternatives to today's imbalanced internet applications. There are already dozens of funded teams around the globe working on alternatives to Facebook, Google, Amazon, Uber, and Airbnb that reward consumers for the value they create. There will be many, many more contenders before winners start to emerge.

As entrepreneurs introduce more and more viable products with blockchain-driven compensation models, consumers will start to see that they can achieve some control. If a particular consumer has been disillusioned with the products they use today, or if they highly value the compensation offered by an alternative model, they may very well convert.

Let me be clear: the practice of using tokens to compensate contribution is extremely nascent. There is not clear regulation or a proven business model in place yet. But initiatives that are eventually successful can build on the backs of large addressable markets. And they could potentially achieve a level of loyalty, engagement, and high-quality contribution that eclipses that of today's models.

THE SHORT JOURNEY FROM EXPOSURE TO EXPECTATION

We can expect that some entrepreneurs will focus their initial work on relatively targeted and specific audiences. We can also expect that once these consumers are exposed to the idea of being compensated for their contribution—whether this contribution is content, or data, or even their attention—they will eventually learn to ask for it. And it is then a short distance to come to expect it.

As this "compensation mindset" becomes more ingrained for these first target audiences, we may see adoption spreading outward, in an epidemic-like pattern, from their spheres of influence (family, friends, community members, colleagues, and so on). We've seen this before in platforms like Facebook, which first took hold with college students; with Airbnb, which first took hold with members of the Democratic National Convention, who were at a loss for rooms in an overcrowded city; and with Twitter, which gained an uptick in traction among SXSW attendees.

WHERE IT COULD ALL BEGIN

Crypto-enthusiasts are an obvious choice. While the number is hard to peg, one popular digital currency exchange, Coinbase, has over 20 million accounts (double the number of brokerage accounts at Schwab).[106] But let's dig a little deeper to examine how innovators could influence broader knowledge, understanding, and adoption of this compensation mindset with another large, global audience. —for example, the 2.2 billion gamers worldwide.

How One Audience Could Influence Adoption

In the debates over where adoption will accelerate, gamers are in a strong position to be an early audience. Games have been using virtual currencies for over 20 years. Users are accustomed to purchasing, earning, and spending in this way. From Playstation Store credits to digital Xbox Live memberships, digital assets and goods are not foreign to modern gamers. Tavonia Evans, the founder and CEO of a blockchain company and mother of eight, explains, "There are a lot of millennials and teens who are very aware of cryptocurrency. The concept is not new to them; they look at it as similar to the virtual currencies they are already using online. And if a match gets lit in this area—well, we all have seen how quickly something small can start a movement."[107]

Gamers also trend technically sophisticated: a recent Magid Media Futures study found that gamers are more tech savvy than the average online user.[108] This could indicate that, if properly motivated, they would be willing to jump in even before user experience (UX) has reached the point of being truly consumer-ready.

A high number of blockchain-based companies will be directing marketing dollars to educate gamers on what a blockchain makes possible. In the last few years, there have been 50 ICOs for gaming-focused projects, from over 20 nations. The top 10 fundraisers brought in over $300 million alone.[109] They include companies that are building products that provide new revenue streams for expert gamers to sell coaching to other consumers, compensate a player for engagement with a brand, or enable gamers to move digital collectibles from one gaming environment to another.

The success of those projects will depend on many factors, and it is likely that a great many will fail. However, all these teams are aligned in their community about the new types of value that come from this new model. Their marketing dollars will drive awareness and interest among gamers, regardless of how many companies gain actual traction.

If entrepreneurs build products and applications that resonate with gamers and they become strong adopters, they could influence the spread of knowledge and trust of cryptoassets as compensation. Once gamers are comfortable owning and using tokens, they may then help to make their friends and families comfortable as well (assuming we have reached the point at which products are consumer-ready). Given the number of gamers, their increasing gender diversity (45% of smartphone gamers and 44% of PC gamers are female),[110] and how globally dispersed they are, this could be an influential force.

There are many other possibilities for specific segments that would be motivated to adopt early—for example, digitally sophisticated populations in need of income (think: students) or frequent contributors to an existing platform if it were to add blockchain-driven compensation features (think: bloggers contributing to a platform like LinkedIn or Medium, or reviewers on a platform like Amazon or Alibaba). Each blockchain-driven business will be motivated to also introduce users to the new kinds of benefits blockchains enable, and familiarize them with its unique forms of compensation—and these efforts, gathered together, could be a massive force. If a trusted, established brand makes a strong move into the space, this could also be the trigger of hockey stick–like adoption (*https://en.wikipedia.org/wiki/Hockey_stick_graph*).

But regardless of where it starts, its diffusion will move in lockstep with the evolution of the technology. There are formidable challenges to come, including the difficulty of identifying best product-market fit, clunky user experience, limited scalability, cryptoasset volatility, and an unclear and rapidly shifting regulatory environment. However, the quality and volume of the human capital moving in to contribute their minds and skill sets to the advancement of the space is staggering. While it will take some time, we are sure to see rapid innovation that gradually chips away at these obstacles.

CONTRIBUTION DOESN'T ALWAYS MEAN HUMAN

As we acquire more products equipped with IoT functionality, these assets can also contribute data or even content, and we could be compensated for this as well. Our car could contribute weather or road condition data, our refrigerators could contribute food data, and a drone could capture video footage. It's not hard to project into a future in which assets like these are making money for us as they contribute value to a digital application or platform.

COMPENSATION DOESN'T ALWAYS MEAN MONEY

Compensation does not need to be seen as strictly financial. In fact, at least in today's world, paying consumers directly for data can reduce their trust.[III] While this perception may evolve as new digital norms do, we can expect that companies will also become clever in how they frame compensation using tokens, perhaps more as "earnings" or "rewards" than currency, and emphasizing how those tokens can be used to get goods and services consumers value over conversion to traditional currencies. There will be a great deal of important experimentation and learning that comes out of this area in the next few years.

TOWARD A MORE BALANCED FUTURE

These new models will give customers a choice. The unblocked customer will be able to share more equitably in the value they create. They will have more control over who gets to use what, and in what way. For example, a consumer could choose to lock the data exhaust flowing from her fitness tracker, or choose to sell it to Nike, Amazon, or a research study.

As more products and services gain traction, they will each make a contribution to training customers that there is a new way of doing things. And as more and more expectations change, a new digital norm could evolve: brands will compensate consumers for their contribution to value creation.

> As more and more expectations change, a new digital norm could evolve: brands will compensate consumers for their contribution to value creation.

But there will be a terminal limit to the amount of value that can be returned to the customer. Our contributions are worth more when shared. A single dataset on a particular consumer is not particularly useful. It is when data is combined across populations and sources, and processed, that useful insights can be extracted. It is an organization's investment in predictive analytics, data scientists, machine learning, and all the supporting infrastructure that makes it possible to unlock these insights. This costs money.

Likewise, a single piece of content from your average citizen, no matter how well composed or carefully written, has limited value. It is the volume of content from many contributors that attracts users. It is an organization's investment in developing an ecosystem of contributors and users, facilitating value-added connection between those contributors and users, and all the infrastructure required to manage and evolve a two-sided platform that makes it possible to drive revenue. This also costs money.

Margins will be compressed, but they will not go away. There needs to be a motivating driver for someone to make this investment (and that someone could actually be the community itself, as you will see Chapter 9).

It is not inconceivable to think that one day kids will be shocked that in the 2010s their grandparents *paid* for Amazon Alexa to sit, gathering data that went straight to a retailer instead of Amazon paying them for the privilege of listening to the family interacting in the intimate space of their own home.

 ## Cautions and Considerations

The shift toward fair compensation presents both threats and opportunities to existing businesses. While some of these cautions and considerations are very future-focused, they are meant to provoke your thinking about what could come. This is by no means an exhaustive list; it provides additional food for thought on how to prepare for this new paradigm.

CAUTIONS

Moving too early or too late

As with any new technology, timing is crucial. With its complexity and rawness, this space will prove particularly challenging to time correctly. Move too slowly, and you could be caught by surprise as a competitor discovers a particularly elegant and engaging way to compensate your customer base, and takes them from you. Move too quickly, and you could end up wasting resources and confusing your customers with an ill-executed strategy, clunky technology, or token they perceive as worthless. Internet incumbents have particularly high stakes—if they move too quickly, they give more away to customers than they need to, and if they move too late, they risk disintermediation themselves. Discover ways to achieve a more accurate barometer of customer readiness and market landscape, such as conducting customer research, participating in think tank–like sessions with a range of experts, and actively engaging through partners, pilots, and other forms of experimentation.

Not taking emerging alternatives seriously

The business landscape is littered with disastrous misfires as companies missed crucial signs of a shift in environment. Let me be clear—I believe the great majority of blockchain-native startups that have raised funds through initial coin offerings (ICOs) in the last few years will fail. And this aspect—compensation— is very difficult to get right. The eventual leaders will have aced the development of an economy, a product that incorporates high-fidelity behavioral economics and network effects.

But some projects will eventually be viable, and teams will launch compelling products. And we can expect the next generation of blockchain natives—perhaps those founded this year or next—to build on the incredible learning, experiences, and development of the first. And so on. Look carefully. Pay attention. Learn. Even if these young companies and their products are rough around the edges, they are getting very wise, very quickly. Understand what they are getting right—and when they are reaching the early stages of traction with your customers.

Throwing the proverbial baby out with the bathwater

Many of the early teams are technology-driven. In these early days, that's essential. But I've talked to many that understood only part of the pain they were solving for potential customers, or didn't have a full understanding of the business hurdles that they would need to overcome to bring their vision to life. These teams will fail. But studying their model, and understanding their points of failure (and what they did get right), is an incredible opportunity to give more clarity and confidence to your own journey in the space. And perhaps you may come across a player that, in "my chocolate and your peanut butter" style, has what you lack in a way that fits perfectly with what you, as a partner or investor, can provide.

Not considering how quickly an established player could move

An established brand with a large customer base could develop their own token off an existing protocol that has been optimized for their space, or even leverage a token that has already established traction elsewhere. If effectively leveraged, either approach can enable them to move very quickly. Their brand could lend legitimacy to the use of a token for compensation, build consumer comfort with the idea of cryptoassets, and spark an uptick in adoption. If you are the right brand, consider these strategies yourself, and if you are not, think through the potential impact of others making this move, and how you might be able to leverage a development like this to your advantage.

The inherent portability of tokens

Tokens—like any form of money—are perceived as valuable when they can be used for the exchange of desired goods and services. The success of newly developed tokens hinges on many factors, but a key driver is the ecosystem of places they can be used to purchase or trade for things of value. The foundations that govern these tokens are motivated to develop a rich ecosystem for them. In simple terms, the more decentralized a token—the more places it can be spent—the more vibrant its economy and useful it is. This means that successful tokens are also portable. They can be earned in one place and spent in another, and the team that developed them doesn't always have control on how that all goes down, nor do you.

This portability, and the potential conversion of all tokens into traditional currency, will intersect with our psychology in a way we can only guess. We have never seen this phenomenon in the wild, at least at mass adoption scale. Harvard Business School professor Thales S. Teixeira points out that content gated by even small, seemingly insignificant payments will give a consumer pause. Even if the value of their time is much higher, says Thales, consumers will take the extra time to find content elsewhere for free instead of paying a few cents for it.[112]

If tokens are perceived as a kind of useful monopoly money that lives and breathes outside of their normal economy, consumers may spend them freely. As they realize they can be converted to cold, hard cash it may impact behavior, at least until they develop new habits. Watch carefully—there is still a lot to learn about how we will behave in this new world.

CONSIDERATIONS

Understand what customers' contribution means to your business

Get a head start on understanding the true business value of what customers are giving you freely today. We are in the infancy of the complex practice of assigning a value to both data and content, and the nuances behind it (such as how the influence of the contributor can impact value). People value different kinds of contribution in different ways, and there will be important demographic differences that need to be understood. Exploring these questions early will give you more clarity to determine where compensation supports your business model and where it doesn't. While much value will be difficult to quantify, you can map relative value to drive focus on what kind of contribution is the *most* valuable to your business.

Practice by studying an area that is more tangibly quantified. For example, if you have an online community, you can examine how to attribute value to the answers that community members give to each other's questions. For example, quantify the cost savings of not having to answer the question with internal staff, and the value of capturing question-response that may have never even been presented through formal channels. Account also for the networked value of the answers—the value of making the answer available to the community forever. Assessments will not be exact, but they will offer directional insight.

Take a baseline of your customers' current mindset

Take the opportunity in this early stage to establish a baseline understanding of how customers *perceive* the value of what they are giving to you today. Where do they assign value, and where are they disillusioned with you or others in your space? This will help you not only find gaps between what your customers feel they are giving and what they are getting, but also be more attuned to changes in this baseline as the space evolves. Also work to understand and track your customers' perceptions of cryptoassets over time, as they evolve.

Find your early adopters and collaborate with them

Identify segments of your customer base that are early adopters of cryptoassets and most likely to be early adopters of competitive alternatives, and bring them into the fold. Research them. Ideate on how to work with them. Collaborate with them to identify insights for how you could leverage the shift before it becomes mainstream.

Find ways to experiment—and learn—early

Grow your knowledge of how different segments within your customer base respond to compensation by experimenting with various approaches, whether blockchain-driven or not. Consider:

- Generating ideas to pilot or trial compensation models that aren't driven by cryptoassets or blockchains (and thus can be executed more immediately) for certain segments of your customer base. You'll learn how they respond and how you need to structure internally to be able to accommodate a compensation model, even before your customer base is comfortable with cryptoassets. Social media players Kik and YouNow, for example, experimented in this way with virtual currency trials on their platforms as a precursor to designing tokens.

- Run a campaign with a complementary partner once they start to gain traction for their token. This could be a campaign that targets your customers who are already using their application or platform, or that encourages their customers to interface with yours.

- Consider an even deeper collaboration through investment or formal partnership with an early player whose target audience intersects with yours, and use their platform, application, and token to gain deeper learnings on how your audience responds.

Examples

The blockchain space provides a rich set of case studies in this dimension. Time will tell if they will work out in the long run, but right now, here are a few projects chosen to whet your appetite for what's to come.

STEEMIT: COMPENSATION FOR CONTRIBUTION

Steemit at first looks like a crypto-centric Reddit. But dig under the covers, and it reveals a thoughtfully developed infrastructure for applications and platforms to compensate contributors for content deemed valuable by a community. Compensation comes in the form of token STEEM, which is also listed on several exchanges and readily tradable. Steemit.com is a first use case, but the protocol and token have also been used for other applications as well, including a YouTube-like site, DTube.

CEO Ned Scott sees a "tokenized internet" as a solution to problems endemic to media today. "Print is dying; ad integration is inefficient, distracting, and generally unwanted by consumers," he said. "It's led to a widespread battle to monetize content. And we've made this monetization easy."[113]

The team gives the analogy of a game system where users compete for attention and rewards by bringing content and adding value to the platform. Governance has been designed to encourage long-term investment in the platform, and the company emphasizes that Steemit is not a "get rich quick" scheme. Most of the authors that are earning high rewards have spent a lot of time in the network building followings, making connections with others, and developing a reputation for bringing high-quality content.

Steemit is launching what they call "smart media tokens," or SMTs, that could allow any social network to reward contributors with tokens for the value they create on a network. The tokens can be private labeled and integrated with a website. Ned envisions SMTs as "an inexpensive, user-friendly, secure way for mainstream businesses to leverage blockchain and cryptocurrency technology without being blockchain experts."[114]

BRAVE: GET PAID TO BROWSE

Brendan Eich is the creator of JavaScript and cofounded Mozilla. Now, he is the CEO of blockchain-based Brave, a company on a mission to "fix the web" by attacking each layer of inefficiency in the browser ecosystem. This new model was designed to deliver more to all the players in this ecosystem—except the middlemen that today take more than half the revenue. They've been eliminated. Both advertisers and publishers get more value, and consumers get compensation for their contribution—whether that contribution is data or attention.

But users also get an immediate benefit in the form of a browser that is safer and faster. Today's browsers take much longer than they could, as ads and trackers slow down the loading of sites. CNN takes an average of 84 seconds. CBS News takes 45 seconds. On blockchain-based Brave, CNN and CBS take 12 and 16 seconds, respectively, by blocking these ads and trackers (which can number in the dozens, and can introduce risk of malware, known as *malvertising*). Then, users can decide if they will let ads back in—for compensation in the form of BAT tokens. Publishers get a better deal by going direct, and users get a share of the ad revenue in exchange for their attention. Users are also promised fewer, more relevant ads through machine learning algorithms that match ads to user interests.

Brave uses *zero knowledge proof,* which means that ads can be verified as delivered without identifying the actual user. In other words, users can remain anonymous to the advertisers, publishers, and any other member of the ecosystem but still earn compensation for their actions.

"We have a horrendous problem with ad clutter," Brendan explains. "It's not just annoying, it's not just slow. It's kind of creepy how it tracks you around the web and promotes things to you. You would hope you'd have some protection for your browser—they should protect you, they are your agent. Unfortunately the top browsers, most of them anyway, have a conflict of interest. They are either directly or indirectly dependent on advertising."

Brendan continues, "Too many parties are taking a cut, so there is less and less for the publishers. *You* should get a cut—your attention costs something. Right now it is priced at zero and you get annoyances, and risk . . . Imagine a world where you have your own dossier—it's your online life, it should be your data. If you own it, then you can give terms of service to the big network superpowers, the walled gardens, and the giant companies."[115]

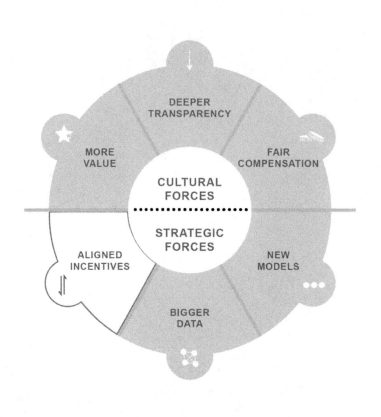

9

ALIGNED INCENTIVES

"There is no influence like the influence of habit."

—GILBERT PARKER

Summary

Blockchains and tokens unleash a powerful new incentive structure that could evolve to craft near-perfect alignment between action and reward. They could become a key tool for capturing attention and shaping behavior. But they also give new power to the crowd, which will, in turn, influence the shape of business.

Tokens are a flexible, high-fidelity incentive mechanism that could be used to shape and reward behavior. Companies will eventually learn how to use tokens to align interests, but it is a two-way equation: the community will also learn they can shape the business.

Tokens have the potential to be leveraged creatively to drive engagement, and could solve some of the most challenging problems facing marketing executives. But tokens will be most interesting when used to motivate an entire community to contribute to advancing a product, a business, or a mission—or as a mechanism for aligning the interests of various parties within an ecosystem.

In fact, by their very nature, successful tokens don't live in silos—they break the boundaries of brand and business. Businesses that want to leverage these tokens will find it demands a shift in how they think about success and will require new kinds of collaboration.

 **The Setting**

THE STEADY EXTINCTION OF THE LOYAL CUSTOMER

Winning the attention, engagement, and loyalty of today's consumers is a continual and difficult battle for marketers. Consider shopping as a microcosm of new digitally driven consumer behavior. The internet, social, and mobile have made "shopping around" habitual. Looking through the lens of search data, Google reports that not only have mobile searches for "best" grown over 80% in the past two years, but there has also been higher growth among "low-consideration" products (apparel, beauty, personal care, dining, food and groceries, occasions and gifts, retailers and general merchandise) than "high-consideration" products (business and industrial, consumer electronics, finance, real estate, travel, vehicles).[116] This indicates consumers are reconsidering brand choices more habitually and more frequently, even for smaller items of less consequence.

The internet, social, and mobile have made "shopping around" habitual.

Consultancy McKinsey found that not only was loyalty ephemeral, but consumers frequently switched brands once they decided to shop. In a recent report, a full 87% of consumers shopped around and just 13% (in the categories studied) were "loyalists." And after shopping around, a full 58% ended up switching brands. When they dug deeper, the report continues, McKinsey discovered how vital it is to be included in the set of brands that first come to a consumer's mind when he or she is triggered to make a purchase decision. Nearly 70% of the brands purchased by consumers who made a switch were part of these consumers' initial consideration set when they started shopping.[117]

These studies show the importance of being everywhere, all the time. But earning initial consideration goes well beyond simple brand name awareness. Shoppers need to have a clear understanding of benefits and value. That means robust and authentic content that elevates products, and brands must dominate not only media channels but social networks as well (especially for millennials, who heavily leverage social media for feedback on buying decisions).

BEING HEARD IS HARDER THAN EVER

At the same time, the marketer's arsenal is losing potency. While there may be more options to reach a target audience than ever before, it has never been more difficult to earn the attention and engagement of consumers.

Harvard Business School professor Thales S. Teixeira studies the "Economics of Attention." Professor Teixeira defines attention as the allocation of mental resources, visual or cognitive, to visible or conceptual objects. Of course, before consumers can absorb advertising or other forms of brand messages, they first need to be paying attention. I recently spoke with Thales about his research.

"The quality of consumer attention has been falling for decades," Thales explained. "Consumers have lost interest in the information content of ads because they can access more and better information on-demand. So, the supply of attention has gone down, while at the same time the number of companies and brands advertising has increased. It's a simple law of economics—when demand goes up in relation to supply, the price goes up."

He continues, "The net result for the CMO is that the cost of attention has been rising. In fact, even after accounting for inflation, it's a seven- to nine-fold increase. That is the biggest increase companies are facing—bigger than wages, health care, and insurance."[118] Figure 9-1 illustrates this trend.[119]

Studies have shown that consumers are exposed to thousands of brand messages a day and switch screens over 20 times an hour. Meanwhile, they are becoming incredibly adept at filtering out what they don't want to see, and more savvy about completely blocking ads altogether. Millennials in particular have developed what seems almost like an evolutionary feature that imbues them with the power of selective filtering to curate their digital-world experience in real time.

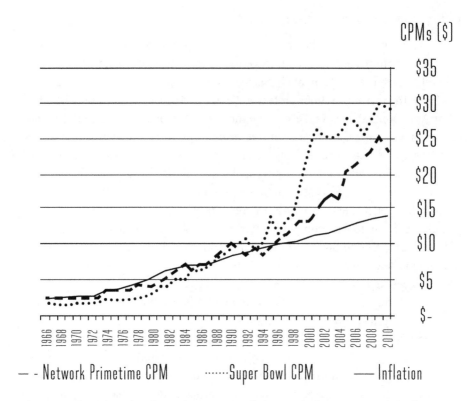

Figure 9-1. The rising price of attention. (Source: Thales S. Teixeira, www.economicsofatten-tion.com.)

NEW TOOLS HAVEN'T ALWAYS DRIVEN ROI

New engagement channels that seem promising at first often are hard to leverage effectively. For example, take a look at mobile apps. In 2013, the Chair of the General Management Program at Harvard Business School, Sunil Gupta, declared apps "the best way to win the hearts and minds of mobile consumers."[120] And many brands invested heavily in apps, often encouraged by agencies that saw an exciting new revenue stream in the work of creating these resource-intensive digital interfaces.

Fast-forward a few years, and few brands have been able to crack the code to drive ongoing engagement through mobile apps. In fact, the majority of users (51%) download *no apps* over a month. Smartphone users spend half their time on a single, top-used app, and spend nearly the entirety of their app time in just 10.[121] So, while apps are indeed an important part of consumers' digital experience, it's very difficult for a brand to earn the position as one of the few that they actually use.

Over a hundred years ago, department store founder and marketing pioneer John Wanamaker declared, "Half the money I spend on advertising is wasted; the trouble is, I don't know which half." Back then, there were very few channels to reach consumers. Now, the marketing landscape is a stunningly complex and ever-changing kaleidoscope of options. Channels that didn't exist a few years ago —native advertising, flavor-of-the-year social platforms, and in-app advertising— now contribute to the fragmentation of marketing team attention and budgets. Even with their tracking tools, analytics, and in-house data scientists, marketers are still guessing. They still can't be sure what they do is actually driving the behaviors they want.

Even with their sophisticated tools, marketers can't be sure what they do is actually driving the behaviors they want.

And it's made much worse by bot fraud and click farms. Bot networks can now be rented by the hundreds of thousands, and they have become quite sophisticated at mimicking humans. The Association of National Advertisers (ANA) reports in their Bot Baseline Report that the economic losses due to bot fraud were estimated at $6.5 billion globally in 2017.[122] Throw in pixel stuffing, cookie stuffing, ad stacking, search ad fraud, ad injections, and domain spoofing (to name just a few tactics), and it's easy to imagine how ad fraud overall will have reached $19 billion in 2018, according to Juniper Research.[123]

LOYALTY PROGRAMS ARE BROKEN

Loyalty programs have been historically been an attractive tool for influencing consumer behavior. In various forms, they have been used by marketers for over 100 years. But it was the debut of airline frequent flyer points nearly 40 years ago that sparked a cultural obsession. This early success spawned loyalty programs across industries as diverse as retail, entertainment, grocery, and hospitality. US consumers hold 3.8 billion memberships in customer loyalty programs,[124] and the average US household participates in 29 different programs.[125] That gives consumers a complex and often fragmented labyrinth of points systems, currencies, redemption rules, and exchange programs to navigate.

Loyalty programs are increasingly falling short of businesses' expectations. A McKinsey study found that 58% of loyalty program members don't cash in their points, claim their vouchers, or otherwise follow through on the offers they've signed up for.[126] And those that don't redeem are more than twice as likely to defect.[127] These programs have proven poor at driving consideration, targeting instead a much smaller (although high-value) segment of customers. And returns have been diminishing. Airlines in particular have been cutting back on their programs because they are becoming too expensive—exacerbated by accounting requirements that mean unused miles weigh down balance sheets.

Businesses are clearly struggling to continually be seen, heard, and understood by consumers and influencers. Where do they turn?

 ## What Blockchains Make Possible

POWERFUL INCENTIVES AT SCALE

Blockchains can enable a powerful new incentive model that can be used to craft near-perfect alignment between action and reward: tokens. There is much uncertainty today about how tokens will be regulated or even taxed, but there are many leaders in the space working to make them available as a strategic tool—and with good reason. Should tokens become mainstream, they could potentially be more effective at shaping behavior and driving action at scale than anything we've ever seen before.

The first blockchain, the bitcoin blockchain, created a secure, decentralized digital currency that, with a clever twist of incentive design, plays a key role in securing the blockchain and making it resistant to attack. Now, we have many blockchains, and many tokens. And these tokens can work to do much more— they can be adapted to incent any behavior.

Elad Verbin, the Lead Scientist at Berlin Innovation Ventures, explains, "Incentive design is one of the killer features of blockchains. Blockchain systems are uniquely able to implement fine-grained incentives tied to complex business logic. They also have the potential to be highly scalable, so they can support giving out incentives in tiny increments (e.g., micropayments), as well as enormous incentives given all at once."[128] Prominent blockchain innovator Trent McConaghy describes it like this: "The blockchain community understands that blockchains can help align incentives among a tribe of token holders. Each token holder has skin in the game. By rewarding them with tokens, you can get people to do stuff. Blockchains are *incentive machines*."[129]

HIT ME AGAIN, PLEASE: WHAT THE HECK ARE TOKENS?

In broad strokes, tokens are a privately issued asset that can hold the same characteristics that all money does: they are fungible, divisible, portable, and durable, and are in limited supply. They exist only in digital form or code, and are secured using cryptography.

Tokens are typically created and distributed through a token sale (which is also used for fundraising) or giveaways (often with the intent of building a community). Often, foundations govern these tokens, with open source rules that anyone can see. To sustain value (beyond speculation), these foundations will need to attract an ecosystem of buyers and sellers that find value in transacting with the token. These are essentially self-sustaining mini-economies, called *token economies*. Today, the "value" of tokens is driven largely by speculative investors, and it will be a difficult transition to move from this "speculative value" to value derived from true utility—there is much debate in the community as to what path this transition will take.

Thousands of tokens have been created so far. While technically tokens could be created by a knowledgeable developer in less than an hour, creating a token that will have sustainable long-term value is very difficult, and it is very likely that the vast majority of these tokens will fail (simply visit deadcoins.com, a site that tracks the fallen, to get a feel for the scale of this challenge). However, those that are intelligently designed, well governed, and attract vibrant "token economies" could be contenders for long-term sustainability. These are the tokens that have the potential to become a compelling new tool for shaping behaviors and incenting engagement.

YOUR TOKEN OR MINE?

Theoretically, anyone can issue a token. However, it's extremely challenging to issue a good token (as defined by long-term utility), and even more difficult to issue an unquestionably legal token in the face of the global regulatory uncertainty surrounding cryptoassets. Add in the complexity that long-term value depends on also building an economy around the token—an ecosystem of places a token can be used in exchange for goods and services—and you can see this is real work. But anyone could use a token that is already in the market and that has a "vetted" design (although few have truly been battle tested yet) and an active token economy. Or, they could use one of the growing number of token-as-a-service companies for a templatized path to a custom token. We have yet to see how consumers will react to the universe of tokens, and even with the market shakeout in the second half of 2018, it is quite possible the sheer number of options thrown their way as projects advance will feel overwhelming or confusing. Bottom line, there is a lot of growing up that needs to happen before we will have clarity on how to best use this new incentive tool. Even with this (large) uncertainty, it's clear this is an important area to watch.

One token can be exchanged for another or into traditional currencies on exchanges that are built specifically for this purpose. Not all tokens are listed on exchanges, and the user experience of signing up and securely using them is intimidating for first-time users. However, there are many companies very interested in making this experience easier, and getting more and more people involved in using and investing in cryptoassets. We will most assuredly see rapid improvement in this experience.

While the universe of tokens is still young, the cryptocurrency market cap was over $200 billion for most of 2018. And as the space evolves, there will be increasing clarity as to which will be winners—essentially those that are successful at attracting consumers, businesses, and other members of the ecosystem to their "movement."

Note that a discussion of tokens can quickly get complicated. There has been a great deal of excitement in the community about special categories of tokens with unique characteristics, like non-fungible tokens (NFTs) and security tokens, for example. For the purposes of this chapter, I am focusing only on one function of tokens: incenting consumer behavior at the application layer. If you are interested in learning more about the fascinating role of tokens in making blockchains work or how it is possible for a digital currency to even have any value at all, I have included resources on my website.

TOKENS BUILD ON A FOUNDATION OF BEHAVIORAL PSYCHOLOGY

Token economies have actually been around for a very long time. In fact, simulated, nondigital "token economies" have been used by therapists as an effective mechanism for shaping behaviors since the 1960s.

In 1958, Dr. Nathan Azrin arrived at Anna State Mental Hospital in Illinois as the new director of treatment to find his new charges unwilling to dress or apply basic hygiene. With his colleague, Teodoro Ayllon, Azrin created the world's first official token economy. It was a system in which patients bartered for tokens by modifying their behavior in incremental steps, and could later exchange the tokens for goods or privileges. Soon, the majority of the hospital's population was dressing themselves, and some had even created a token-exchange store on the ward where token holders could trade their earnings for coveted items like lipstick.

Token economies have since become one of the most successful approaches in applied psychology and are used in education, couples therapy, military training, employee supervision, prisoner management, addiction treatment, athletic coaching, and parenting. According to the *Encyclopedia of Mental Disorders*, a token economy refers to a behavior modification system that utilizes some form of token to encourage the increase of desirable behavior, and the decrease of undesirable behavior.

Now, with the advent of cryptoassets, token economies will infiltrate our digital experiences to reach a scale never seen before. It is yet to be revealed what happens if this tool is easily accessible to any marketer. And despite broad use in their pre-crypto form, there has been very little research in the wild that would help us project how these systems will interact with our psychology when applied with this scale. Watch closely.

FINE-TUNED CALIBRATION—AND IMPACT

Tokens, when tied into a digital interface, can be very finely calibrated to incent behaviors that drive new levels of engagement and action. They have three key attributes that work in concert to deliver this new, powerful incentive model:

High reward relevance

Businesses have historically been limited in the kind of rewards they could offer consumers, with many resorting to loyalty point or service credits. As this space evolves, consumers will have the flexibility to use tokens they have earned to buy an increasingly broad range of goods and services. Tokens could potentially be portable between applications and even platforms. Consumers could even convert them to cash they can hold in their hands, if available in a growing number of exchanges focused on this purpose. This means they can tailor their reward to be more meaningful to them.

More precise targeting

Tokens are not only highly divisible, but also can be easily targeted to micro-behaviors. Rewards can be focused on driving small, discrete tasks, or even used to influence the shaping of broader behavior by continually rewarding very small actions. (First introduced by behavioral psychologist B.F. Skinner, *shaping* is the process of reinforcing successively closer and closer approximations to a desired, or targeted, behavior and can be a powerful method of influence. It is this concept that drove the initial idea for Dr. Azrin's first token economy.) Over time, as practitioners learn more about how consumers interact with their application or platform to earn tokens, they will be able to incent "quality" micro-behaviors at higher and higher fidelity. As the practice evolves, it is likely we will see the earning of tokens pegged to actual impact as well—for example, the success an influencer has on getting his or her followers to take action.

Immediate gratification

A fundamental component of effectively influencing behavior is immediate reinforcement of actions with rewards. This instant feedback loop could be made easier with tokens (versus waiting for a transaction to clear or a monthly statement, as in the case of miles or points). The reward can be embedded directly in a digital interface so that users can see the results of their actions, as in a gamified system.

THE POTENCY OF TOKENS + GAMIFICATION

In fact, the practice of using the triggers, stimuli, and approaches pioneered in games will be an important tactic for all businesses, regardless of industry, that want to influence behavior with tokens. Non-gaming industry professionals call this practice of using gaming fundamentals to drive engagement outside of an actual game *gamification* (a term that can make true gaming industry insiders cringe). Gamification is nothing new. It's a well-worn and proven strategy in a broad range of industries. MySugr uses it to help manage diabetes, Duolingo uses it to teach language, and even Facebook deploys gamified campaigns to help brands engage consumers. All of these examples give us that familiar, lovely zing of dopamine (a hormone that makes us feel good) by rewarding us for specific actions. And they trigger serotonin (which can boost mood) when we think about past successes, such as looking at badges we've earned.

But game designers have long held a unique and extremely effective tool in their arsenal. It's a mechanism that hasn't been broadly accessible to industries like health care, education, and social media: virtual currency. Game designers have spent years working to shape consumer behavior with a rich range of in-game transactions—all fueled by virtual currency. They have learned how to drive engagement and revenue, no matter how good a player is or where they are in the game. They have even learned how to use virtual currency to help build communities. They have learned how to keep "in the game" and to drive habit. They have built best practices around what works and what doesn't when it comes to creating new economies that motivate and reward users' behaviors. Recently, social media players like Kik (instant messaging) and YouNow (livestream video chat) have experimented with in-app virtual currencies (and both have designed tokens).

When they hit the mainstream, tokens could be even more potent than an in-game virtual currency, and applicable to a much broader audience. In fact, the combination of tokens plus gaming fundamentals could give a range of businesses across industries the potential to tug more deeply at our psychology than ever before.

The combination of tokens plus gaming fundamentals could give a range of businesses across industries the potential to tug more deeply at our psychology than ever before.

In our modern, digitally driven world, we are an increasingly receptive audience. As Mary Meeker explains in her 2017 Internet Trend Report, millennials and Generation X have been gamified since birth. They've become wired to respond to the gaming mindset, such as the feedback loops and desire to progress to higher levels and achieve mastery. In Mary Meeker's words, "Games are now foundational to digital success."[130]

MORE POWERFUL, ALIGNED COMMUNITIES

But the power amplifies by an order of magnitude when applied to an entire community. Blockchain entrepreneurs could use tokens as levers with which to influence a community's direction of movement, and motivate community-level action. It is here that some of the most disruptive use cases are sure to originate. Tokens align the incentives of a user and a community, offering the possibility to reward actions that contribute to network value and community cohesion. Token holders also have "skin in the game"—the value of the token is driven by the size and engagement of its community and overall ecosystem. They have a vested interest in increasing token value, and supporting the participants in that token's ecosystem.

Tokens can also be used to align the interests of a B2B ecosystem of businesses. They can be designed to drive productive contributions and positive behaviors even from a diverse range of businesses in a way that delivers value back to the ecosystem and all its members.

But blockchain-era communities will also have the power to exert great impact on the business itself. Because tokens are often designed to be portable, communities will have a new tool with which to wield their collective power. If a business is not serving a community, or violates the ethos or values of a community, that business could be abandoned en masse, along with all the economic weight that community represents. Companies that can find ways to align their business models to values and beliefs of a community's will find themselves in a position to better tap its potential power.

BLURRING THE LINES BETWEEN BUSINESS OWNERS AND PARTICIPANTS

On a token-driven platform (imagine a tokenized version of Amazon, Facebook, or Uber), the lines between participants can blur—all participants, whether buying or selling, consuming or contributing, would benefit from the increasing value of the network. This raises the possibility that token holders may act as promoters, working to refer and engage others, and growing the overall value of the network. Historically, businesses based on network effects struggle to get to the critical mass that makes a network truly valuable. Amazon, Facebook, and Uber derive much of their value from the size of their network. Tokens could, if the network is designed well, help propel a business past this classic dilemma; with everyone getting a share of the value created, all participants are motivated to make the network successful.

KJ Erickson, the cofounder and CEO of Public Market, a tokenized ecommerce protocol, believes that these centralized-network-effect businesses are primed for displacement. "As network-effect businesses grow, the value of participating and the cost of switching becomes higher, and so they naturally drive towards monopolies," she explains. "All for-profit companies have a fiduciary duty to serve shareholders, and so they extract as much profit as possible through huge fees—understanding that even if network participants are frustrated, they have few alternatives. I argue that the network effects of tomorrow will often be built around decentralized, tokenized ecosystems with no distinction between network participants and network owners. They'll capture the value of the network for participants without charging 'rent,' in the form of fees and data. It's a better outcome for everyone—and if well designed, these decentralized networks could even supplant some of today's most powerful companies."[31]

James Glasscock, a founder of both a blockchain consultancy and a crypto venture fund, describes a vision for a new balance of power. "In the current system, the incentives are not properly aligned for the good of the community. The incentives are aligned for shareholders. But isn't this backwards since the count of the community members that use these services far outnumber[s] the count of shareholders? Think about it, Netflix subscribers outnumber Netflix shareholders, Facebook users outnumber Facebook shareholders. Blockchain can help switch this paradigm and better align the interests of the shareholder and the customer."[132]

Implications: Program the Incentives, Program the Behavior

Clearly, blockchain-driven tokens are in their infancy. Today we can only speculate how we will behave with broad exposure to multiple token economies, when tokens become more easily exchangeable for traditional currency, and when they become integrated into a greater share of our digital lives. It is also uncertain whether we will become confused or develop "token fatigue," overwhelmed by all the tokens that are thrown our way.

It is, however, likely that we will go through several phases as we learn about tokens, and figure out what role we want them to play in our lives. We may start by discovering them, experimenting with them, and then eventually simplifying —curating a portfolio of tokens we care about and to which we are willing to dedicate mindshare. It is this select set, perhaps, with which we create habits and loyalty, eventually incorporating them into our daily lives. Perhaps the order changes, or the cycle repeats continually. Perhaps communities gravitate to favorite tokens or suites of tokens. But in some way our relationship with tokens will settle into some kind of cadence over the years to come.

Regardless of how this evolves, it is clear that tokens have the potential to trigger and interact with our psychology at a chemical level. It is clear they hold power. It is clear they could shape behavior at many levels. There is no doubt: this is an area to watch closely. Watch carefully how it develops, and conduct your own research to understand your customers' mindset around tokens, and how that changes over time. Experiment yourself with using token economies, and experiment—thoughtfully—as a business. But for now, let's unpack some of the areas in which tokens could have impact.

DRIVING ESCALATING COMMITMENT

It's a fact of every business: different segments of customers want different levels of engagement. Some just want a transactional relationship, to make a purchase and move on. Some want to believe in a business, and may spend great time and effort giving product feedback, making suggestions, evangelizing, and otherwise contributing to its success. And some fall in between. Blockchains and tokens in combination are flexible multi-tools capable of delivering tight-fit incentives for all. Token-based incentives will be versatile, easily scaling from rewarding a micro-behavior to incenting business-changing contributions.

They could also be used to cultivate a committed relationship from something that started much more casual. As tokens accumulate, users will likely take notice—suddenly, a balance earned through small, barely noticeable actions is worth something of value to that individual. This can offer a pivotal moment for the relationship between a business and a customer. It presents the opportunity for nurturing customers from casual users to more devoted customers and even promoters of the business. And this effect could escalate quickly. Because the value of the token theoretically rises with the value of the network, the more tokens a particular individual holds, the more vested they are in the success of the business, and the more they want it to increase in size and vibrancy. A simple reward could thus evolve into a currency that individuals actually personally care about.

They may care about it simply because they (eventually) could exchange their balances for goods and services they value, or convert it to local currency they can use at the grocery store. But there is also the possibility for something more. It's been well documented that today's consumer desires more "meaning." Tokens or token campaigns could be tied to social causes or brand missions that help a consumer feel they get meaning from their interactions with that business. The more aligned a brand is with an individual's values, and the more the individual sees the brand as helping them appear as the person they want to be, the more likely a business will be able to spark this effect. For this reason, it's quite possible we see many businesses of the blockchain era flex very closely to the macro (and micro) values and desires of their customers.

STOKING COMMUNITY THROUGH TOKENS

These same principles can be applied at a community level, and in fact, it is at this level that tokens will reveal their true superpower. A business could use tokens to tap into an existing community and incent that community to move in a direction that helps the business. Or, it could use tokens to foster the growth of a new community. Regardless, with the right circumstances they could be used to unleash baking soda-and-vinegar–like reactions that make change happen quickly—whether they are small actions that add up to something big, or are used in the form of bounties to motivate large-scale actions that drive the business forward.

USING TOKENS TO SHAPE INDIVIDUAL BEHAVIOR

Highly versatile, tokens will likely be used by brands and businesses in creative new ways to incent awareness, drive engagement, and trigger action—areas that have been increasingly difficult for marketing departments to crack. While the rules governing the token and any changes are typically baked into its design at birth, the token itself can be used very flexibly. They could be used, theoretically, to reward ongoing behavior such as social sharing, going into a store, converting a friend, completing a profile, achieving a new level of mastery, interacting with ads, or just using the product. Or they could be used in sophisticated single-use campaigns that integrate other technologies—making a purchase of something specific, sharing an image that includes a certain product, or interacting with an augmented reality experience on a package or label.

Blockchains could help advertising carry more impact. As discussed in the previous section, before consumers can absorb advertising, they first need to be paying attention. Consumers could be paid to watch ads, or to interact with them —even be rewarded when they make an immediate purchase. As more consumer-ready applications gain traction, they will offer a platform for brands to launch creative, context-aware advertising campaigns that reward consumers on their terms. For example, a retail brand could reward students who complete a course in an online degree program, or give gamers a reward when they reach a certain status in a gaming application.

This new incentive model also holds interesting possibilities for marketers to experiment with honing the granularity of their campaigns, as the space evolves. For example, if a consumer or influencer has been willing to make additional data available and verifiable, it could be used to target very specific customer profiles to take an action. Imagine a futuristic scenario, for example, in which an automotive company hopes to convert recent university graduates to their brand just as they start the next phase of their lives. They could deliver a generous promotion with assurance that they were verifiably being offered and redeemed by only these graduates—without the brand having to obtain or verify the actual data themselves. Or perhaps a new meal delivery service is looking to optimize operations by increasing penetration of a specific neighborhood—they could offer significant bounties to those who refer verifiable neighbors that convert to long-term customers. One could also imagine a future in which there is barely a middleman at all—individuals share a profile of the kind of advertising they would like to consume, and brands can interact directly with them, with both parties receiving high value.

INCENTING NOT JUST ACTION, BUT IMPACT

A key twist is that rewards could be tied to measures of quality. The definition—and measure—of quality will depend, of course, on what the business is trying to achieve. But the traceability of impact and results could influence the entire practice of measuring marketing ROI. One could imagine incenting the amount of time spent on an activity; how frequent the interaction, transaction, or share; or how many votes a response to a question receives from a community.

Over time, we are sure to see applications that help marketers make a direct correlation between amount of reward and the amount of value contributed to an application or platform—for example, a blog post that gets a high number of claps, likes, shares, and traffic could get a larger reward than one that doesn't. Or brands could take this a step further—by rewarding "highly regarded" content (measured in a similar way) that makes positive mention of a particular product. B2B companies could incent customers who are also product experts to provide quality support to their community's questions by highly rewarding answers that are completed in a certain timeframe or that receive a certain number of likes. A health insurance provider could tie rewards to the sustained maintenance of weight, and an auto insurance provider to the sustained adherence to speed limits.

THE NEXT-GEN INFLUENCER STRATEGY

Long before social, marketers used influencer strategies. For 20 years, the Milk Processor Education Program capitalized on the influence of celebrities, athletes, and social icons with the "Got Milk?" campaign. With the advent of social networks and platforms like Instagram, YouTube, and Twitter, people could go from relative obscurity to huge followings and influence from within the comfort of their own home. These influencers can command a lot of authority and trust with consumers. Seventy percent of teenage YouTube subscribers say they relate to YouTube creators (influencers who have met certain criteria on YouTube) more than traditional celebrities, and 40% of millennial subscribers say their favorite creator understands them better than their friends.[133] A single nod to a product or service from a key influencer can trigger instant excitement. Brands are becoming more adept at building relationships with these valuable advocates, and better equipping them to tell brand and product stories on their behalf.

What happens if tokens become a tool for brands to incent influencers? You can imagine the same dynamics that could motivate consumer behavior being applied to influencer armies. Rewards could be targeted to specific activities, or the quality of content as measured by shares or likes. Already, blockchain entrepreneurs are launching projects that focus on incenting influencers, with token rewards for "proof of contribution." Many of these early solutions feel experimental, although they already work to solve problems of verification, negotiation, micro-payments, and a currency that transcends borders. Larger social media companies are also getting involved and are sure to push the boundaries of how brands can incent influencers more efficiently, and with more transparency about results than ever before. When more evolved, they could provide a mechanism for truly leveraging even micro-influencers at massive scale.

The technology may also enable more creativity in influencer campaigns. Influencers by their very nature are masters of community engagement and viral tactics, and hold the potential to be a creative force supporting a brand's objectives. Conceivably, tokens and blockchain-driven validation could enable brands to incent purposeful creativity—aligning influencers' on-the-ground innovations with a brand's mission by rewarding the achievement of certain metrics. In essence, blockchain functionality could boost influencers to influence with more impact.

USING BLOCKCHAINS TO ENSURE QUALITY

But blockchains make it possible to go further than simply verifying and tracking metrics that indicate impact. They can go deeper, to verify the contributor is a real person. Since the dawn of digital marketing, marketers have long tolerated noise in their results from fakes, frauds, and now bots. Blockchains can certify that contribution is linked to a specific identity, and the reputation that identity has built over time. They even have the capability to verify additional data that a contributor has opted to add to their identity, such as locations, credentials, group affiliations, and other attributes. Because all of this data can be verified by a blockchain without divulging the real-world identity of the contributor, it can significantly prevent bad actors and fraudulent activity without compromising privacy.

Another way blockchain entrepreneurs drive the quality of an exchange or interaction is through a mechanism called, in crypto-speak, *staking*.

With staking, the individuals or parties involved put up tokens as a form of collateral. With this skin in the game, they are more incented to follow through to produce the promised outcome, whether that's providing a good or a service. If everything goes well, these stakes are returned to the original contributors. If it doesn't, they can be redistributed according to the rules of that protocol (and there are typically arbitration channels to deal with disputes). While there is still a lot to learn about this approach, it could evolve to be a powerful tool to incent behaviors that add value to a network.

Blockchains also have the potential to solve some of the advertising industry's biggest challenges, and blockchain entrepreneurs are swarming to this space. They are developing decentralized ad platforms and consent-based ads, and pairing up with ad industry R&D groups in consortiums to prevent fraud. The level of innovation that we will see in the next few years is sure to change the shape of the market. Many of these innovators are focused on developing transparent and secure marketplaces in which advertisers can validate directly that they are getting what they are paying for; this would indeed be a breakthrough in "truth in advertising." However, we will also see a range of new functionality that leverages token incentive models to garner attention and increase engagement from consumers—consumers that are verifiably real people, not bots.

BUT WHERE DO YOU START?

Knowledge of cryptoassets among the general population is currently very low. But this will not stop businesses from experimenting with the use of tokens. It may take some time, but best practices will eventually emerge to match consumers' readiness. The journey will likely start by framing tokens as something a consumer understands already, like a loyalty point or a reward. Consumers could accumulate and even use tokens without a need to understand the full extent of how they function or the richness of what they do—or even without knowing that these are cryptoassets at all. As more and more businesses incorporate tokens, and collectively invest resources in educating the general population, it is quite possible that one day in the near future we will see a rapid uptick in adoption of cryptoassets as a whole.

AGILE STRATEGIES, SMARTER MARKETING

Astute marketing teams may learn that tokens not only give their consumers feedback loops but also give the marketers themselves useful insights. With a proliferation of options for marketing spend, better clarity into what actually drives ROI is a highly attractive prospect. Marketers will be able to observe with higher fidelity and traceability how effectively a particular incentive triggers a specific action at a certain time or in a certain context. Tokens could be used very flexibly to tune behaviors, and the most effective teams will be those that have the unique skill sets to use agile strategies of rapid experimentation, measurement, and execution—and that have the skill sets to analyze and learn from the data these experiments produce. Over time, these teams could leverage these learnings to improve efficacy and even, one day, to optimize marketing budgets.

REINVIGORATE THE LOYALTY PROGRAM

Another area that is receiving a great deal of attention from blockchain entrepreneurs is loyalty programs. One day, we could hold tokens as loyalty "points," and combine those from a variety of brands into a single unified wallet. These rewards, even if multiple "currencies," could move without friction on a single platform. Consumers would not have to manage a maze of different program restrictions and redemption policies, and could potentially be more actively engaged with these valuable wallets of cross-program loyalty points than they are with today's fragmented and scattered programs.

Brands could gain visibility not only into how consumers earn loyalty points, but also into how they respond within the freedom of a larger redemption marketplace, potentially driving new insight on customer behavior. Consumers could even be incented to make different choices within that marketplace at different times.

We can also expect structural changes to how loyalty programs work. Brands may strike partnerships or create coalitions to develop "loyalty networks" that both meet their business objectives and give consumers a form of points that they value more highly than what they have access to today. New partners could be rapidly added to these networks without today's complexity, making it easier for loyalty programs to stay fresh and even to partner with complementary emerging brands that don't have the infrastructure or resources to support a traditional loyalty program partnership.

In fact, the idea of a formal points "partner" may one day fade away, to be replaced by a vast ecosystem of merchants of all sizes. Marketplaces of granters, earners, sellers, and buyers may even emerge, as may consumer-to-consumer point exchanges. As the idea of a formal loyalty "program" begins to dissipate, we may see a replacement that looks more like a series or network of highly targeted, and increasingly tailored, ongoing loyalty campaigns.

As loyalty programs collide with blockchain capabilities, relatively feature-rich loyalty incentives could be offered by just about any size or maturity business. No longer will extensive program development or the buildout of a complex support infrastructure be necessary. Industries that were never able to effectively leverage old reward point structures may find new opportunities in this next-gen version. Service providers will likely spring up to assist businesses with every aspect of these loyalty campaigns, making them "turn-key accessible" to virtually every merchant, organization, or even home-based seller.

Brands will need to keep a close watch on the evolution of the loyalty points space so they can effectively respond. While early, one could imagine that consumers may begin to expect rewards at every turn—every ad they watch, every share they post, and at every point-of-sale transaction. This could depress the value of an endorsement ("he's doing it just because he's getting rewards"). Because having multiple partners on a single platform increases the value of the rewards on that platform, there may be great pressure to join a network in order to remain competitive. Consumers may develop distaste for the lock-in that typifies today's programs. But if these next-gen loyalty networks become commonplace, the competitive advantage of any one brand's approach may diminish. Over time, consumer interaction with these programs could look less like loyalty and more like a transaction-level preference for whomever happens to be offering the best reward at the time.

Brands will need to think very carefully about how to design and participate in these next-gen programs to ensure they effectively reinforce the relationship customers have with their particular brand. There could be benefit to brands by moving early to develop a blockchain-based loyalty platform that is attractive to both their business and their customers. Early movers could set a precedent for the governance of these new networks, the design of the incentives, the regulation of who owns the customer and has access to their data, and the rules for the program. But while there are many highly regarded brands that have put out a press release or other indicator that they will use tokens in a loyalty program, actual implementation must move in lockstep with the maturation of the space.

THE POWER OF PARTNERSHIP

It is true not only of loyalty programs that the more opportunities for redemption, the more valuable it becomes to the consumer. This is true for the use of any incentive—the more places a token can be used, the more utility value it holds. For this reason, blockchain-based tokens are most powerful when tied to a thriving ecosystem of participants and partners.

To be a "success," tokens have to earn liquidity in the marketplace, and connect to a thriving ecosystem where they can be directly earned and spent. While thousands of tokens exist today, there will be a much smaller number that gain long-term prominence. They may be optimized for different uses—there may be a dominant token (or a set of several) for media, another for education, and yet another for gaming, for example, but regardless, the winners will have a booming ecosystem and vibrant mini-economy. Watch carefully and be deeply thoughtful in picking teams, making alliances, and selecting platforms.

But do partner, wisely and often. Partnerships will be an important component of success to businesses in a blockchain world, and the successful businesses of tomorrow will become increasingly adept at navigating these alliances to mutual gain. As we evolve to a more collaborative relationship between customer and business, we could also evolve to more collaborative relationships among businesses themselves, aligned by a common mission and vision for the customers they serve.

> *Partner wisely and often. Partnerships will be an important component of success to businesses in a blockchain world, and the successful businesses of tomorrow will become increasingly adept at navigating these alliances to mutual gain.*

The Beauty of System-Wide Alignment

When orchestrated well, tokens could be used to align all stakeholders toward a common goal to drive the organization forward. This includes not only individual customers and networked communities of customers, but the ecosystem of partners and even employees and investors as well. The lines separating the roles of these contributors could blur as motivations and actions move in concert. Applied especially against missions that advance society, this is when these potent incentives turn beautiful—and could bring great long-term success to the organizations that master it.

THE DANGERS OF A COIN-OPERATED WORLD

From a social science perspective, I cannot emphasize enough the grave responsibility that comes with this powerful tool. There is a flip side of token-fueled, gamified technology. One day, we may all be interacting with multiple token economies on a daily basis. If and when this happens, we will need to be more mindful about how we humans stay in control. The feedback loops, the immediate gratification, and the manipulation of micro-behaviors that tokens enable (especially combined with gaming fundamentals) mean that tomorrow's applications could be plugged more directly into our chemical circuitry. They may constantly reward us for participating, and could become addictive in nature. We will need to work harder to make sure the technology is serving us—versus us serving it.

We can use gamified applications to help us exercise more effectively, eat more healthfully, learn new job skills, build important sources of income, and connect more deeply to our communities—or we could let them alter our belief of what's important. We've seen how hard it is to strike this balance with Web 2.0 (think of the teen who starts to tie his sense of worth to the number of Instagram followers he has). It will be harder as we are surrounded by more and more token economies vying to influence our behavior.

As you deepen your exploration of this space, my hope is that you will be thoughtful about the implications of the technology and your work. Importantly, there is a strong argument for this approach from a coldly quantitative perspective as well. In the blockchain era, the businesses that will thrive are those that do right by the community. Every community is composed of many individuals, and their stakeholders—parents, peers, and partners—who will all be watching to see who is serving their interests best now, and for the future.

Throughout your journey, there will be opportunities to make decisions that impact your customers' lives. I believe there is always an option to choose a direction that more symbiotically supports customers' health, success, and happiness. And while at times there are short-term hard costs associated with this choice, the organizations that follow this path will enjoy longer, stronger relationships with customers, stronger communities, and long-term business results. This kind of symbiosis, in fact, will be a key driver of the new collaborative relationships that will typify this next era.

 ## Cautions and Considerations

New incentive models present both threats and opportunities to existing businesses. While some of these cautions and considerations are very future-focused, they are meant to provoke your thinking about what could come. This is by no means an exhaustive list; it provides additional food for thought on how to prepare for this new paradigm.

CAUTIONS

Overestimating (or underestimating) the value of tokens to the consumer

In this early stage there are a lot of unknowns about how tokens will be valued by a consumer. Today, much of a token's "price" is determined by speculative investing activity. But until tokens have reached broader acceptance from both consumers and merchants, we will not understand their true, nonspeculative value. While a token may look like it has a certain value associated with it, today that is only the value for someone who knows how to exchange it for other cryptoassets, traditional currencies (also called *fiat*), or the limited goods and services currently available for that particular token (if any). Research your customers' mindsets to understand how they perceive token value, or experiment with incentive campaigns for a token's already-enthusiastic users. And conduct lots of research to understand how this changes over time as the market evolves—perceptions could change rapidly.

Trying to explain too much or too little

Just as most consumers don't understand the inner workings of your loyalty programs or what happens to get a PayPal payment from their account to yours, they will not understand the ins and outs of how tokens work. To the consumer, many of the details will be—and should be—opaque. Incentives should be communicated in a way that is exciting and attractive, and introduces near-zero friction.

At the same time, make sure that more information is available for those who want and are ready to know more. The blockchain movement has high standards for open sourcing everything: code, governance, even how money is spent. Don't make it look like you are trying to hide a cryptoasset. Make sure that those who want to understand more can.

Treating customers like a social experiment

Consumers are not rats. But if you overdo it on rewarding for small tasks before you know the nuances of how to do it right, they may feel like you think they are. Companies need to learn the nuance, for their particular industry, of giving both large and small context-aware, value-added rewards to different demographic and psychographic segmentations of customers, in different settings. At this stage, this is the work of pioneers—there are no best practices, and there are no guardrails. However, you may be able to be a part of establishing them, or can leverage the specialists who are sure to emerge.

CONSIDERATIONS

Understand what quality engagement and content means to you

This early stage is also a good time to more deeply understand what kinds of engagement results in business value, and what that value is. Gallup research has found that customers who are fully engaged represent an average 23% premium in terms of share of wallet, profitability, revenue, and relationship growth over the average customer.[134] But what does engagement mean in your business? What specific triggers or actions could potentially be encouraged through incentives?

While it may prove elusive to quantify value for many forms of engagement, you can map out the relative value of specific actions and events that trigger a customer to more deeply engage with your product or brand (i.e., specific enough to be reflected in code). You can also map out "signals of quality" for influencer, social, or community content to better understand what drives value in that area. This kind of analysis can help you home in on what incentive models may be most compelling to experiment with first.

Understand how your community, ecosystem, and mission intersect

You've seen how in the blockchain world, power comes from aligning the interests and values of community and ecosystems. Study your universe to identify what drives your customers, what drives your partners, and where these interests intersect. Use this filter to give you a compass with which to assess other potential partners or members of your ecosystem.

Find your crypto-savvy customers and collaborate with them

Identify segments of your customer base or influencer network that are early adopters of cryptoassets, and bring them into the fold. These early adopters will likely have a unique profile and many characteristics may not be extensible across your broader customer base. However, they can help you bridge two worlds: your brand and the world of token economies. Talk to them, learn from them, and brainstorm with them. You will likely generate insights for how to start experimenting in the space.

Use someone else's application or platform to run test campaigns

Grow your knowledge of how to use token-based incentives by testing campaigns on a blockchain application or platform that is gaining traction with your customer base (using their token). While not every company will be able to find an appropriate partner at this early stage, new players will continually emerge. Start by putting together a list of the kinds of companies that could be a potential fit, and keep watch on the space as it develops. Once you find a company that is a fit, work with their team to get practiced with different ways to target different kinds of behavior, and gain some early insight on how to measure the return to your business.

Examples

Entrepreneurs are using incentives to shape and align behavior across a diverse set of use cases. Time will tell if they will work out in the long run, but right now, here are a few projects chosen to give you a glimpse of just some of these.

SWYTCH: INCENTING GLOBAL-SCALE ADOPTION OF RENEWABLE ENERGY

A sophisticated team from investment banking, energy trading, and academia came together to create Swiss nonprofit Swytch to incentivize the world to adopt renewable energy at scale. They saw that while billions have been spent by governments to incentivize renewables, overall success has been limited. Carbon emissions continue to hit record highs and the threat of climate change looms larger every day. The team is developing a blockchain-based platform that seeks to verify and reward the production of sustainable and renewable energy through the Swytch token. By capturing data directly from IoT and smart devices and through market aggregators, Swytch can create immutable proof of production and dynamically allocate tokens. Swytch aims to serve as a globally standardized incentive for producers, and allow consumers to validate their own sustainable actions.

The team aims to address key systemic issues that have held back the broad adoption of renewable energy: the lack of a global, easily tradable incentive mechanism; the difficulty of verifying and securing production data at the source; and the dearth of quality public data on where and how renewable energy is produced. The team has been cultivating partnerships from cities and corporations to build interest in the initiative. Eventually, they envision incenting consumer actions, such as the use of an electric vehicle.

"We hope to accelerate the switch from fossil to sustainable energy, but in a highly equitable, decentralized manner," explains founder John Henry Clippinger. "I think it is a very reasonable aspiration. Solar and battery power is getting cheaper and more decentralized, and people can be incentivized to not only transition, but actually produce and monetize their own energy. We want to make it as easy to develop your own solar energy business as it is to buy a car, and we want to open that up anywhere in the world. This not only creates a new infrastructure, but changes two fundamentals: the source of the energy and the source of value generation. Blockchains can help us move to this concept of the 'prosumer,' in which people are both producers and consumers of value. It's a very different world."[135]

MOBIVITY: ALIGNING AN ECOSYSTEM OF BRANDS AND CONSUMERS

Mobivity Holdings Corp. touches 30 million Americans and tens of millions of transactions weekly through a proprietary platform that helps restaurant and retail brands such as Subway, Round Table Pizza, and Smashburger better understand customer behavior across thousands of brick-and-mortar locations. I sat down with CEO Dennis Becker to learn how his company, which is investing in a blockchain-based infrastructure, was thinking about the technology. "We see blockchains as an architecturally superior way to unlock new business models that solve problems these brands face," he said. "It can serve as an enabling infrastructure that makes new kinds of interoperability possible. It can open up opportunities that no one has ever before attempted because they would be a logistical mess."

Dennis walked me through multiple layers to explain these opportunities. He started with a view into how blockchains can align the behaviors of an entire ecosystem of supply chain and food service operator brands. "Billions of dollars are moving from brand to brand to fund joint marketing," he said. "But because their systems are proprietary and the data lives in silos, there is very little visibility into what is actually working, and very little control once those dollars go over the wall. It's like a multibillion-dollar shadow economy." Blockchains could provide an infrastructure that sits between brands, providing an interoperable data, accounting, and payment layer that could trace the redemption of a joint promotion directly to an individual franchise—and compensate them immediately. "By making it possible for these brands to talk to each other technically," Dennis went on, "by giving them visibility into the same data, it can help bring them closer and align them on their value proposition." This blockchain-driven infrastructure can also help companies that "have no way to leverage customer relationships across an umbrella of brands because each has its own centralized, proprietary data stores and infrastructure."

Dennis then walked me through the customer view. "There is an opportunity to create a more trusted relationship with the consumer, giving them more control, and giving both brand and consumer more value." He described how consumers could choose to let a brand know a little bit more about them in exchange for more targeted, personalized offers. "Let's say I want to try out 'smart offers,'" he said. "I could let a brand look at my location or other data, and so when they reach out to me I can get more value out of it—more of what I want." So, a coffee purchase this morning, followed by a sandwich at a different merchant this afternoon, could fuel a personalized discount for dinner tomorrow, with each transaction informing the brand, the consumer, and the consumer's profile. The data could be stored in a "personal information wallet, not on a brand's servers, and I could turn off a brand's access whenever I want to."

"But," explained Dennis, "it's still very, very early." His company is developing blockchain infrastructure in parallel with their existing platform so that "when business users are ready to experiment, the infrastructure is already there," ready for them.

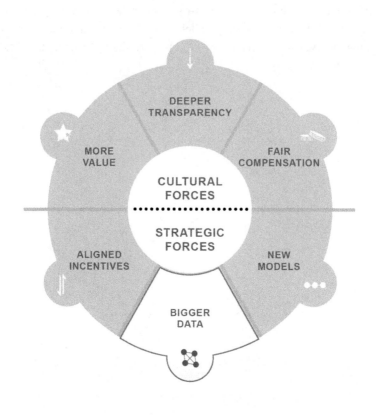

BIGGER DATA

Hiding within those mounds of data is knowledge that could change the life of a patient, or change the world.

—ATUL BUTTE, MD, PHD, PROFESSOR

Summary

Blockchains could one day open a broader, deeper data layer than has ever been available. However, because it would no longer be proprietary, organizations would have to work harder than ever to extract competitive advantage from that data.

Blockchain technology holds the potential to unleash more comprehensive data—data that could drive deeper insight, and help to realize big data's promise to advance business and society. However, it comes with a key tradeoff. "Ownership" of the data shifts from organizational silos to the individual contributor, who, in the vision of blockchain entrepreneurs, will be able to safely "vault" a great range of data, including, potentially, new datasets that they had not previously been willing to make available.

Decisions to use or sell that data would also be increasingly controlled by the contributor. Those organizations that learn to operate successfully within this new paradigm could access a new breadth and depth of data to improve products, market smarter, and discover insights that may very well change our world. However, when fewer datasets are proprietary, businesses will have to work harder than ever to sustain competitive advantage.

 The Setting

BUSINESSES FUELED BY BIG DATA

We live among a business landscape obsessed with big data. For years a diverse array of companies has relentlessly dug into building out their data stores and predictive analytic capabilities. It's not just internet giants, but companies in industries as broad as retail, agriculture, health care, education, and transportation. They've accelerated data collection, from credit card swipes to location tracking, entertainment preferences, biometrics, and social media connections. Data fuels decisions in the C-suite, marketing, product development, finance, production, human resources, and research and development.

Some businesses are even investing billions in strategies to get as much data as they can about consumers' health, location, preferences, and behaviors. Google bought Nest, Facebook acquired WhatsApp, and UnderArmour has made multiple acquisitions to become one of the largest digital fitness companies in the world. These investments have been driven in part by an assumption that the organization collecting the data owns it, and has unfettered access to its use—that the one with the most data will win.

FALLING SHORT OF THE BIG DATA PROMISE

Companies are doing amazing things with data. T-mobile cuts customer churn, Walmart stocks stores based on predictions of what will sell, and Kaiser has improved patient outcomes. But today's insights are only as powerful as the data silos in which they sit. Each business works to develop its own data view—data it gets from customers, acquisitions, partnerships, and data brokers. But the resulting pool is still filled with an incomplete picture of a customer or condition, and data of variable quality and cleanliness.

The real promise of big data is realized when data is broken out of corporate fiefdoms. When data scientists talk about the most promising contribution big data could make to our world—things like fighting hunger, slowing climate change, and developing personalized medicines—they are talking about data that's bigger, better, cleaner, and richer than what we have today. They are talking about breaking data out of silos so they can discover the insights hidden within this vaster data ocean.

Even companies with much more modest goals of building better products, deepening understanding of their customers, and identifying new markets crave much more holistic—and more accurate—data than they have access to today. Their holy grail is a unified data profile on customers.

FIGHTING THE IDEA OF OWNERSHIP

But the very idea of a corporation owning our data is under attack. Certainly, we've granted them permission, in the reams of legalese we rarely review when signing up with a new company, and we've expanded that by ignoring the legal updates filling our email inboxes. And we've given freely: Facebook, the largest online social network, has collected 300 petabytes of personal data since its inception[136]—a hundred times the amount the Library of Congress has collected in over 200 years.[137]

But it is becoming increasingly obvious that these organizations are poor stewards of our data, and it's hurting us. An employee at an Anthem health insurance subsidiary opened a phishing email and, because the company had failed to patch a known vulnerability, 80 million member and employee records were stolen. Equifax traced the theft of Social Security numbers and other sensitive information for 143 million Americans to a software flaw that could have been fixed. And the misuse of Facebook data by Cambridge Analytica is surely not going to be the last scandal that drives attention to the danger of allowing companies unfettered access and permissive usage of consumers' data.

The public's awareness of this threat is growing. But they have little choice but to hand over their data if they want access to modern basics like credit, health care, and social networks. They may not trust these companies to be good guardians, but they don't have an attractive alternative.

Regulators are starting to step in with power the public doesn't have. General Data Protection Regulation (GDPR) is a new European Union law with strict requirements on data protection and privacy that corporations have been scrambling to meet. GDPR focuses on ensuring that people who use online services know not only exactly what data those companies will take, but how they put it to use.

After the Cambridge Analytica scandal, Facebook CEO Mark Zuckerberg was summoned to Congress, where he was grilled for 10 hours by nearly 100 legislators in the House and Senate. It's still unclear what regulation will come of the growing data privacy inquisition, but it is clear the pressure for change is intense. Representative Billy Long of Missouri told Zuckerberg, "You're the guy to fix this. You need to save your ship." While even Zuckerberg said regulation of his industry is "inevitable," David Vladeck, former director of the US Federal Trade Commission's Bureau of Consumer Protection, said, "We do not have an omnibus privacy legislation at the federal level. We don't have a statute that recognizes generally that privacy is a right that's secured by federal law. And that puts us at the opposite end of the spectrum from some of the other major economies in the world."[138]

This same movement to protect citizens' privacy can also make companies reluctant to try to find a way to share data, even if doing so could lead to a positive outcome for an individual patient, or for broader society. We can see this quite clearly in health care, where laws like the United States' Health Insurance Portability and Accountability Act (HIPAA) provide important protections, but make it harder to realize the promise of such lofty initiatives as personalized medicine, in which a person's genetics, environment, and lifestyle can help determine the best approach to prevent or treat disease.

Andy Coravos is passionate about how advancements in cryptography—of which, she emphasizes, blockchains are just one aspect—combine with advancements in data science. She is the CEO and cofounder of Elektra Labs, a company working at the forefront of digital medicine (specifically, biomarkers and sensors). In a recent conversation, Andy emphasized the tension that exists today between the two arguments of "we need privacy," and "we need sharing."

"What matters most," she explains, "is data governance. If I am sick, I want my doctor to have access to my medical records—I don't want them to be private. What we need now is more secure sharing, more control, and more governance."[139]

Across the spectrum, it is clear that pressure is building.

IOT FUELS THE FIRE

Much of the scrutiny from both consumers and regulators so far has focused on data created, retyped, or reposted by humans. We are about to see an explosion in new classes and types of data coming from the billions of IoT devices that will be surrounding us, many of them measuring and reporting on everything from how we move to our biometrics and even our emotional state. As mentioned previously, Gartner estimates that more than 20 billion connected "things" will be in use by 2020.[140]

IS IT TIME FOR A NEW DEAL ON DATA?

In 2007, Sandy Pentland first proposed a "New Deal on Data" to the World Economic Forum (WEF). Sandy is one of the preeminent thinkers on data. He was named a world's most powerful data scientist by *Forbes*, is a founding member of Google's advisory board, created and directed the MIT Media Lab, and is on the board of the UN Sustainable Global Partnership for Sustainable Development Data.

Through multiple discussions at the WEF, the New Deal took shape. The key insight, he said, is that, "Our data are worth more when shared. Aggregate data—averaged, combined across populations, and often distilled to high-level features—can be used to inform improvements in systems such as public health, transportation, and government."[141]

The cornerstone of the proposal was that to have a successful data-driven society, we must have the guarantee that our data will not be abused: ownership of data must be returned to the people. The New Deal puts people at the center, not corporations: "The current personal data ecosystem is feudal, fragmented, and inefficient. Too much leverage is currently accorded to [organizations] that enroll and register end users. Their siloed repositories . . . contain data of varying qualities; some are attributes of persons that are unverified . . . For many individuals, the risks and liabilities of the current ecosystem exceed the economic returns . . . Personal privacy concerns are thus addressed inadequately at best, or simply overlooked in the majority of cases."[142]

Ultimately, the Chairman of the Federal Trade Commission (who was part of the working group) put forward the US "Consumer Data Bill of Rights" (which has not yet resulted in actual controls), and the EU Justice Commissioner declared a version of the New Deal to be a basic human right.

But the New Deal considered ownership the minimal guideline. "There needs to be one more principle . . . to adopt policies that encourage the combination of massive amounts of anonymous data to promote the Common Good." The New Deal continued: "to enable the sharing of personal data and experiences, we need secure technology and regulation that allows individuals to safely and conveniently share personal information with each other, with corporations, and with government . . . we must promote greater idea flow among individuals, not just within corporations or government departments . . . the entities who should be empowered to share and make decisions about their data are the people themselves: users, participants, citizens."[143]

The New Deal envisioned a more highly functioning digital economy: a world in which people could choose to share data—thus making big data safer and more transparent, as well as more liquid and available. It anticipated an environment in which true data-driven breakthroughs would be possible, by breaking data out of silos where nobody even knows it's there, and making it available to data scientists while concurrently protecting the person who provided it.

What the New Deal on Data did not include was a solution for how to make this possible.

WHAT'S COMING NEXT COULD CHANGE EVERYTHING

While it has moved slowly, it's clear that the cry for giving data ownership back to the people has been building. Consumers are more aware, and regulators have begun to mobilize. But there hasn't been a technology that could enable a real alternative. Until now.

With blockchains, an answer is possible.

 # What Blockchains Make Possible

WHO REALLY OWNS THE DATA?

Blockchains set loose a tectonic shift in the idea of data ownership. This will be a two-edged sword for companies fueled by consumer data. One edge sharply limits the access businesses have to data. The other could give some organizations bigger and better data than they've ever had before.

It starts by putting the consumer at the center.

YOUR VERY OWN BLACK BOX

Imagine this: one day, you could safely place an anonymized, encrypted version of your identity data in a "black box" on a blockchain. You could choose to have a trusted third party verify that your identity is a "real" person. You could also choose to tie different datasets to this "prime identity." For example, the data flowing out of your connected home could be gathered in a "home" subidentity, and you could create subidentities for your connected car, commerce, banking, academic accreditations, health care records, social networks, and so on. You have essentially created a personal data vault. Your data has not only become yours, but it has become much more secure—and much more useful to you.

There are many emerging companies that are seeking to become a trusted protector of user data and identity data. In a banking relationship, the bank holds your money, but does not spend it at their discretion—it is yours and you decide how it is spent. With an "identity" bank, a user could safely store their verified identity (or an anonymous proxy of their identity) on a blockchain. You could choose how it is used. The vault could properly function as a safe, universal "key" for identity, and you could approve specific applications to access it and use it.

CONSUMER AT THE CONTROLS

In this vision, you choose who sees and uses your data, granting access only as necessary. Whether this party can attribute the data you share to your actual physical world identity is up to you. And you can even choose to sell your data to a brand, or donate it to a research study you support. Blockchain entrepreneurs term this *self-sovereign identity* because it lives outside of the sovereign of any central organization or state—the sovereignty comes from the individual.

Only what's needed for a specific purpose would be shared. Today, when you go out for a drink with a friend, you may be asked for an ID. You hand a stranger, some guy leaning against the door of a bar, a lot of personal information: your full name, home address, license number, birth date, height, weight, and eye color. But all they really need is a single data point: that you meet the drinking age requirement, yes or no. With a blockchain-driven black box, you could divulge only what is required for a specific digital interaction. And users could grant—or revoke—access to a specific company on a need-to-know basis.

For convenience, you may choose to cluster the data in your black box into different profiles that you share with different organizations. Just as you may act differently with your friends on the weekend than you do with colleagues in a meeting, you may have what some blockchain identity companies are calling "avatars." You might have a private avatar for managing private affairs, family, and wealth; a business avatar for managing bank accounts and loans; and a social media avatar for managing the data that you share with your social networks. There are several pioneering companies developing a vision for making this an accessible, easy experience for users. There is a long road ahead, however, to develop both the technology and governance that truly protects users. As Meltem Demirors has said, "Self-sovereign identity sounds good, but the implementation will likely be the battle of our lifetime."[144]

SECURING AND PROTECTING THE DATA

This vision is also more secure than today's corporate "honeypots" filled with millions of records that invite continuous cyberattacks. Not only is your data in its own vault, it is kept private through various cryptography approaches.

The spread of data is controlled as well. Today, data you don't even realize has been gathered about you is scattered across databases across the world owned by companies you can't name. With this blockchain vision, individuals could audit what data has been collected, and trace how it has been used. Not only could just your relevant data be made available to a third party, but in addition technologists have made great progress on solutions to enable a third party to identify patterns in encrypted data without decrypting it first (essentially, enabling data science to unearth insights without "seeing" the underlying data or compromising the privacy of those who contributed it). This is a powerful evolution in what is possible with data.

THE POTENTIAL OF NEW, POWERFUL DATA LAYERS

As we discussed earlier, big data holds the promise of great advancements in business and society. However, with organizations considering data they "own" as proprietary, data scientists are typically limited to insights only as powerful as the data in their organization. Today, breaking data out of these silos would violate increasing regulation and privacy norms, and increase risk of compromise and attack. But as users control more of their data, the concept of a new universal "data layer" arises. In this vision, the data lives in the data layer, but is accessible —as needed and if permission is granted by the contributor of the data—across applications and digital interfaces. Over time, this layer could become a trusted repository and source for the data of millions—or billions—of users and devices.

In the hopes of many blockchain natives working in this space, the data layer is interoperable across platforms and protocols. Because the data would not be exclusive to a particular application, this could have significant impact to companies whose products use data to lock in their customers—if this future is realized. You may have invested a great deal of effort, for example, in developing your LinkedIn profile. While it is easy to cut and paste the text from a colleague's recommendation, you cannot similarly transfer the veracity of that recommendation—that it came from a real person who wrote it about you. That is something that only LinkedIn can provide. However, in the blockchain future, elements of reputation like reviews, endorsements, and networks could theoretically be made portable, changing the drivers of competitive advantage for some companies (and there are blockchain entrepreneurs who have already introduced early versions of products that do this).

THE BLOCKCHAINS THEMSELVES ARE PUBLIC DATA LAYERS

Blockchains by their very nature are public and auditable (with so-called "private" blockchains being accessible only to a defined community). This means that the data residing on a (public) blockchain is available to all. Different protocols will take different approaches to obscuring the data, or placing some data "on-chain" and other data "off-chain" with an encrypted link that alone renders it usable, but there is still data to be had for anyone who chooses to inspect it. This is of special interest to those looking to perform analytics on token economies, but may have other uses as well.

AT THE STARTING LINE

We are still in the achingly early days of developing the technology to support this fascinating but futuristic vision. Many of these data types must abide by regulation (like health data) or involve the coordination of many parties (consumers, new trusted third parties, and other businesses), presenting additional complexity to making this vision a reality. Importantly, the entire vision hinges first on consumers broadly adopting blockchain-based identities (the "vaults"). While there are easily hundreds of projects angling to serve various markets, they face an arduous journey to establish trusted relationships with consumers. Expect it also to take a long time for technical and legal issues to be worked out.

But there are great volumes of financial and human capital pouring into the space with the goal of bringing this concept to market. Early use cases may focus on data of little consequence or with targeted and likely highly technical communities (a great deal of focus, for example, is being put into exploring some of these ideas through the lens of artificial intelligence, with its insatiable thirst for large datasets to be used in "training" machines). But over time, innovators will achieve breakthroughs that collectively move us in this direction. And there are entrepreneurs who are inching toward working proof of concepts even with sensitive data, such as health data.

THE TWO-EDGED SWORD OF THE BLOCKCHAIN DATA STORY

This visionary shift in ownership carries a mix of consequences for the data-driven corporation. Those that depend on their stores of consumer data for competitive advantage will have to rethink how they retain their position. This includes companies that use data to lock consumers into a platform (as social media does today). On the flip side, the accuracy, the depth, and the breadth of data available could skyrocket. Corporations could also be relieved of the massive risk—and cost—of being a guardian of sensitive data. And those that are incurring a great cost to verify identities for new customers today, such as banks, could significantly reduce those costs by offloading this to reliable third parties.

Implications: Rethinking the Rules of Competition

BIGGER, BETTER DATA

> *One of the first steps to promoting liquidity in land and commodity markets is to guarantee ownership rights so that people can safely buy and sell. Similarly, a first step toward creating more ideas and greater flow of ideas—idea liquidity—is to define ownership rights.*

> —DANIEL "DAZZA" GREENWOOD, ARKADIUSZ STOPCZYNSKI, BRIAN SWEATT,
> THOMAS HARDJONO, AND ALEX "SANDY" PENTLAND
> IN "THE NEW DEAL FOR DATA"

Google's research chief Peter Norvig famously said, "We don't have better algorithms than anyone else; we just have more data."[145] And study after study has shown that more data can beat better models. It's one of the reasons that today, power resides with those who own the most data.

The blockchain era could change this balance.

While there is still much work to be done—from technical development to the emergence of cross-platform standards to, importantly, broad ecosystem adoption—there is a great deal of attention and investment from technology industry heavyweights as well as smart young players. In this view of the future, the data stored in consumers' personal vaults would be more accurate and more holistic than what is tucked away in today's corporate silos. But the key shift for organizations is that they will no longer own it—the consumer does. Data that used to be a competitive advantage could become a commodity. What was once available to one organization could now be accessible to many. Instead, power will shift to those who can tap into the most data, and can gain insights better and faster than others.

Those organizations that can figure out how to get to this bigger (and better) data have the potential to drive deeper insight—and finally realize the true promise of big data to advance business and society. Or, simply to build better products and do smarter marketing. Blockchain-era datasets could potentially be:

Better quality

In a study of over 2,000 data and analytics decision makers across 10 countries, KPMG and Forrester Consulting found that just 38% have a high level of confidence in their customer insights (and only a third seem to trust the analytics they generate from their business operations). Yet the vast majority say these insights are critical to their business decision making.[146] Because the usefulness of a data vault to a consumer is higher if it is accurate, individuals will be motivated to ensure the accuracy of their data. And, because of blockchains' unique ability to immutably validate data, organizations could have greater confidence in the integrity, accuracy, and provenance of data, whether it is coming from human or machine.

Deeper

If the adoption of blockchain-based identity becomes mainstream, and consumers perceive blockchains to be a secure, value-added alternative, there is no limit to the depth of data they may eventually contribute. Businesses could incent consumers to share data on psychographic characteristics or personal interests and needs. Consumers may even make personal data available they would never dream of sharing with a company today. Wearable sensor technology can now measure tone of voice, movement, gesticulation, and emotion. Once this technology breaks out of the lab and into our day-to-day lives, it could be used to understand relationships and behavior at a very intimate level. For the right incentive or mission, consumers may offer this up to organizations for their use. "People are okay about sharing data if they believe they'll benefit from it and it's not going to be shared further in ways they don't understand," explains Sandy Pentland. [147] This data could be offered up in a way that contributes to the cause but holds back actual identity, protecting individual privacy.

Broader

Likewise, as comfort levels increase, users could contribute a greater range of data. Click and search data may be joined by social network, health, fitness, car, and home data. Blockchain technology will be coming of age in concert with the imminent mainstreaming of IoT—a synergistic pairing. As consumers awaken to the troves of data these growing volumes of devices collect, blockchain functionality could help them feel comfortable that the data won't bring them harm. Identity systems on a blockchain could ensure a safe place for the data, and open up the possibility that it can later drive value back to the consumer whose actions created it, if they chose. As described in the "New Deal on Data," giving "customers a stake in the new data economy . . . will bring first greater stability and then eventually greater profitability as people become more comfortable sharing data."[148]

More unified

The unified customer profile has become a holy grail, ever-elusive, for many marketing departments. This coveted holistic view could reveal who a customer is, what they want, and when they want it with such granularity that marketers could present just the right offer at just the right time to trigger action (even if they can't tie this profile to a specific person). That's quite a power. In the blockchain era, some companies could get closer to this tantalizing prospect. Perhaps they attain access to massive volumes of data from the new broader, deeper data layer (and successfully use advanced analytics against them). Or, they gain such deep trust from customers that they are able to achieve access to key datasets within the personal identity vault. And these offers could operate with a more symbiotic ethos than is possible today—data could fuel the discovery of offers that customers actually want instead of being bombarded with offers that just clutter their world.

THE VISION OF THE DATA MARKETPLACE

As more and more individuals, machines, and organizations use blockchain-based identity systems, a kind of global data commons could surface. As more contributors and types of datasets feed this data commons, it would attract businesses seeking to access it, and data marketplaces could emerge. Whether driven by consortiums of established enterprises or newly established blockchain natives, these services will facilitate the buying and selling of data between individuals, organizations, and even machines. With transparent pricing and usage tracking, these data marketplaces could become efficient business models for data creators, and we could imagine that some businesses or consumers will discover creative ways to drive revenue from them (for example, a drone enthusiast who maintains an entire fleet to gather and sell weather and image data). This would thus attract more data sellers—and activate powerful network effects to grow the value for all parties.

THE REDEFINITION OF COMPETITIVE ADVANTAGE

As data becomes more of a commodity, accessible by many, it starts to tear apart our conception of what competitive advantage is in a digital world. This could trigger power transfers that we couldn't have anticipated just a few years ago. No doubt these changes will build ever so slowly at first, but eventually, category by category, they will bubble up through enough of our institutions to reach the proverbial tipping point. And at some point it could happen: no longer will data itself be a competitive advantage.

Where, then, is competitive advantage to be found?

DATA SCIENCE QUALITY COULD BE MORE IMPORTANT THAN EVER

In 2008, DJ Patil and Jeff Hammerbacher sat down for lunch in a Palo Alto cafe. The two men were struggling to build out teams that could find value in the vast amounts of data that the young companies they worked for—LinkedIn and Facebook—were throwing off. Over broccolini, DJ asked Jeff, "Hey, this thing we do —what do you call it?" Neither knew what title to give HR for their open jobs. "It wasn't a statistician," DJ told me, "or an economist, or a research scientist—and business analyst sounded too much like Wall Street." By the time they finished lunch, the two had found a new candidate: data scientist. DJ and his team then ran a test: they listed the same open jobs under different titles. "We ended up hiring only the people who had applied for the data science jobs. The applicants were really cool and clever, and didn't fit any mold—we had a rocket scientist, and a former brain surgeon," DJ said with a laugh.[149]

By 2011, in Santa Clara, California, O'Reilly Media gathered data scientists for their first industry event, the inaugural Strata Data Conference. There were 1,400 attendees. In 2012 an entry for "Data Scientist" showed up on Wikipedia, and three years later, DJ Patil became the first Chief Data Scientist of the United States.

Over the last decade, data science has gone from an obscure practice to one of the key forces driving decisions in conference rooms across the globe, industry after industry. The best teams are able not only to answer key questions with insights found in the data, but also to take broad expeditions to discover questions in the data itself that no one has yet thought to ask.

The blockchain-era shift away from proprietary data makes the quality of the science performed on the data more important than ever. As data becomes commoditized, the data arms race will no longer be only about who has the most. Instead, it will be about who is best able to use it. This means being so good at it that you have the ability to extract insights that others can't see from the same vast troves of data. And it means having an ability to act effectively on those insights.

These two dynamics have proven to be very difficult for businesses to get right. While some companies have developed admirable prowess, most have struggled. And indeed, it is exceptionally difficult.

It of course requires hiring top data science talent. While this work and the tools to support data science have become quite sophisticated, many businesses are still scrambling to find enough people capable of doing high-quality work. But even the best insights are useless if the business can't act on them. Actionable insights require tight collaboration between the data scientists and business-people across divisions. It requires working together to bring business context to the data and ensure that exploration is focused on solving fundamental business problems. And even if the organization and culture are structured to make this possible, it won't be effective unless executives and managers have achieved at least a basic level of data literacy, or they won't be comfortable making decisions on data over the age-old practice of experience and gut instinct. While some divisions have always been data-centric and may be predisposed to this way of thinking (finance), others have more recently made the transition (marketing), or have barely begun (human resources).

A data advantage is thus not only about who can build the best data science teams supported by the best data science tools, but who can develop a strong data culture. The Chief Data Officer (CDO) is an emerging C-suite role that will help to increase data sophistication across the business. Gartner estimates that by 2021 the office of the CDO will be considered a mission-critical function in 75% of large enterprises.[150] In the blockchain era of bigger, broader, deeper data, those who discover and mobilize around insights more effectively than competitors will be those that pull ahead.

THE POWER OF RELATIONSHIPS

There is one angle that could give the select few access to proprietary datasets. That angle is trust.

Today customers almost blindly trust businesses with their data. But as they become aware of the risks of doing so and the emerging blockchain-fueled alternatives, many will become more thoughtful about what they give away. In a blockchain world, businesses will have to earn customer permission to obtain data. Just as a healthy friendship builds trust and a foundation for increasingly intimate sharing over time, a brand that consistently demonstrates it is worthy of trust could be granted more intimate knowledge of a customer than competitors.

Trust means consistently returning value to customers in exchange for what they have provided. It means making their lives easier, richer, or more efficient. It means an organization demonstrates it is a worthy steward, capable of protecting data, as a trustworthy friend would protect a secret. And it means interacting consistently and predictably over time. In return, the most trusted brands may find they can get customers to progressively divulge more of themselves directly to them.

THE IMPORTANCE OF MISSION

In our digital world, there are a lot of products and services that are made better through data. They may be as starkly important as the delivery of more personalized health care, or as lightly consequential as a product recommendation. New users of Goodreads, a book rating and discovery application, have been known to invest hours in cataloging and rating books in order to get targeted recommendations for what to read next. Consumers have demonstrated great willingness to share data when they know it will be used in ways that help them.[151]

> *In the blockchain era, it will be more important than ever to develop and operate by a mission that clearly communicates value to customers.*

In the blockchain era, it will be more important than ever to develop and operate by a mission that clearly communicates value to customers. Customers will get to choose if and with whom they share data, and so convincing them of their role in achieving a mission they both understand and desire will become an important marketing skill.

This dynamic is one of the most acute aspects of the new, more collaborative customer relationship that will be required for success in the age of blockchains. To get there, businesses need to not only deeply understand customers' desires and needs, by segment, but also do the hard work to align their interests with those of their customers, ensuring that both parties are truly benefiting from the data that is being collected.

For many companies, this is a difficult self-examination and challenging re-alignment. However, it has never been more urgent. Customers have become much more sophisticated at spotting inconsistencies between brand claims and the experiences they have day to day with a brand—and projecting them out to the world via reviews or social media. The purity with which a business operates to its mission will be a key measurement that customers use when deciding if they are going to share data.

Organizations focused on social good initiatives could find themselves with an advantage. Believers will, for the first time, be able to contribute data to a cause without risking privacy. What this opens up—from traffic management to disease prevention—could be staggering. As people start to see positive results from population-level data donation, one day giving data may become as standard a practice as giving cash to a favorite charity is today.

GROWING AWARENESS OF THE VALUE OF PRIVACY

While many consumers have a vague awareness of the value of privacy, few do anything to retain it. This is especially true of millennials, who came of age in a world characterized by an extreme lack of data privacy. However, we can anticipate that with all the marketing dollars that eventually will be channeled into teaching consumers about the value of protecting their data, they will have a stronger grasp over its importance. While they may end up being quite willing to hand data over for compensation, it is likely to be a much more conscious exchange than what is happening today.

A SHIFT THAT PRESENTS NUANCED CHALLENGES

There are many other implications of this massive shift in the concept of data ownership. For example, platform loyalty could decrease. Today, users that have invested time into building reputation and networks on a platform are held hostage to that platform—leave, and it's lost. The more data customers own in a portable data layer, the lower the switching costs to move to an alternative. Smith + Crown's head of research, Matt Chwierut, explains, "The barriers for a user to exit LinkedIn or Facebook are very high. Many blockchain protocols are trying to have lower barriers, and build in interoperability of blockchains and tokens into their platform. So users could transfer their data, and value, more seamlessly than they can today."

Companies may also have to deal with a loss of visibility to a single customer's digital lifecycle. As more data gets put into personal vaults, it will be more difficult to get perpetual access to a customer's digital movements, or to stitch together behavior patterns across digital interfaces. Businesses that use questionable harvesting techniques will also find it harder to use those tactics.

KNOW THY DATA, KNOW THYSELF

Consumers may be charmed by new services that could become available as they strategically allow access to more data. Already, the data consumers provide helps to drive, in part, better digital experiences. In her 2018 internet trends report, Mary Meeker speaks to how data-driven personalization drives growth and helps internet companies, from Nextdoor to Spotify to Facebook, to make low-priced services better. But, she warns, it also attracts the attention of regulators, introducing a "privacy paradox."[152] If data is self-sovereign, consumers could theoretically safely give services access to more data, and get even better experiences in return. If they can safely provide location data to applications they wouldn't normally allow, they could get new context-aware offers and services. One can imagine how recommendation engines could deliver far more resonant results by leveraging deeper, richer data, even without identifying the consumer. Imagine a movie recommendation app that has a history of not only the movies you liked, but your physiological reactions to them as well (from, for example, Apple Watch heart rate measurements, or eventually, dopamine, serotonin, or cortisol measurements from devices that track hormone levels). Using your data along with anonymized data from other people with similar profiles, it could offer up movies that would make you weep, make you laugh, or get your heart to race with a great deal of reliability. Companies, too, could benefit, with better targeting and higher engagement. Tim Berners-Lee, who has been developing a new platform that works with the existing web, called Solid, believes that the principle of "personal empowerment through data" is fundamental. "Data should empower each of us," Tim explains. "Imagine if all your current apps talked to each other, collaborating and conceiving ways to enrich and streamline your personal life and business objectives . . . you will have far more personal agency over data—you decide which apps can access it."[153]

It's also conceivable that services may arise that enable individuals to commission their own data science. As a culture we spend a great deal of time and money on self-help and self-examination. In the blockchain future, people could accumulate and have easy access to a treasure trove of their own data—a lifetime (or even multiple generations) of health records, fitness metrics, even sentiments or emotions. No one is more motivated to find patterns that could unlock the best-fit cancer medicine, psychotherapy, or retirement plan than the person who needs it. It's conceivable that we will see high-end services or software that offer analysis and recommendations based on the comprehensive profile in a personal data vault.

ENABLING A NEW WAVE OF INNOVATION?

As blockchain-driven identity and data businesses mature, more data than ever before could be accessed by a wider range of organizations. This could be the missing piece to unlock the true economic potential in big data. It could conceivably catalyze a new wave of data-driven innovations that could change the way we work, live, and play—or even the trajectory of entire populations. But this next data arms race will also be much more difficult to successfully navigate than anything we have ever seen before.

Cautions and Considerations

The shift in data ownership presents both threats and opportunities to existing businesses. While some of these cautions and considerations are very future-focused, they are meant to provoke your thinking about what could come. This is by no means an exhaustive list; it provides additional food for thought on how to prepare for this new paradigm.

CAUTIONS

You are behind in data science

If there is a gap in your data science capability in relation to competitors, you are likely already well aware. In the blockchain era, a shortcoming in data science could be especially dangerous, as competitors use truly big data to outsmart you across the board.

Hiring a few smart data scientists and turning them loose on your data is not enough. Truly great data science must be enabled from the C-suite. To deliver insight that makes a difference in your business, the work needs to be viewed as a strategic business initiative, not a technical project. A strong data science program requires focus, placing data scientists effectively in the organization, and enabling decision makers across the organization to act on insights by increasing their data literacy.

Entering the blockchain era with a trust deficit

Trust has always been important, but the blockchain era will amplify the negative effects that come from a lack of it. If you are already struggling to gain or retain customer trust, this could be a pivotal moment. Mobilizing now with a focused initiative, driven from the top, could help to build credibility before blockchain adoption goes mainstream. Start by articulating values and ethics that are closely connected to the core business, and formal systems for measurement. In a gross oversimplification of what is a very complex evolution, success will depend on deep management commitment, enterprise-wide discipline, link to incentive structures, training, transparency, and tracking.

A business model reliant on proprietary consumer data

If the lead is yours to lose, be alert to which segments of consumers are making the transition to blockchain-based stores of data, and with what kind of data. If your business has historically depended on this kind of data, you may have a lead in data science expertise and data culture. Use your lead to leverage the new breadth and depth of data more effectively than others—if the vision of data marketplaces is realized.

CONSIDERATIONS

Boost your data culture in advance of blockchains

There is no need to wait for bigger data to become available (which may take many years). Start the hard work of developing your organization's data capabilities now so you are better prepared when the time comes. The field of data science has advanced greatly in the last few years, and best practices have emerged for building data science capabilities, increasing data literacy across an organization, and forging collaborative relationships between data scientists and the business. Study them, and develop a strategy to grow your data skills that starts with C-suite sponsorship.

Tap into the state of blockchain identity work

Explore new blockchain applications that offer consumers identity and data ownership as they launch. Examine them from the viewpoint of your own role as a consumer. Identify which approaches make you feel secure, and your own willingness and ease with which you contribute data. This will help you spot the moment user experience is refined enough to more broadly appeal to consumers, just before adoption spikes.

Work on your relationship

Conduct research to understand the areas where your organization is trusted, and the areas where you are not. Do the difficult self-examination work to understand the origin of your organization's shortcomings and consult outside experts to tell you straight what it would take to transform untrustworthy to trustworthy.

Look especially for opportunities to demonstrate to customers how you give them value via the data they contribute to you. Market this value and put in place frequent feedback loops so the idea of getting value in return for what they provide is continually enforced. In the years it will take for adoption to take hold, you have an opportunity to create a foundation of trust in your customer relationships, if you are willing to take on the investment.

Take a critical look at your mission

Mission statements can be worthless, or they can hold powerful galvanizing power for an organization. How does yours stack up? Are your customers and their needs and desires at the core? In what ways do you operate to this mission, and in what ways do you fall short? A well-crafted statement that builds on the heritage and belief of your organization and has the support of leaders and managers across the organization will help you win customers to your cause—whether it's social good or building a better product—and increase their willingness to continue to share data with you directly.

Examples

Identity and data are at the heart of so many blockchain projects, and this is probably the hardest area to select just a few examples. These two serve as just a glimpse at what entrepreneurs are working on now.

UPORT: TAKE BACK CONTROL OF IDENTITY

At the crux of the concept of bigger data, and indeed much of the vision of a decentralized future, is self-sovereign identity. There are easily over 100 projects focused on this, but for their vision to be realized, the industry will likely need to adopt some standards. The Decentralized Identity Foundation, which now counts nearly 60 members, focuses on just this.

uPort is one of the members, and is focused on building an open standard protocol layer on top of which any digital transaction can happen—but with self-sovereign protected identities. The team aims to enable a world in which a user can truly own their own identity and all the data associated with it, and establish a reputation for that identity. They do so by verifying key components of that identity (such as via reputable, certified authorities), for which the identity receives credentials or "claims." When the identity is used for an application, it is the consumer who grants the permissions, and dictates who can access which pieces of data. Everything from friend networks to browsing and purchase histories could be eventually incorporated into this self-sovereign identity. And "identity" doesn't have to be a human, either. It could be an organization, a device, or a bot, enabling all sorts of new business models.

I sat down to talk with Rouven Heck, the cofounder of uPort. "If we want to truly empower people to own their identity as well as their data, it must be interoperable," Rouven said. "I believe there will be not just one identity company that will dominate the market, as we saw big players like Facebook and Google dominate the Web 2.0 world. Particularly because identity is so critical, I believe we are only successful if we achieve global standards. When you send an email, it doesn't matter what server or device you use. That's why we're focused on building an interoperable identity layer. Standards and protocols, ultimately, should be blockchain agnostic."

Rouven imagines a world in which blockchain-based identity gives the end user new kinds of value, and eliminates the friction we have become accustomed to today when we sign up for a new product or service. "You could walk into a bank or insurance company, and you could choose to share reputation data that would enable them to make a fast decision to offer you a financial product. Or, you could decide to share your purchase history with a shopping site—without revealing who you actually are—and get custom recommendations. You could establish all kinds of trust and get all sorts of valuable interactions and experiences without middlemen."[154] Various organizations are conducting pilots with uPort, and Zug, Switzerland, has even begun a pilot program to offer citizens access to a new suite of e-government services by using their uPort identity.

Other identity players include Evernym (which is building its own identity blockchain and is tied to the Sovrin Foundation, which counts as partners heavyweights including Cisco, IBM, Deutsche Telekom, and Workday), Solid (a project led by Tim Berners-Lee, the creator of the World Wide Web), and Blockstack (which has an ambitious plan for encouraging the development of consumer-focused services built on identity).

OCEAN: UNLOCKING MORE DATA

Trent McConaghy has been a prominent blockchain innovator for years, but his first love, he says, was AI. For years he had hoped that the blockchain and AI worlds would collide—and they finally did in 2016 when he realized that all roads led to the same place: the problem of data. Specifically, said Trent, "Latent value lurks everywhere in the data—enterprises have plenty of data but don't know how to make it available to the world. Startups know how to turn data into value using AI, but they're starving for data . . . Society runs on data, yet much of it is controlled by a handful of companies with more power, resources, and reach than most nations. That's a problem." Trent founded Ocean "to give society equal opportunity to access data through a new kind of data marketplace."[155]

The Ocean Protocol team is led by top-tier experts in big data, blockchains, artificial intelligence, and data exchanges. Their focus is to make more of the world's data usable by enabling it to be shared and sold in a safe, secure, and transparent manner. This is particularly important to advance AI, which will affect nearly every sector of the economy in the coming years, including advertising, finance, health care, retail, automotive, energy, transport and logistics, and aerospace. AI requires vast volumes of data to be trained effectively—models have limited accuracy and usability without appropriate data. But a small handful of organizations have accumulated both massive data assets and AI capabilities. The Ocean team saw these organizations as potentially becoming so powerful, they could endanger a free and open society. The protocol aims to unlock data to enable more for more equitable use and outcomes of data.

Their solution hinges on safe sharing and their belief that data is locked up because sharing has been too risky. Ocean Protocol is a business, technical, and governance framework that is brought together to serve the needs of all stakeholders in the data ecosystem. Ocean ensures payment to the provider, using Ocean tokens, while guaranteeing control, auditability, and transparency to everyone. "If we do this right," said Trent, "the marketplaces can even handle a data commons, where data is free to use, yet you are rewarded if you contribute to the commons. This can complement paid data; free and paid can work hand-in-hand, making each other stronger."[156]

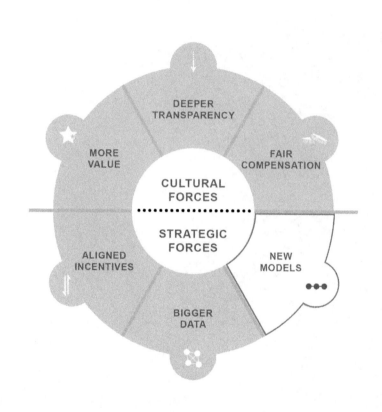

NEW MODELS

The worst place to develop a new business model is from within your existing business model.

—CLAYTON CHRISTENSEN

Summary

Blockchains open up the possibility for unprecedented business models driven by decentralization. These new models flip the rules for what it takes to be successful, will influence today's incumbents, and could drive new competitors to power.

The success of decentralized models will be driven in great part by how powerfully an organization attracts the support of the crowd and an ecosystem of partners. This changes the dynamics of what drives dominance—but it will be a long road of trial and error to determine how to drive sustainable long-term revenue from these new models. We may see a shift, in many areas, to businesses that trade margin for scale or operate under new structures designed to return more value to a community at large.

FLIPPING CONVENTIONAL WISDOM

Every one of the examples we have looked at so far, of course, represents a new business model. But the models we're about to look at deserve their own dedicated section. This is because these models have a tendency to flip and twist conventional wisdom of what an effective business looks like, and it takes some study to understand the implications. Eva Kaili, the member of the European Parliament who chairs the Science and Technology Options Assessment panel, asserts that these emerging blockchain-driven models could "democratize value chains, remove transaction costs, optimize the allocation of resources and risks, expand social inclusion, and improve the quality of services and products we receive as customers and as citizens."[157]

Much is still to be learned about these models, and the next few years will bring an explosion of experimentation in the quest to find a path to both disruption and profitability. This tension may feel familiar. As with the early days of the internet, the sustainability of a new model is not always clear. Do not make the mistake of writing them off for this reason. While many businesses that attempt these models will fail, some probably spectacularly, as a whole they could collectively impact the way we work and live (think about how players like recently public and high-valuation Dropbox, Spotify, and Snapchat have struggled to crack profitability—even as they played a role in changing our world).

The territory we're about to enter gets a little muddy, but also a little more exciting as we look at how blockchain technology can enable new industries and merge and transform existing ones. What follows is a high-level tour and is by no means exhaustive; it is simply a glimpse of where things are headed. We are at the beginning, and it will be fascinating to watch how innovators will improve and build on these models, and which new ones will emerge over the next decade. But each theme I'm covering represents an embryonic movement, and as it evolves, it will morph and shift, be pulled into different industries, and cross-pollinate with existing models—and each will lend its impact to the new expectations of the unblocked customer.

EXTREME PEER-TO-PEER

I start here because it is the idea of pure peer-to-peer exchange of value that has inspired so many blockchain pioneers. In Chapter 6 we saw how the unblocked customer will demand more from middlemen, and how we will see a next-gen middleman emerge. We explored examples like Open Garden and Decent. But "extreme peer-to-peer" models warrant an additional spotlight in any discussion of new blockchain business models.

Extreme peer-to-peer envisions the near-total extraction of the middleman, to be replaced by a self-governed community, with users interacting with other users and the community through the safe haven of the protocol's code and governance. It is these structures that give the entire community guardrails for interaction, and facilitate contracts, payments, and reconciliation. There are many entrepreneurs looking at using this approach for social media, news, and exchange of goods, among other areas. But let's take a look at this approach through the lens of two areas that have a large and direct impact on our quality of life, day to day: commerce and transportation.

Peer-to-peer global commerce

OpenBazaar is looking to create a world of truly open commerce with no middleman between buyer and seller, and zero fees. Merchants, currently small businesses from over 30 countries, create their own store, and do not need a bank or credit card processing—all transactions take place with cryptocurrency.

Especially for ecommerce executives, who know consumers abandon carts at a whiff of friction, OpenBazaar is easy to eschew. It's clunky, and it's awkward. The platform only uses cryptocurrency. Until recently, users have had to download a full node, and interact only through a hard-to-use desktop app (beta mobile versions were recently launched). Cofounder Sam Patterson helps to set expectations: "Existing centralized marketplaces like Amazon and eBay have had decades to build up an impressive suite of features for their users . . . it will be a long time before we are as feature-rich as the big platforms."[58]

However, OpenBazaar provides a fascinating vision of how a community could one day chip away at existing incumbents. You see, this is not a company; it's not even an organization. It's free, open source software. It was built to provide everyone with the ability to buy and sell freely. In fact, no one has control over OpenBazaar. Each user contributes to the network equally and is in control of their own store and private data. The creators envision an ecosystem of developers offering value-added services that work with OpenBazaar (for which these developers could charge), which also incents them to advance the OpenBazaar code itself. Success for the participants—including the creators—comes from the increasing value of the overall ecosystem. The creators founded a company, OB1, that is looking to develop and offer add-on services for both buyers and sellers, but doesn't expect to have any proprietary advantage over competitive developers

—every contributor benefits when the ecosystem expands with new members, adding value to the overall platform.

Peer-to-peer ride sharing

New ride sharing models have rapidly grown to change the way we move around cities over the last decade. Many of us think today that we are using a peer-to-peer model when we get in a Lyft or an Uber. We are, after all, exchanging currency for a ride from someone we have never met, even if that exchange is governed by a platform. However, blockchain models imagine pushing peer-to-peer to new levels. Israel-based La`Zooz developed a vision to use a blockchain to deliver more sustainable, smarter, and more collaborative ride sharing than has ever been possible. The team envisioned ride sharing with a mission: to maximize existing transportation infrastructure and vehicles through a direct peer-to-peer exchange. Uber drives revenue by extracting high fees from both sides of a two-sided network, and does not synchronize the desired routes of driver and passenger with the intent to benefit the extended community.

In contrast, La`Zooz is user-driven, with the community collectively deciding what to reward each contributor through the support of sophisticated protocols. It was designed to help people that need a ride to find an empty seat in a vehicle going the same direction, giving the provider a "fair fare" (set by the community) and reducing miles driven across the universe of vehicles and users. Shay Zluf, who helped to create La`Zooz, sees a chance to make mobility more sustainable: "Thousands of empty car seats haven't experienced any tush for years. Our road space and transport expenses are mostly used to move empty seats from one place to another. It's time to change that."[159]

THE BIG FLIP AND "SUPER PLATFORMS"

In the blockchain community, there is much talk about "fat protocol, thin apps." This concept—illustrated in Figure 11-1—was pushed into broader awareness in August of 2016 by then–Union Square Ventures analyst Joel Monégro through a post on the company's blog.

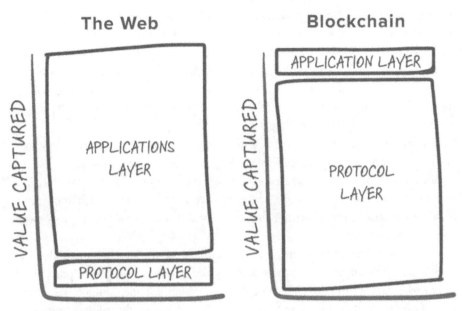

Figure 11-1. Fat protocol, thin apps. (Source: Joel Monégro, Union Square Ventures blog.)

In the pre-blockchain internet, applications carry all the power. This is why today, we see quite a few "winner-take-all" markets dominated by giants (Amazon, Facebook, Uber). While the protocol layer (TCP/IP, HTTP, SMTP, etc.) produced immeasurable amounts of value, it was the companies that created applications, collecting and leveraging vast troves of data, that were able to capture this value in the form of revenue. Venture capitalists learned that investing in applications produced higher returns than investing in protocols, and that's where the money and focus went. The protocols were "thin" and the applications were "fat."

In contrast, in the blockchain world, this thesis (which is yet to be definitively proven, and is somewhat controversial) promotes a reversed relationship. Value concentrates at the protocol layer, and only a fraction of that value is channeled to the applications layer. These are "fat" protocols and "thin" applications. This happens because shared data layers (as we explored in Chapter 10) are at a meta layer, not the application layer.

The introduction of cryptoassets also fuels the flip. Tokens make it possible to monetize the protocol layer, incentivizing protocol development, as well as functioning as a tool to increase protocol adoption. Even entrepreneurs that create nonprofit foundations to manage a protocol stand to benefit if their protocol wins, assuming they hold a good deal of the token (as the ecosystem and utility of the protocol expands, so does, theoretically, the value of the token). While there was no business model for internet protocols, money and resources are now pouring in to the development of blockchain protocols. It will be fascinating to watch how this investment—which has never happened at this layer at this magnitude—will feed new breakthroughs that will impact us all, eventually, downstream.

What are the implications of this direct flip? In addition to making protocol-layer entrepreneurs potentially very wealthy, it now puts the user at the center. Applications built on these protocols are like constellations of compatible products or services, each providing a specific function for the user. Each application accesses the same secure, private data layer. And this access is turned on—or off —at the user's discretion.

With user data in an open and decentralized network rather than siloed in individual applications with access gated by large companies, new applications have lower barriers to entry. This enables a more vibrant and competitive ecosystem of products and services on top of this protocol and its shared data layer.

James Glasscock, a founder of both a blockchain consultancy and a crypto venture fund, describes it like this: "In the future decentralized world of applications, there may be no 800-pound gorillas like Facebook and YouTube. They will be replaced by 800 gorillas that are one pound each, operating across different sectors with microeconomic fairness for all participants, including audience, creators, widget providers, curators, analysts, writers, and much more. Those smaller gorillas," James continues, "are going to solve different issues within their respective ecosystems. They're going to be hyper-focused on providing solutions to their niche cohorts. And they will be independently profitable—this is a game changer."[160]

But these smaller players would theoretically access something more by plugging into a fat protocol, and it's vital: because in the blockchain world good protocols attract ecosystems, even niche players could get the benefit of network effects by building on top. People using applications on that same protocol would already have their information in the shared data layer. They already use the tokens. For them, it could be practically frictionless to add one more thin app into their lives. When larger companies start plugging into that ecosystem too, network effects only get amplified more. Everyone benefits.

Joel summarizes it like this: "The market cap of the protocol always grows faster than the combined value of the applications built on top, since the success of the application layer drives further speculation at the protocol layer. And again, increasing value at the protocol layer attracts and incentivizes competition at the application layer. Together with a shared data layer, which dramatically lowers the barriers to entry, the end result is a vibrant and competitive ecosystem of applications and the bulk value distributed to a widespread pool of shareholders."

He also warns that "many of the established rules about building businesses and investing in innovation don't apply to this new model and today we probably have more questions than answers."[161] For example, to bend your mind a little more, different protocols could be interoperable, as innovators work on things they call "cross-chain atomic swaps" and other hard-to-wrap-your-head-around terms.

Despite this uncertainty, this is where entrepreneurs and investors are heading. There is a general feeling in the community that eventually models will emerge that enable profitability at the application layer, although very different models than those today, and that this will incent further innovation.

Blockstack is a startup with a particularly ambitious mission: to create a new internet for "decentralized apps" where users own their own data. They encourage users to get started by installing the Blockstack Browser, and envision developers creating an ecosystem of applications on top of it (and they have a handful available today). Users access the apps through the browser and a single account (much like Google products work today), but retain ownership of their own data (unlike with Google). Users give (or revoke) explicit permissions to their data. Information is encrypted and stored on users' personal devices. There are no middlemen, no passwords, and no data silos to breach.

Eric Ly, the cofounder of LinkedIn, is building a new protocol called Human Trust Protocol, or Hub. Hub uses a cryptoasset, the Hub token, to incentivize users to verify and build reputation. Eric sees reputation as key for creating economic value for users. With reputation, he explains, we have a sense of why someone, or something, is valuable. With a good reputation, users can gain more opportunities, command higher premiums for their products and services, and get more cooperation from others. "We want to get that piece right for users," he explains.

The Hub token lets users earn trust as a result of successful interactions. Verifiable and portable across applications, users own their own reputation data. To demonstrate the utility of the protocol, Eric and his team have built Hub app, a professional network where users connect in communities and marketplaces. The app integrates with the protocol to deliver more trustworthy engagement and opportunity than nonblockchain platforms can deliver. However, Eric envisions developers using Hub wherever reputation is important to interaction, evolving the ecosystem of apps over time. "We see Hub being used for anything from sharing economy to online communities and even messengers—anywhere that people interact in a larger context with people they don't know." He continues, "It would be really great if we could rearrange economic mechanisms so the benefit of reputation data is redistributed from centralized corporations to the edges, where the users could benefit from the value of this data—that is a pretty big thing to happen, and it would be neat to be a part of that transformation."

AS THINGS GET SMALLER, VALUE GETS BIGGER

There is an Alice in Wonderland–like spell flowing through the blockchain space. As you get deeper, you spot it in many different areas. Time and time again, a common theme emerges: things are shrinking and it makes new things possible. We just saw that as applications shrunk in respect to protocols, they could deliver more value to the people using them.

Blockchains and cryptoassets lend themselves extremely well to breaking down pieces of something into fragments—I call this effect *atomizing*—and providing immutable verification and tracking of that something, embedding terms and conditions with it, or enabling trades with it. They also make even small transactions possible and worthwhile. Micro-payments are an incredibly important use case and are integrated into many projects. We'll likely see an evolution in micro-lending as well. But, with the assistance of complementary technologies, there is not much that can't be atomized and used in new ways, whether it's a house, a work of art, or even airspace. What follows are a few diverse examples of how atomization manifests. As you spend more time in this space, keep an eye out for this shrinking effect; you will spot more. Here are just some of the interesting—and diverse—areas in which this concept is emerging.

Education: atomizing credentials

Years ago, I conducted an in-depth study of what was holding back broad-scale adoption of exciting new technology-enabled education solutions. One barrier, specifically in higher ed, particularly frustrated me: the lack of a trusted cross-platform mechanism for tracking, verifying, and thus using "micro-credentials," certification that a specific course has been successfully completed. There was no widely accepted way to certify that someone had gained knowledge or a skill without the wrapper of the familiar, widely accepted, but expensive and time-consuming, degree. New, technology-driven courses were available to give high-quality, low-cost (or even free) content to anyone who could access an internet connection. But their utility, and thus value, was limited without universally accepted recognition that the course was indeed completed successfully. And if this could be figured out, it would help so many that didn't have the money or time for a full degree. Blockchains promise a solution.

Learning Machine, which we met in Chapter 7, uses Blockcerts, an open standard, to establish a lifelong learning record. The team sees education as a critical pathway for upward mobility and economic improvement—and credentials earned on that journey serve as important markers of skill, competency, and accomplishment. But education providers don't always have a secure way of issuing these credentials that students can take with them and build upon. With Blockcerts, student data ownership is attainable: learners can receive their official records in a digital format that is tamper-proof and immediately verifiable by others.

While the initial use case is focused on verifying traditional university degrees, the protocol could be leveraged to support micro-credentials and the "unbundling" of education. "Not all micro-credentials need to be on a block-chain," explains Learning Machine Vice President Natalie Smolenski, "but any skill or experience that needs to be verified with a high level of certainty, across space and time, should use a blockchain. For many people without access to higher-level degrees, or those switching careers or fields, micro-credentials may very well be the most valuable credentials they achieve over a lifetime, and being able to own and independently verify those credentials anywhere can mean the difference between stagnation and access to opportunity."[162]

Insurance: atomization of time and space

A discussion of new blockchain models is incomplete without a close look at insurance. As we saw in Chapter 10, blockchain-driven identity can be the corner-stone of many new businesses and models. Insurance is also a great enabler. Gopi Rangan is the founder and general partner of the first insurtech–focused venture capital firm in Silicon Valley, Sure Ventures, is an adjunct professor at INSEAD, and has coauthored over 30 patents. We sat down over a glass of wine to explore how the combination of blockchains and insurance could change lives.

Gopi painted an eloquent picture of how insurance, something many of us think of as—I'll say it—boring, is actually a crucial safety net for society that makes it possible for all people to aim for long-term prosperity and key to sup-porting our universal quest to maintain a high quality of life over time. Pooling and distributing risk among a community makes the entire community better off. "The quality of life of one individual does not descend, for long, by a single unfortunate event," Gopi explained. "Instead, they are supported and protected."

One of the challenges in the industry is that the need for protection changes not only from person to person, but over time and circumstances too. Insurance products have been relatively rigid—you can insure a car, but it's much harder to insure it just in those moments you need the insurance, or find someone willing to insure something of much lower value—say, a computer or a bike.

Blockchains (along with a new flood of IoT-driven data that can be used to calculate risk and monitor assets) could make it easier for insurers to offer granular protection that flexes and changes with individual needs. It drives costs down and enables unique identifiers, immutable tracking, and contracts that can be executed without a human—making it possible to make insurance work for smaller and smaller things or periods of time.

In a blockchain future, it could be possible, for example, to get insurance just for those times when you take that bike and computer outside of your home. It also makes it easier to integrate that insurance into an ecosystem, offered as an add-on service to a range of products. "It could influence us to be more open to sharing," Gopi explained. "Now you can lend that bike to a neighbor without a worry. As a community we are better off—it brings us together."[163]

There are dozens of teams clustering around many different segments of the insurance industry, including micro-insurance. For the newest approaches, it's still early and the work has the feel of science experiments. It's likely the insurance industry first gains the most significant experience with blockchains in the areas where the pain of today's model is most significant, like title insurance. But new business models will come, stoking macro shifts across the insurance value chain and potentially realizing, pulling from Gopi's vision, a higher quality of life.

Atomization of business

With the internet came new opportunities for an individual to launch a business. All of a sudden, the average citizen could take a special skill, capacity in their house or car, or a unique personality and point of view, and turn it into revenue. The growth of the freelance economy, the debut of the sharing economy, and even social media influencer models have enabled people to make a living— sometimes a very good one—without working for a traditional company.

Blockchain technology could give individuals a plethora of new tools and access to marketplaces that they could leverage to diversify income, even build a personal enterprise—continuing the trend toward micro-businesses. We've already looked at a few ways this could happen. We saw how people could make money off their "data exhaust"—all the data passively flowing from their devices and digital interactions. The way the sharing economy could expand to a houseful of assets. Even how normal browsing behavior could be monetized.

But there will be an explosion of other models that bring revenue to an enterprise of one. They will unlock new value for skills that were previously unmonetizable. They will create more efficient markets for things that were lying dormant and unused but now can be easily bought or sold. There will be many blockchain companies that seek to provide vibrant marketplaces that enable this future, and it could change the dynamics for many businesses today.

Matt Chwierut of Smith + Crown speaks to this new world: "Where it gets really interesting is in the specific mechanism of compensation," he said. "A platform can facilitate a peer-to-peer exchange: I sell a good or service to a buyer on the other side, and blockchains enable a very efficient payment rail. They can exchange a range of cryptoassets, or even be compensated through newly issued tokens or bounty 'rewards.' People could own their own business models. Take content, for example. An individual could sell their content as a subscription, make it advertising-based, make it sponsor-based where endorsement is embedded, or even focus on earning some form of token rewards. Regardless, blockchains open up the possibility for micro-actions and micro-contributions to be compensated in a variety of ways, and new value to be captured and given to the individual. Tokens can substantiate value that previously couldn't be substantiated."[164]

Platforms will offer their own tokens or use one that has built momentum elsewhere, but an individual—perhaps an artist or a filmmaker, or a small business—could also release their own private-labeled token to obtain funding and use in their own ecosystem. There are blockchain companies that are working to templatize the approach of issuing a token, and there are a growing list of artists, musicians, and filmmakers who have done so.

Solo developers could use the fat protocols described earlier to more easily create and monetize new applications. If she picks the right use case and protocol, a developer could have a fast path to network effects and no longer has to develop enough trust with a user to earn their data—it all lives in the shared data layer, and she can deliver value to users without even knowing who they are.

We probably can't predict all the new businesses-of-one that could come out of blockchain technology, but this is sure to be one of the most interesting areas to watch.

Atomize—and liquify—assets

There is a call among some enthusiasts to "tokenize everything." Often, what they are talking about is the ability to use tokens to exchange fractions of a large asset, which can then be used to open up new sources of capital or sharing models. Any "real-world" asset can be tokenized. Fine art and real estate are two favorites and there are dozens of projects that are working on many aspects of this, often in ways that look very similar. But, ultimately, these kinds of projects envision the release of billions, even trillions, of dollars of illiquid assets into liquid marketplaces that could be invested in or exchanged by anyone. Some believe this could upend the entire financial service industry, and herald a new system that is more transparent, liquid, and accessible. There are fascinating experiments happening today with this approach and many in the financial services industry are carefully watching what new financial instruments will take off via this new paradigm. This will be an interesting and fast-moving area to watch, one that could impact the very idea of ownership and access to capital.

PROGRAMMABLE ASSETS

Another related area that has captured the attention of insiders, although still in painfully early days, is the concept of programmable assets. Visionaries see leveraging blockchain functionality to make it fast and easy to intricately tune financial instruments—and see a world in which this capability becomes core to all new kinds of products and services.

Spencer Bogart is a partner at Blockchain Capital, one of the oldest venture investors in the blockchain technology sector. We sat down to talk about what he is observing in this area of development. "From a corporate perspective, programmable money and assets is one of the most exciting areas right now. For the first time, you have digital native assets built on digital native infrastructure, and this makes it possible to do all sorts of interesting things."

For example, the transaction of an asset could be programmed with a "time lock," in which a party can specify that asset can't be spent until a time in the future. Or, they could specify a "multi-sig" requirement, ensuring a transaction won't take place until a certain number of signatures are registered from a pre-specified pool of signers. Or any other criteria that could be programmed in code. Some entrepreneurs are even exploring ways to make productive use of capital with nearly zero counterparty risk, a concept that Spencer describes as "absolutely mind-blowing from a lending perspective."

"You can do all these things using the legacy financial world, of course," Spencer explains. "But it takes great time and effort. In this new world, you can reduce the work to a couple lines of code—this could unleash all kinds of novel uses that we've never seen before. It's an extension of Marc Andreessen's thesis that software is eating the world—software may also take over the way we move anything of value."[165]

MACHINES WORKING TOGETHER TO SERVE US

An enthralling futuristic vision is when the machines use a blockchain network to exchange value, autonomously and machine-to-machine, in order to make our world run better. In conjunction with IoT and new mobility technologies like connected cars or drones, blockchains could play an important part of enabling a new way for both people and things to move through the environment. Jessica Groopman of Kaleido Insights shares, "Machine-to-machine blockchain models, especially, are fascinating. There is such an opportunity for something good to come out of it." With built-in token incentives, the movement of people and things through the environment can be optimized in exciting new ways. Jessica's partner at Kaleido Insights, Jeremiah Owyang, adds, "When everything around us that is inanimate becomes animate, the world becomes alive around us."[166]

Blockchains could help various devices and machines to interact more easily, and more securely, through the use of verifiable identities. For example, a drone could deliver a package to a lockbox, with the lockbox verifying if the drone is "safe" and opening, automatically, to receive the delivery.

Jessica shares another example: "A local government could incent how you move around the city with tokens"—and these tokens could be exchanged directly from machine to machine to optimize use of infrastructure. Dovu—a blockchain startup backed by InMotion Ventures, Jaguar Land Rover, and Creative England, a fund backed by the UK government—is developing a protocol that could be leveraged for just this. The company is starting with a solution for seamless payment across transport services: one secure global token for riding a bus or train, or renting a bike or car. Users will have the option to sell the data produced by their vehicles as they use them—whether they are rented or owned. For example, smart cars are predicted to generate up to 25GB of data per hour. That data can be useful for identifying traffic congestion—and tokens could also be used to incent alternate routes or modes of transport to help traffic get flowing again. If you take the bus or walk instead of driving, for example, that action could be rewarded with extra token. But over time the technology could be leveraged to incent actions that mean smoother flow of both people and vehicles within the infrastructure we have today.

The DAV Foundation is a nonprofit based in Zurich, Switzerland. The team, coming from heavyweights like GM, Ford, SAP, UPS, Nasa, Google, and IBM, is building a network powered by the DAV token. DAV could be integrated into any vehicle, which creates a connective tissue among cars, drone, and ships, for example. Autonomous vehicles can then discover, communicate, and transact with each other—without human intervention. This means that the owner of any vehicle could buy or sell transportation services that employ that vehicle. I sat down with DAV's thoughtful cofounder, Joe Lopardo, to talk about his vision. "Right now," Joe explained, "I own a vehicle that is just sitting in my garage 96% of the time. If you fast-forward 10 years, that vehicle could be autonomous, and I could put it to work for me when I'm not using it. If I'm going on vacation for a week, I could set parameters for use—let's say I don't want it to go farther than 50 miles from my house. Then I set it free. In that week, it could deliver passengers, supplies, whatever. It would know when it needs to go to a charging station, or if the tire pressure is low, and could negotiate a rate and pay for these services on its own—without me or any other human getting involved." Obviously, Joe points out, there are regulatory and infrastructure constraints right now, but with DAV, a token could ultimately move anything, anywhere.[67] In collaboration with Skysense, Inc., the foundation has been working on a proof of concept using a fleet of drone charging stations. Certain drones are now able to access a network of charging stations in northern Italy, using the token to bid for electricity from charging pads based on price and location.

The vision extends to moving goods through a supply chain. "Imagine," says Joe, "an autonomous 18-wheeler driving from California to Pennsylvania. That route could be optimized so it could unload packages along the way to smaller vehicles, also autonomous. It's like UPS or Amazon does today, but not only without the human drivers—it's with no human intervention at all."

While mobility is a particularly interesting application of machine-to-machine, any IoT device or connected machine is a candidate. We've long heard talk of IoT-enabled refrigerators that can let you know when you're out of milk. What about a future in which the fridge not only knows the milk is out, but also negotiates the best price from various vendors, orders it for you, pays for it on your behalf with tokens, and all you have to do is take it off your doorstep and put it inside? (Although we could take it even further, with a connected lock on your front door allowing a range of service providers to come inside and put it in the fridge for you, along with the insurance in case they break something in your house while they're at it.)

SOCIAL-ALIGNED MODELS

One of the most appealing themes to come out of blockchain models is in the area of social good. Blockchains could help individuals, companies, and governments "see" the real impact of their actions. And the feature set of blockchains and tokens could enable many, many ways for businesses and individuals to align on shared values. Social good could be baked into a protocol or a token (for example, there are many blockchain projects that, through their governance, channel funds to a treasury or pool, which is distributed according to voting from the community). Individuals could show their support of an initiative by choosing to engage with the businesses and brands that use a mission-based token. In this way, day-to-day micro-decisions by individual consumers could conceivably fund real impact. Or, tokens could help drive specific actions.

One surprising example of this is The Plastic Bank, which was founded in Vancouver in 2013 with the mission to stop ocean plastic by gathering a billion people together to monetize waste. Scientists predict there will be more plastic than fish in the ocean by 2050. By compensating people for the plastic they gather, primarily in developing regions, the organization prevents the flow of plastic into our oceans. A blockchain is used to track the entire cycle of recycled plastic from collection, credit, and compensation through delivery to companies for reuse. Tokens are thus used to jointly tackle ocean plastic and poverty.

Various teams are working on projects to enable more transparent funding of development projects. In regions in which funding can be siphoned off through layers of "middlemen" (with some being outright bribes), or are frequently abandoned midway, there is hope that the trust via blockchains can encourage investment in crucial infrastructure.

The potential for societal-level impact is tantalizing. I am optimistic that we will see many exciting and far-reaching developments in this space. My personal hope is that many of these projects will eventually evolve into a virtuous, self-propelled feedback loop. That organizations will see the value of baking in elements that serve society, and will deepen their understanding of how this drives more sustainable long-term businesses.

PART III

UNLEASHING AN UNBLOCKED FUTURE

12

WHERE TO BEGIN

Standing in the middle of the road is very dangerous; you get knocked down by the traffic from both sides.

—MARGARET THATCHER

Now, Where to Begin?

You've seen how this new technology will bring far-reaching change, and also the great uncertainty of when. Few organizations are prepared to deal with this level of ambiguity. And many will, understandably, hesitate to go through the pain change requires. Jeremiah Owyang, a founding partner at research firm Kaleido Insights, created an innovation council to help large corporations innovate with new technologies. "In many cases, large companies are resting on their laurels, dependent on multimillion-dollar product lines," explains Jeremiah. "They may be led by senior execs who will retire in 10 years. They are not given the right incentives to make radical changes. These companies have to feel some pain, or have something scare them, before they are ready to take action." But by then, it may be too late. "When blockchain technology catches fire," Jeremiah warns, "it will go faster than a company can catch up."[168]

Companies that want to thrive on the other side of blockchain disruption do not have a choice: they must learn how to learn, rapidly and effectively, to navigate through it.

Organization Models Birthed from Disruption

Disruption has become a perennial challenge. Many wise and celebrated organizational researchers have devoted their careers to developing methodology to help organizations cope.

One of the most tantalizing concepts for dealing with ambiguity came from Peter Senge, who, in the 1990s, popularized the idea of the learning organization with his book, *The Fifth Discipline*. This concept means that a company uses organization-wide learning to continually transform itself for competitive advantage. In a learning organization, Peter explains, "People continually expand their capacity to create the results they truly desire, where new and expansive patterns of thinking are nurtured, where collective aspiration is set free, and where people are continually learning to see the whole together."[169]

While it has proven difficult for organizations to embody this ideal, the concept—and increasing necessity—of learning as a tool to achieve competitive advantage in an unpredictable environment has remained attractive. With blockchains, learning is the first big challenge, and that learning is not "one and done." The environment is shifting constantly, and new twists on the technology and new innovations are continuously debuting. And with the level of human and capital investment in the space, this is only going to accelerate. With blockchains and many other accelerating new technologies, there has never been a more important time for the organization to learn how to learn, continuously.

Another increasingly popular response to the threat of digital disruption, especially among the world's largest corporations, is to create an innovation program. These programs can take on many forms and flavors, ranging from dedicated corporate incubators and outposts to light-touch innovation "tours." In fact, Jeremiah Owyang identifies 10 different types of corporate innovation programs. But no matter the approach, they are all focused on tapping into the juice of innovation, and facilitating its flow into the minds and products of a company.

Tales of success continue to stoke interest in innovation programs, from Volkswagen's collaboration with university researchers to Walmart's rapid experimentation and prototyping. But the majority of large companies struggle to find the right model to propel their organization to sustainable innovation. It's proven to be extremely difficult to bridge new opportunities to the organization at large. These programs tend to push the responsibility of innovation to specific groups, whereas long-term business-changing innovation has historically been most successful when it becomes a way of business—an essential part of the culture.

Analyst firm CB Insights recently released a State of Innovation report, with the results of a study of nearly 700 corporate strategy executives. When asked, "How at risk is your company of disruption by emerging technologies and companies?" fewer than 4% said they were not at risk. But despite deep fear and talk of disruption, companies were investing in the small stuff—nearly 80% focused their resources on iterating on the status quo rather than on disruptive risks, even though 85% said innovation is very important. High-performing companies were more likely to be first movers, invest in disruptive projects, and build cultures of innovation across functions. The report also found that corporate propensity for building over partnering or buying was a key factor in slowing down innovation.[170]

IN THE BLOCKCHAIN ERA, THIS IS NOT GOOD ENOUGH

These trends are particularly worrisome at this moment. We are slowly, but steadily, approaching a flood of blockchain disruption. Large organizations will need to find a way to effectively experiment with, pilot, and innovate on the application of blockchain technology to their business. And because the real power of blockchains is activated when the technology is used to align and facilitate exchange within an ecosystem, the companies that will best leverage it will be those that understand how to partner.

ISOLATE OR INTEGRATE?

But there is value in first getting to know the technology yourself. And speed, agility, and iteration—attributes so essential to learning to apply a new technology—are easier in small, focused teams. It's not surprising, then, that this is how many companies are starting. Jeremiah Owyang reports seeing a lot of this kind of experimentation. "I have talked to teams that are not even aware that another business unit is doing something with blockchains until the press release comes out," he said.[171] Blockchain entrepreneurs have also shared stories of corporations that were studying their work closely, watching and evaluating whether to skirt legacy infrastructure completely by creating a totally new venture that functions outside of the organization at large—and its constraints.

TIME TO RETHINK INNOVATION

But, for the corporation, the biggest step forward will come from projects that reach far and wide, touching current processes and systems. And this requires diverse, cross-functional skill sets. To be successful, projects will need to connect true business and user needs to the vibrant innovation that's coming out of the blockchain landscape. And that requires domain expertise from across the business. This is why as this wave approaches, it's a great time to take a close look at your platform for innovation, and examine carefully what is working and what is not.

It's also a good time to look at how you build knowledge across the organization. As we saw with data science and the importance of increasing the "data literacy" of a company, it will be vital, as the technology becomes more widely adopted, to increase "blockchain literacy" as well.

Corporations can take a look at how Fidelity Investments has been raising blockchain literacy. A unit of the company, Fidelity's Center for Applied Technology (FCAT), is tasked with exploring how new technologies could impact customers' lives. Four years ago, FCAT created an incubator to study blockchain technology and established a "Bits and Blocks" club that anyone in the company, globally, can join.

The club offers different ways for members to learn, and they can pick and choose how they participate. The team developed a curriculum that helps club members tailor content to their knowledge. An employee with no experience could enter the "101" track, while developers with prior knowledge can access more advanced "301"-level content. Local meetups provide a forum for members to gather in person. There is an online knowledge center. Monthly "office hours" give anyone an open forum to ask questions of FCAT's blockchain incubator team. And, a speakers' series brings in luminaries such as Ethereum-cofounder, Vitalik Buterin, Lightning Labs CEO Elizabeth Stark, and others you've met through these pages, such as Meltem Demirors and Lou Kerner. Now approaching 3,000 members, the club has increased blockchain knowledge across the organization.[72]

This focus on learning is paired with a willingness to experiment with purpose. Fidelity CEO Abby Johnson surprised the press by announcing in 2017 that the company was using excess compute capacity to mine bitcoin. Fidelity employees can use bitcoin to pay for coffee in the firm's Boston headquarters. Fidelity's charity arm has been accepting bitcoin donations for years. And the company has partnered with San Francisco–based exchange Coinbase to enable customers to view the value of their digital currency from the Fidelity website. The company looks at this experimentation as a way not only to learn more about what's going on, but to take a temperature of market demand.

Teams also need to acquire knowledge quickly to be able to astutely discern, among a confusing panorama, where blockchain technology can truly move the business forward and where it adds unnecessary friction and complexity. In the buzzy enthusiasm for the new powers unleashed by this technology, many companies are making mistakes in this area, piloting a blockchain where an old-school database could be more effective. It takes knowledge to determine when to dig in and when to call bull, and teams will need to build it quickly.

Education will be the key tool for assessing the best time to make a move. There is recognition, in the words of one executive, that "whatever we build today will probably have to be changed again." Some encourage finding a single area a company is comfortable with, no matter how small, and then moving on it to get applied experience and real data. Others make the conscious decision to drag their feet just a bit longer. Either approach may prove to be prescient, but regardless, wise companies will make moves now to *educate* their forces and to *experiment*, so they are poised to recognize the moment of clarity as it emerges—and are prepared to strike.

> *Companies will educate their forces and experiment with this new technology—sooner rather than later.*

Human resources thought leader Josh Bersin offers a path forward with his perspective on "agile organization models," which he observes "are starting to go mainstream." He points to research from Deloitte that shows "redesigning our organization to be more digital and responsive" is now the number-one human capital trend around the world (59% of companies rate this as "urgent"). Josh maps out how agile organization models, in which dynamic and diverse teams assemble quickly to focus on a specific outcome, contrast to traditional models.

This new organization model, according to Josh, is structured by projects, squads, and teams instead of hierarchical business functions. These structures assemble (and may stop) quickly, and are organized by assignment, tasks, and "expert roles" instead of traditional job descriptions and titles. People may even work on multiple projects, tapped for their specific skill, instead of holding a traditional, functionally aligned position.[173]

HETEROGENEOUS COLLABORATION REQUIRED

This new model also offers a structure for bringing diverse skill sets together to focus on a common goal. In the movie *Ocean's Eleven*, George Clooney's character recruits a diverse team of specialists, each with a unique ability and disposition to pull off the perfect heist: rob three casinos at once. To do something that's never been done before, you need to take calculated risks—and this kind of heterogeneous collaboration is crucial to bringing an ambitious goal into the realm of the possible. In her book *Building the Future*, Harvard professor Amy Edmondson speaks to how large-scale systemic innovation calls for "big teaming": intense collaboration between professions and industries with completely different mindsets.[174] This is especially essential when it comes to blockchain technology.

For those who choose to move early, it means getting in on the ground floor and being a part of shaping the structure at a foundational level. The technology is new, and the way that humans will interact with the systems built on it is still hypothetical (although informed by generations of economic and social science). If you do want to get skin in the game early, bring heterogeneous skills to the table. In addition to engineers, cryptographers, and blockchain developers, consider consulting economists, public policy experts, behavioral economists, social scientists, and even game designers. Build a working team of opposites that mashes up your own domain experts with complementary skills and approaches from diverse specializations to forge thoughtful innovations. Even if your focus is learning versus acting, creating a think tank of your best thinkers and an *Ocean's Eleven*–type team of specialists could be a high-return investment that helps you more quickly and effectively focus your exploration within this complex and important space.

As the space evolves, we will see more people holding new titles and role mashups. Companies will start hiring token economists. Traditional disciplines will emphasize new skills, such as those represented by the seemingly at-odds title held by lawyer and blockchain specialist Diana Stern: Legal Innovation Designer.

EFFECTIVE AND DIVERSE

But how do you lay a foundation for success when your team is characterized by diverse (and often divergent) perspectives? Without existing relationships or previous shared experience, it can be a challenge for teams to even identify a best next step, much less a path forward.

I asked Amy Edmondson what advice she would share with organizations that are starting these efforts. "You have to recognize that there will be failures—small things and large things will go wrong along the way," Amy explained. "So companies need to first step back and really understand the potential opportunity. If you don't have a strong sense of what might be possible on the other side, you will not weather the storm ahead very well." Secondly, Amy continued, "Organizations need to recognize where they lack expertise or vision internally—and reach out for help to external people or organizations who better understand this future to get up to speed." Finally, "Leaders can't be shrugging their shoulders if someone asks them why this is important. They must have clarity, and an elevator speech on why this matters. What is at stake? What is the opportunity?"

Ideally, this elevator speech paints a powerful but abstract picture of the future, instead of a photograph, explained Amy. Something so new can come into focus only as the team makes progress—you won't know exactly what it will look like until you get there. Importantly, this approach leaves space for others to contribute their expertise. "When creating a terrifically interdependent new initiative," Amy emphasized, "you have to leave room for others to make their contribution."

But how do you align a team with a deliberately vague future vision? "The answer lies in the concept of purpose," Amy explained. "Vision is the 'what,' but purpose is the 'why.' It could range from the desire to provide more value to customers, staying relevant in a changing world, or even being on the leading edge of what's possible." Regardless, the technology—whether it is driven by blockchains or not—is simply a means to an end, a way to help fulfill that purpose.

The next challenge is to create opportunities for people to come together to share their ideas. Amy has seen a methodology called *charrettes*, originating in architecture and urban planning, become more widely used across sectors. "It's an effective way to plan for any multifaceted challenge," she said, "such as improving K–12 education or stroke care—anytime you need to pull together experts from different domains." The charrette is a focused and intense planning process that brings these diverse contributors together, lasting anywhere from a day to a week or more.

Members may share a meal or an activity together before they begin formal planning, to establish some connection. And then the work begins. The key to success is careful curation and facilitation. It requires being deliberate about creating the context, setting the stage, proactively inviting participation, and making room for productive and thoughtful responses. It requires being thoughtful about establishing a psychologically safe space to share ideas and ask questions. It requires frequently slowing the conversation down to ensure that members understand each other. The word *platform*," for example, means something very different to an architect than it does to a software engineer.

Facilitation can help close the conversational loop—one person says something, and everyone checks for understanding. It can help to sort those ideas that have the most practical strength versus those that may be interesting, but don't yet have a path forward.[175]

Blockchain-Era Table Stakes

Several key tenets will characterize those organizations that connect more directly to success with this technology. While only the beginning of what it takes, these attributes will emerge as crucial.

OPEN MINDSET

No one can do blockchains alone. It's an ecosystem and a community-driven technology that requires collaboration to be effective. Wise companies are opening up their approach to innovation at levels that may have been unthinkable a decade ago. The accelerated pace at which innovation is occurring makes it critical to effectively tap into what's happening outside the organization, both in the blockchain community and among potential partners. As the technology has evolved, dozens of consortia have sprung up, focused on everything from round-tables where contributors simply share their learning and perspectives to fully integrated test beds for new blockchain projects.

Consortia arise naturally as a consequence of the technology itself. The greater the number of users, the more valuable the technology is to all of them. These network effects can motivate competitors to collaborate, and to create shared standards and governance structures. Some consortia have made notable progress thanks to the outsized commitment of a single leading player, such as with Hyperledger (IBM is providing a significant part of the codebase), or via the sheer volume of companies involved. However, switching from a competitive to a collaborative mindset is, not surprisingly, very difficult. It will take time to see projects move into production and to be adopted broadly.

FIRST, SEARCH WITHIN

One place to start a quest for internal knowledge is to mine internally for sometimes hidden pockets of passion and expertise. Blockchains, in particular, are a subject that captures the hearts and minds of a diverse range of people, and you may well have more resources inside than you think. They could be anywhere in your organization. Perhaps they are spending their weekends studying blockchains or investing in cryptoassets because it interests them. It may be, as John Oliver spoofed on *Last Week Tonight*, a few rogue people scattered around, like that "one guy in your office who [won't] shut up about it...who's been annoying everybody with his 'you got to get into bitcoin' #@$% for years."[176] Or maybe they have advanced degrees in cryptography or economics, even if they aren't using them in the work they do for you today. Use LinkedIn to find them if human resources can't help you. Give them a structure or platform, time to explore, a way to connect ideas to others in the organization, and a conduit for being heard by decision makers.

CONNECT THE NODES

A big part of this structure is connecting the pockets of interest, exploration, and learning across the corporation. Delegating blockchain efforts to a consortium and the few people across an organization who are working with that consortium will not be enough long term. Blockchain technology can drive benefit to multiple areas of the organization, from back-office divisions to marketers, in both top-line opportunity and in cost savings. Ultimately, focused efforts will need to be paired with broader, more dispersed learning across the organization. In each area of the organization in which blockchains could have impact, wise organizations will cultivate learning and foster connections between these "nodes." An organization can benefit by facilitating and encouraging connection points from these nodes to the blockchain community, and mechanisms and structure for pulling knowledge back inside and sharing it across all nodes in the organization.

PUT THE CUSTOMER AT THE CORE

But regardless of how well you have stocked your teams with well-balanced and diverse expertise, the make-or-break mindset is, bar none, that of the customer. Bring in domain expertise from every area in which the business touches customers. Even consider models that bring customer input more continuously into the learning process, from qualitative and quantitative research to more involved advisory programs. For years, companies have been working to "bring the customer into the boardroom." As this next era takes shape, perceptive companies will bring the customer into emerging blockchain programs.

Research firm Kaleido Insights cofounder Jessica Groopman frequently points out this imperative in her conversations with corporations exploring blockchains. "Perhaps this is stating the obvious," she says, "but I just need to emphasize, companies can't forget the customer experience. How are they ensuring the blockchain user experience is well thought-out for any customer-facing application, whether that is for a nurse, a lawyer, or an end consumer? These are the core principles of good design and consumerization of applications, and they are just as relevant here as they are in any other digital experience—perhaps even more."

Consider internal customers as well as external. Jessica also advocates for the importance of planning for hybrid architectures. In her view, blockchains will not replace existing structures and infrastructure overnight. Rather, they will evolve alongside incumbent systems and existing standards, complementing, then supporting, and then making certain workflows irrelevant. "Bring in the folks that will be impacted by technical changes," she says. "Maybe they are the sys admin or the product manager. It is important they are bought in, but can also help ideate on top of the direction."[177]

Change Agents in Action

There are many leaders working tirelessly in the blockchain space to educate individuals, teams, companies, and community groups about the dawning blockchain era and the opportunities it offers. The two executives discussed next are leveraging their deep personal expertise to educate their organizations about the potential in this technology.

LYDIA KREFTA: SHARED KNOWLEDGE DRIVES INNOVATION

Lydia Krefta discovered blockchains on the job. Principal Product Manager at energy company Pacific Gas and Electric Company (PG&E), Lydia was working on an initiative to examine how changes to the grid like the growth of electric vehicles and solar on rooftops might impact PG&E's business model. Phase I of the project was data collection and analysis; Phase II was evaluating pilot projects that could refine PG&E's capabilities to adapt to changes in the industry. To evaluate each emerging tech initiative, Lydia created a chart that ranked each according to its nascency and its potential value. When the team had their results, there was a clear winner.

"Blockchains were super nascent," she says, "but had really high potential—far more than anything else on the list. I could already see not just how they could impact PG&E, but the entire energy industry—and so many other things outside of the energy industry as well. That was my aha moment. It was clear this was technology we should be paying attention to."

At that time, Lydia knew little about blockchains other than what her own analysis had revealed. A self-described "knowledge gatherer," she plunged into an omnivorous study. "I'd stay up at night and read article after article," she says. "I didn't understand half of what I was reading, so then I'd go read more. Bitcoin, Ethereum, open source software, peer-to-peer transactions, hashing, smart contracts...you name it, I followed every lead, and I could not get enough. My husband felt like he lost me for a few months while I was really digging in and getting comfortable understanding the tech."

At PG&E her first hurdle was convincing people to pay attention to a technology that was still so new and unproven. But Lydia had an ally in leadership who was as excited about blockchains as she was. Together they came up with a plan to fund research. At that time 50% of Lydia's role was focused on electric vehicles, and as they left the meeting where they learned they'd secured funding, her coplanner asked how she'd like to spend the remaining 50% of her time. "And I was like, 'Blockchains, definitely!'" says Lydia. Thus Lydia built a brand new role for herself on a walk to the elevator. And within four months, she says, "It went from 50% to 150%."

One of the first things she did was form a blockchain learning group for anyone in the organization who was interested. "The initial effort was grassroots and scrappy," she said. "People learned about it through word of mouth." The first meeting drew six to eight people, including a director and a vice president Lydia invited to make the group official and to signal the importance of the work to the employees who chose to participate. They dubbed themselves the Blockheads, and gave themselves four months to gather use cases and figure out how to evaluate them. Part of their methodology included determining which use cases did *not* require a blockchain. "One of the things we asked ourselves was, 'Is this really an issue that a blockchain can solve, or is this a process issue?'" Lydia says. Once they'd identified a top 10, they set to work testing the use cases.

Because they were coming at this from a business standpoint, the Blockheads did a mini–business case for each use case. They intentionally targeted use cases that would help the company solve "now problems," rather than problems 15 years down the line. Then the team came back together and mapped out each use case according to how PG&E defines value: 1) growth: how can this help create new products and services? 2) affordability: how can this help cut costs and make PG&E more operationally efficient? Their aim was to choose the top use case from each of the categories. The two winners had to be viable and reflect the company's values, but they also had to earn the team's excitement and enthusiasm.

Lydia says they were surprised to find more viable use cases in the affordability category than they anticipated, but finally chose one. In the growth category, one in particular stood out: putting carbon credits for electric vehicles on a blockchain, which would incentivize charging at times when the grid is particularly green. "This one aligned perfectly," she says. "We could pursue our mission of a sustainable energy future by promoting electric vehicle growth, the team was super motivated, and all the key players across the organization were behind it. The transportation team was gung ho, and leadership was convinced because our choices reflected PG&E's values around sustainability and affordability."

The hunger to learn about blockchains has only intensified, and in response Lydia has launched three levels of education. The first is the Blockheads, who are still going strong. The second is a series of "lunch and learns" where anyone in the company can come learn for an hour. "We cover what a blockchain is, how it impacts the industry, and what PG&E plans to do with it," Lydia says. Demand has proven high, with employees from all areas represented, from Gas Operations to the Customer Care team to Energy Procurement. And the third is a half-hour address for those in leadership. Requiring more than a year to develop, Lydia uses this presentation to educate leadership on what blockchains are, give them an introduction to how it works, and explain why PG&E is paying attention to it.

And when a diversity of minds and a diversity of knowledge bases come together, new solutions or even new breakthroughs are generated. "I understand blockchains really, really well in its general applications and implications," Lydia says, "but I'm not a subject-matter expert in, say, demand response or energy efficiency. But there are others out there who are, and my hope is that by going out and talking to the people who are experts in their areas I can get them to understand the potential value-add of blockchain technology. Those experts will find the hidden use cases and solutions I would never know to look for." And this is already happening. After nearly every "lunch and learn" or internal course, people approach Lydia and suggest high-value use cases.

For leaders who are considering blockchain education in their own organizations, Lydia strongly recommends finding advocates from both the grassroots level and from leadership. "I wouldn't have been able to do what I'm doing at PG&E if I didn't have both," she says. A leadership presence is key to signal support to employees that are investing their time—and so is finding the people who really care about it. If you're working with a team who isn't very engaged while trying to apply new technology, you aren't going to get anywhere. But an excited team will dedicate themselves above and beyond."

For executives responsible for long-range planning, Lydia recommends joining a consortium. "It's incredibly helpful to have a consortium working together to develop a blockchain technology that makes sense for your industry," she points out. "You can see lessons learned from what other people are doing so you don't have to do every use case yourself." A consortium doesn't necessarily have to be organizational or even industry-specific, either. "Really, sharing the development is the whole point," Lydia says. "Blockchains are inherently a distributed technology. Everyone benefits when knowledge is shared."

> If you get in on the ground floor and learn it now, you can actually shape how this technology will impact your industry.

"We had a lot of work to do in educating decision makers to understand the potential impact of the technology and separate that from the potential risk," she says. "We wanted to shift the mindset from 'We can't do that *because of* x, y, and z,' to 'We should try it, but we'll *watch out for* x, y and z.'"

"Initially there was fear about how blockchains could disrupt the industry or introduce new risks, and one instinct in the face of fear or risk is to ignore the unknown. We took the view that if you get in on the ground floor and learn it now, then you can actually shape how this will impact the industry, rather than be left behind and have it hit you on the side of the head like a bag of bricks in 10 years."

DIANA BIGGS: FROM CYPHERPUNK TO ENTERPRISE INNOVATION LEADER

Diana Biggs saw firsthand how the money system was broken while working in microfinance in western Africa. In a city with two ATMs, one of them always broken, consumers had few convenient options for accessing money, and using a traditional service like Western Union to send and receive money required hefty fees for each transaction. There had to be a better way.

When Diana moved back to the States in 2013 to run a startup jointly based in New York, San Francisco, and Nairobi, mobile payment systems in the US were improving, but the artisans she worked with in Africa were still paying steep fees to move money around. "If we have the internet," she remembers thinking, "why can't we have global money?"

As a member of the cypherpunk movement since the early 90s, Diana was more familiar than most with digital capabilities. "I'd first heard of bitcoin in 2011," she says, "but didn't pursue it then because I didn't think it applied to anything I was doing. But the more I learned about its underlying technology, the more blockchains seemed to hold potential application in a variety of systems that weren't working—not just money and ecommerce issues, but health care, supply chain, and even inequalities in society, where it seemed like the people in power weren't doing the right thing for individuals."

Like many, she dove in deep with her exploration of blockchains, and very quickly got caught up in the excitement of the burgeoning movement. "It really felt like the early internet days," she says. By late 2013 she was attending bitcoin conferences and forging close friendships with many of its major players, from bitcoin core developers to the cofounders of Ethereum, who used her New York flat as a crashpad.

Eventually recruited by HSBC to start a new team focused on digital innovation, she continues to be fascinated by how technology can be used to promote financial inclusion and transparency, and how it can solve the problems that always vexed her—like making it easier for people everywhere to access and move money. "I felt that taking my background in mobile financial services and my passion for financial inclusion and then combining that with digital payments, open innovation, blockchains, and AI, especially at a large organization like HSBC," she says, "is how I could be most effective."

And when Diana says "large," she means *really* large: HSBC has more than 38 million customers in 67 countries, and 229,000 employees, which makes organization-wide educational efforts a formidable challenge. But Diana insists that large organizations "absolutely need to be prioritizing learning and getting themselves ready" for the massive changes that emerging technologies, and the resulting changes in our relationship with technology, will spark once they reach scalability. To that end she has implemented a number of creative educational initiatives at HSBC, including a lunchtime master class, a breakfast series called Innovation Mornings that brings in external speakers to talk about different aspects of tech, and internal websites with discussion boards so people can ask questions and share ideas and information on anything from AI to blockchains to data science. These initiatives are open to all employees, and Diana has found that it's not just technologists or digital specialists who are fascinated by these emerging technologies and show up for the classes, but people from all areas of the organization, including risk, compliance, operations, the C-suite, and even individual branch employees.

"It's amazing to see people from such diverse roles getting excited and actively engaging in blockchain technology and thinking about the possibilities for where it could go," she says. "Part of the importance of my group's role is to make sure people feel empowered to be a part of all this new learning, and empowered to find ways to innovate in their own areas. Innovation is about breaking silos—and all of this works especially well with blockchains because they are inherently about collaboration and transparency and empowering users."

To help employees network and collaborate across such a large organization, Diana and her team have created company events that include time for networking, internal tools like the discussion board, a weekly email so employees can share the projects they're working on and collaborate more effectively, and a monthly innovation forum so people from each part of the bank can share and discuss what they're learning. They also actively create a culture that encourages experimentation. "New technology means new potential opportunities. But it also carries equally new potential risks, as well as new experiences—and people need to work with this technology to really understand all this," she says. "So we make sure we're promoting a safe space, a sandbox environment, for creating hypotheses, identifying which tools are best, and testing and experimenting."

You can be tech agnostic, but if you don't test and invest now you'll ultimately be left behind.

Diana says everyone needs to accept that technology in general, not just blockchain technology, is changing things, and companies have a responsibility to keep pace. "You can be tech agnostic," she says, "but you need to test and try and invest, or you will ultimately be left behind." And though blockchains are still relatively new, Diana points out that "things are now starting to move into production and get real, and if you aren't experimenting now you'll miss out on a lot of valuable lessons."

Her advice for organizations looking to jump in? "Start investing in the future today," she says. "Don't write off new technologies like blockchains and think it's all fraud or fad, or that it can't work in a regulated market. That's a comfortable response today that could quickly become very uncomfortable."

13

CORPORATE INVESTING IN BLOCKCHAINS

The blockchain is really going to change dramatically the whole nature of investing and saving in the future.

—MYRON SCHOLES, NOBEL LAUREATE, ECONOMICS

Corporate investing in emerging technology is not a new strategy. Indeed, the few decades have seen leading multinationals introduce active strategies to participate in external innovation. Blockchains obviously offer a new wave of disruptive opportunity for organizations that have expertise, a vision for how the technology will shape their market, and the access to make smart strategic investments. However, blockchains are also poised to influence the way a wider range of corporations invest and raise capital.

The Challenge and Opportunity in Early Moves

There is strong motivation to understand and navigate investment opportunity even as it is still emerging. Together, Alison Davis and Matthew Le Merle, coauthors of *Corporate Innovation in the Fifth Era* and highly active investors and advisors in the blockchain space, have researched how leading innovators such as Alphabet, Amazon.com, Apple, Facebook, and Microsoft invest in innovation. Alison is also a board member and advisor to some of the oldest and most active blockchain investment firms, while Matthew is Managing Partner at Keiretsu Capital, an early stage investment network with over $750 million in funding and active investment in the space. Over dinner, the two shared their perspective on the corporate investment opportunity.

"It's a familiar pattern," Alison explains. "When disruptive innovation arrives, it unleashes enormous value, but that value is not necessarily captured by the incumbents. In the industrial era, enormous wealth was created and transferred to new sets of people—the industrial tycoons and the financiers that backed them. Today we are all very fortunate to be living in the midst of a time of more disruption, innovation, and new technologies than any other humans have ever experienced before. New breakthroughs are unleashing new sources of value that are being captured by early entrepreneurs and the venture investors who back them—and this is especially apparent in the blockchain investment world."

Matthew sees many similarities between this moment and the early days of internet investing. He describes how when disruptive technology changes the world, early rounds of investing deliver far superior returns—but accessing these returns comes with great challenge. "Most people don't even know what questions they should be asking," says Matthew, "much less have enough exposure to identify a strong project or company."[178]

So how are executive teams and corporate venture arms investing in this new area of emerging technology?

Three Investment Strategies for the Corporation

Blockchains offer new layers of investment opportunity for the corporation—and not just for the business looking to build their own disruptive capabilities. Because blockchains are also a key driver in creating what some are calling an entirely new asset class—cryptoassets—they hold the promise for new portfolio diversification and access to capital.

We are already seeing new activity in three areas:

- Building capability via strategic investment
- Diversifying portfolios via cryptoassets
- Raising capital via tokenization

In this chapter, we'll discuss each in turn.

INVESTING IN DISRUPTIVE CAPABILITY

While it's a move reserved for those with depth in the space, some companies are making bold plays to invest directly in blockchain companies. A 2017 CB Insights report found that corporations participated in over 140 equity investments since

2012 and that the number of active corporate investors was fast approaching the number of active venture capital investors. While the financial services industry was the first to make direct blockchain investments en masse, investment is starting to come from a broader range of industries. Japan-based SBI Holdings, Google, Overstock.com, Citi, and Goldman Sachs were the leading corporate investors, according to the CB Insights report, with Overstock.com even building out an internal blockchain-focused venture and development team, Medici Ventures, that holds the broad mission of advancing the technology.[179]

Consortiums have also sprung up as a major conduit for corporate exploration in the space. Arguably those with the most momentum today are Enterprise Ethereum Alliance, Hyperledger, and R3. Enterprise Ethereum Alliance (with 500 members) and Hyperledger (with 270 members) have joined forces to collaborate on bringing standards to the space, while R3, which has a heavy focus on financial services, has more than 200 members.

As the market evolves, we may see more corporations make moves to acquire access to resources and IP, or to leverage the second mover advantage discussed in Chapter 5. Regardless, successful moves will require not only deep acumen in the technology, but also a strong vision for how the technology will shape the future.

DEBUTING CRYPTOASSETS IN PORTFOLIO STRATEGIES

In October of 2018, David F. Swensen, Yale's chief investment officer (known as the university's Warren Buffett because of his investing success) surprised the financial community when news broke that he'd invested in multiple cryptoasset funds through the endowment. A report was published less than a week later attesting that Harvard, Stanford, and MIT were also investing in cryptocurrency and crypto-related projects through their own substantial endowments. These moves were seen as a signal of growing acceptance of cryptoassets as an alternative asset class among institutional investors.[180]

Organizations that seek to actively introduce blockchains and cryptoassets into their portfolio strategy have a few approaches to choose from. Direct investment in cryptoassets is certainly one approach, but this requires a great deal of sophistication in the space, and the industry still needs to mature to fully support the demands of institutional-grade custody. To ease diversification, firms have created indexes and baskets as the industry awaits the emergence of the first exchange-traded funds (ETFs).

But with the space so early in its evolution, many institutional investors seek more active navigation. In addition to established hedge funds moving into the space, a whole new breed of crypto-native fund has sprung up to serve investors looking to incorporate the sector in their portfolio strategy. Matthew Le Merle draws a parallel to the early days of the internet. "Smart people disagree about what is going to happen in the future of this space," he says. "You need to cast a wide net through quality diversification."[181]

Spencer Bogart, a partner at one of the oldest and most active venture investors in the blockchain technology sector, Blockchain Capital, explains, "The technology holds the promise to change the world in profound ways, to create new markets and entirely new business models," he says. "But it's complex. It can take 6 to 12 months of full-time deep diving in to really understand the impact of just bitcoin. And the number of people that are trying to form companies, the number of teams that are looking for ways to push this industry forward, it's astounding. On any given day, we are seeing 20 to 30 inbound investment opportunities. It's a massive undertaking to navigate through the change and complexity."[182]

USING TOKENIZATION TO REMOVE FRICTION FROM CAPITAL

Over the last few decades, investment markets have systematically applied technology to make capital raising and investing more efficient—that is, faster, cheaper, and more liquid. Today, most markets are driven by real-time technology platforms. However, there is a glaring omission: key aspects of the private equity market.

There have certainly been some advancements toward changing this, at least for small capitalization private companies and real estate deals. For example, the US introduced new crowdfunding regulations in the JOBS Act, and similar approaches have been introduced in Europe and Asia. As a result, investors have begun to experiment with direct investing in companies and projects via crowdfunding platforms.

Tokenization is a strategy that could take this process one step further. Pioneers working on this approach envision a world in which illiquid assets are encoded into tradeable tokens that are represented digitally on a blockchain. This would enable fractionalized and theoretically more liquid forms of ownership (friction is reduced if an asset is easier to trade, increasing liquidity). This could also open access to new kinds of investors. For example, enabling fractionalized ownership of a building could open up a new pool of investors that would not make a multimillion-dollar investment in that building, and make it easier to more broadly diversify a portfolio.

Digital tokens can also be programmable via smart contracts, opening new models for raising capital for projects under development by issuing "shares" in the form of tokens to finance an initiative. This approach could potentially be more efficient than today's methods. It could reduce the (extremely high) cost of middlemen to perform such transactions today, and eliminate territorial and even temporal barriers.

This approach was used by blockchain teams seeking to raise capital for their projects by way of tokenized initial coin offerings (ICOs), also discussed in Chapter 5. Many of these teams got ahead of themselves: they didn't have a clear purpose for their token or certainty of whether their tokens were securities (which requires adherence to securities regulation). Some teams even created fake projects to maliciously obtain funds. Nevertheless, billions of dollars were raised through this process—at minimum demonstrating how capital could be raised via tokens, and spurring a great deal of investment in further developing the process.

Expect to see creative applications of this approach from both established financial services leaders and new players. Many of today's innovators are actively working with regulators to develop compliant models that will make tokenization accessible to a broad set of corporations. Mason Borda founded a company, TokenSoft, to support the complex compliance requirements of global companies looking to leverage token models. "For the last few years, we worked primarily with blockchain-first companies," he says. "But at the beginning of 2018, this shifted. Now, banks and corporations are coming to us to understand how to leverage asset-backed token models, and there is a lot of experimentation going on. They're seeking to leverage blockchain infrastructure as a more efficient model —and they're making fast progress."[183]

A New Frontier for the Corporation

While much of this book is focused on how blockchains will change the shape of business, they will also influence how the corporation invests. Leaders are already focusing attention on the space, whether in the hopes of more efficient capital formation or the potentially outsize returns that come from disruption. Investing in this type of high-risk and emerging space requires the same skills and strategies that apply to any other area of emerging technology, but with additional challenges: shifting regulation, a complex and fast-moving landscape of projects and companies, and the difficulty of institutional-grade custody. It's especially crucial to align with expertise as you develop your strategy.

14

THE BIG SMALL PRINT

Throughout this book, I have called out challenges that the space, and anyone looking to work with the technology, will face. These are big challenges, but as I have emphasized, there is a great influx of resource directed to address them. Like so many others that you have heard from in these pages, and that you will hear from as you continue your journey, I am optimistic that the future holds breakthrough after breakthrough that will ultimately resolve many obstacles. I don't believe we know enough to accurately predict where these breakthroughs will come from. However, I do want to leave you with a focused list of warnings, all in one easy-to-scan place, to remember as you take your next step, whatever it may be.

Be Skeptical

Blockchains are sexy at the moment, and that's creating a blockchain blind spot. They're being built in to all sort of visions that really require nothing more than a database or that would be better off centralized. Question if a blockchain is really needed or if you are falling for the "blockchain trap." Does a blockchain solve a real problem? For this use case, do you really need a database to which multiple parties can write? Is there a lack of trust among these parties? Is there truly no third party that these entities would trust? If the answer is no, you don't need a blockchain, end of story. Instead of looking first to blockchains, challenge yourself to find a solution without one.

Don't Write off the Toys

In this adolescent phase, a lot of use cases may look like toys (for the curious, look up Cryptokitties, an application that became crypto community lore when it "broke" Ethereum in December of 2017). We'll see a lot of innovation happening in such strange places as digital collectibles. However, the learnings that can come out of these spaces—in everything from user experience to identity to how users leverage portability to overcoming scalability challenges—is very, very real. This is the time to try out these use cases yourself, and think big about how they can be extended to other applications.

Don't Overestimate Who Cares about Privacy

Some blockchain entrepreneurs are hinging their businesses on converting users that care about privacy. While many care at some level, massive segments of our population have been inoculated to the idea of privacy, even as privacy-related scandals make headline after headline. This may change somewhat over time, but broad adoption will quite likely take something else—a massive groundswell in scandals, or the perception of top side benefits like compensation.

It's Nothing without Network Effects

This next era is about ecosystems and community. If you can't find a strategy to build network effects, you are on the wrong path.

The Best Technology May Not Win

In the hallways of Silicon Valley you may hear the refrain, "Design is the new engineering!" Indeed, design and marketing are the cornerstone of adoption—and without it, a great project can be DOA. This is the time to involve the marketers, designers, and UX specialists, and those who crack this challenge will be in a good position to break open the dam holding back broader adoption.

Nothing Matters without Scalability

Good user experience and network effects aren't possible without scalability, and this is one of the biggest barriers in the technology today. Incredibly innovative and mind-blowing approaches are under development to address this challenge, and more will spring up. Keep a close watch.

Identity Hasn't Been Solved

So much of the blockchain era vision starts with identity. Blockchain entrepreneurs get this and are in a race to figure out who will solve the challenge of establishing trusted, widely adopted identities complete with third-party attestations. A complete answer has not been discovered, and its pursuit is deeply complex. Watch this closely—a great deal of the vision can't be realized until this is solved.

Token Instability Hasn't Been Cracked

Cryptocurrency prices are all over the map. There has been a great deal of work (some of it controversial) on developing *stablecoins,* a cryptocurrency tethered to a more stable asset such as a commodity, and they continue to be an area of great interest and exploration. In fact, nearly 60 stablecoin projects have received more than $350 million in financing.[184] Some companies are setting up foundations that issue multiple token currencies, one to be used for appreciation, and another to be used for transactions. But this whole remarkably complex area of cryptoeconomics—and how a small team of entrepreneurs can build a functioning mini-economy that acts as its own central bank (without all the tools available to a central bank)—is still in its infancy, and the fundamentals are not widely understood.

Consensus Mechanisms Are an Ongoing Battle

Because this book is not meant to be technical, we didn't spend much time on consensus mechanisms. This is an important area to understand—and watch—as you take the next step in your blockchain journey. "Consensus" is how all the nodes on the network agree that the state of the blockchain is correct, and how the blockchain is updated. Consensus mechanisms should be designed so that no single entity could control or derail the blockchain—and this is the most difficult part to get right.

There are many forms of consensus being explored, but no clear winners: we need a lot more work and testing in this area. "Proof of work" is the consensus mechanism that the bitcoin blockchain uses. It is the most battle-tested approach, but it also uses an incredible amount of energy as computers around the world race to solve cryptographic puzzles (as described in Chapter 3), and is vulnerable if one entity could control more than half the network's computing power (called a 51% attack). For blockchains to become more broadly adopted, we will need consensus mechanisms that are both proven and efficient.

We're Still Figuring out Governance

These new networks are driven by baked-in governance. But we don't have many examples of how these networks will function when millions of users get involved. Where will they break? How will they be gamed? We need better answers to these questions in order to develop efficient and effective decentralized governance mechanisms that function as intended. We may see some spectacular fails in the future, and will gain many new insights to behavioral economics along the way.

But Above All, Maintain Vigilance

We have so much yet to discover about how to work with this technology and how it will impact our personal and business lives. Scan the horizon continually to identify new threats, opportunities, and challenges as they emerge. Develop a robust network of trusted thought leaders and vetted specialists to help you stay informed of shifts as the area further develops.

15

BRINGING IT ALL TOGETHER

Key Questions to Help You Compose Your Next Step

We've covered a lot of ground through these pages. We've explored how blockchains work. We took a deep-dive into the core fundamentals that will drive change in a blockchain future. And we tapped into the vision of entrepreneurs and pioneers in the space.

Now what? What do you do when you return to the office tomorrow, or next week? This chapter is a rundown of key questions to ask yourself and your management team as you take your exploration of the blockchain opportunity to the next level. Depending on how complex your organization is and where it is on the journey, some questions may be straightforward, but others may be unanswerable until you've done some digging. Regardless, exploring these questions will drive clarity around where you need to focus your attention. The questions are organized into three dimensions, shown in Figure 15-1:

- Assessment
- Aspiration
- Action

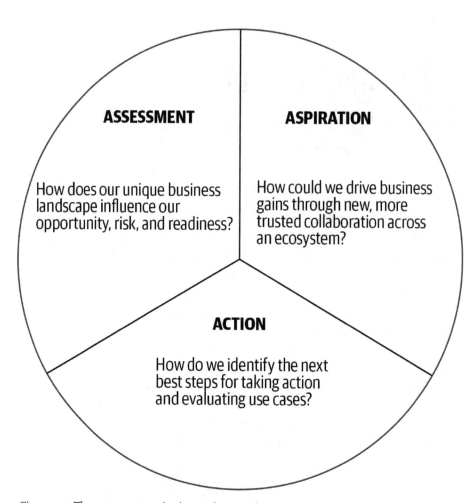

Figure 15-1. The assessment, aspiration, action questions.

ASSESSMENT

How does our unique business landscape influence our opportunity, risk, and readiness?

BROADER ECOSYSTEM	• What industry-wide challenges could be solved by the attributes blockchains and related technologies offer? What blockchain-native companies are attacking these challenges? • Which organizations are exhibiting leadership in our industry and related industries, and what can we learn from their work? • How are we collaborating with the broader ecosystem (whether directly in our industry or beyond), and how should we formalize this collaboration? • What consortia and partnerships are gaining momentum? Which are aligned with our values and mission?
COMPETITORS	• What approaches are established competitors and new, disruptive companies that are targeting our market taking? What can we learn about their successes and failures to date? • What claims are they making? Are they credible? • In what circumstances could their work become a threat? In what circumstances do they become a potential partner? • Where is our business model most dependent on proprietary customer data? How do our customers measure the return on providing that data? • In what parts of our business do we serve as a middleman, and how do our customers measure the value of that service? • What parts of our business model would suffer disruption if competitors could fractionalize ownership of the product or services we provide?
INTERNAL ORGANIZATION	• Where and who are the people across the organization who are exploring the opportunity in blockchains? Where are our gaps? • What projects or initiatives are already under way? • How are we connecting knowledge within our organization today, and how could we formalize this collaboration?
EXTENDED ENTERPRISE	• What projects and initiatives are our partners evaluating? Which align most closely with our values and mission? Which are positioned to address a key pain or challenge we also face? • How can we formalize collaboration with the clusters of knowledge within our partner ecosystem?

ASPIRATION

How could we drive business gains through new, more trusted collaboration across an ecosystem?

REDUCE FRICTION	• Where do high-toll middlemen serve as a proxy for trust in our ecosystem? • Where do cross-border or cross-organization business processes carry high friction and/or risk? • Where is fraud most costly to our business? • How could a decentralized business process increase efficiency for participants or customers?
FIND TOP-LINE OPPORTUNITY	• How could we deliver additional value to our customers by extending and more tightly integrating our business processes or elements of the customer experience beyond "inner circle" partners? • Would there be benefit to us in leading the development of more collaborative ecosystems, or the cocreation of new markets enabled by the technology? • Where could the attributes of decentralization most align with our corporate values and mission? • How could we enable customers to exchange value within their own networks? • How could fractionalized, programmable, and/or more liquid forms of our products or assets drive benefit to our customers or business model? • How could decentralization pose a threat to our business model, and how could we use decentralization to reshape our market ahead of others doing so? • What role do we want to have in the broader ecosystem as this technology matures?

ACTION

How do we identify the next best steps for taking action and evaluating use cases?

RAISE LITERACY	• In what functional areas would we benefit from raising our understanding of the blockchain opportunity? • How could we increase collaboration among executives, technologists, and subject-matter experts within the lines of business to identify strong potential use cases? • How can we best assimilate knowledge from the external blockchain community into our organization?
DEVELOP FILTERS	• Do we have the range of expertise on our evaluation team to accurately assess potential, including technology, customer, and relevant domain expertise? • Will our evaluation team be able to objectively determine if a nonblockchain solution will be more effective than the early stage blockchain (and related) technology available now? • Are we aligned on the criteria against which we will evaluate potential use cases, and a horizon for expected returns? • Are we prepared to invest the resources and funding to truly explore compelling use cases, should we identify them?
MOVE STRATEGICALLY	• Which potential use cases are aligned with the values and mission of our organization, and are likely to gain executive sponsorship? • Which use cases are positioned to demonstrate the real capabilities of the technology to key stakeholders across the organization? • How can we lower the barrier to entry for our chosen use cases to assess feasibility and/or demonstrate returns more quickly? • Which use cases could be extensible to other applications and areas of business to increase return on investment?

Afterword

THE OPPORTUNITY AND THE HOPE ARE HUMAN

The time is always right to do what is right.

—MARTIN LUTHER KING, JR.

I did not dedicate this book to my children lightly.

After many months of writing and editing, I printed and read my entire manuscript on paper for the first time. I noted, with irony, that moving this book about bleeding-edge technology from pixels, where it had lived so long, to a stack of paper that I could hold in my hands helped me reconnect to what I'd written. From my first glimpse of the alternate future that decentralization could trigger, I have believed *this* is an important moment in our collective history. But as I turned that last page and slipped on my shoes to take my dog for a long-needed walk, I was feeling this even more deeply.

I hadn't made it one block before I ran into a neighborhood dad. This man was practically dripping children. He had a baby cradled in his arms. One twin toddler was trying to untie his shoe. The other was wrapped around his leg, and her friend was using his belt to anchor a climb up his leg. "Hey!" he shouted from across the street. "When should I buy bitcoin?" Word had been getting out in my neighborhood that I was writing about blockchains, so I had been frequently peppered with questions while walking the dog.

As I approached, the three toddlers dropped what they were doing en masse and turned their attention to my dog. Good thing, because this time, my Dear Reader, I added a swear when I whispered, "It does *not* matter," a little too fiercely, in his ear.

I hope you see, after reading this book, that focusing on cryptocurrency speculation is missing the point. Over the long arc of time, a shift toward decentralization could have a far more profound impact on those children, now climbing all over my dog, than their dad attempting to time the cryptocurrency market.

We have arrived at a moment in our history in which our destiny—the destiny of humanity—is now irrevocably intertwined with technology. But the systems we create today are capable of becoming bigger than their creators. And once unleashed, they may take on a form we did not intend or predict. *If we want to influence the shape of our future, we must—actively and with intent—shape technology.*

The difference—whether the postscript on this technology will be a story of societal advancements or of freedoms lost—will come from the actions of individuals. Individuals code the protocols, lay the structures, develop the governance, bake in the algorithms. In this space and time, we do not understand all the implications of our actions, and that is why we must move forward thoughtfully and carefully. It is up to us whether we build freedom or suppression into the technology. Whether we will build something that will connect us or we will be the architects of our own fragmentation. Whether we will use this technology to transcend barriers or forge further division.

We can no longer afford to create without a long view of the horizon.

Fred Ehrsam is the cofounder of Coinbase, a company backed by top banks and the NYSE, that aims to bring cryptoassets to the masses. He eloquently shares an important warning: "We are birthing into existence systems which transcend us. In the same way democracy and capitalism as systems determine so much of the emergent behavior around us, blockchains will do the same with even greater reach. These systems are organisms which take on lives of their own and are more concerned with perpetuating themselves than the individuals which comprise them. As technology stretches these systems to their limits, the implications become more pronounced. So we'd be wise to carefully consider the structure of these systems while we can. Like any new powerful technology, blockchains are a tool that can go in many different directions. Used well, we can create a world with greater prosperity and freedom. Used poorly, we can create systems which lead us to places we didn't intend to go."

He continues, "We have the opportunity to create vastly different power structures and program the future we want for ourselves."[185]

Ian Bogost, a professor of interactive computing at the Georgia Institute of Technology, writes in *The Atlantic*, "The technology has been hailed for its potential to usher in a new era of services that are less reliant on intermediaries like businesses and nation-states. But its boosters often overlook that the opposite is equally possible: blockchain could further consolidate the centralized power of corporations and governments instead."[186]

Will this be technology versus humanity, or will it be technology for humanity?

It is up to us to decide. *We* can solve problems. *We* can bake humanity into the code. *We* can work to make sure this new movement ferries us toward a more equitable, just, and progressive future.

> *We all have the ability to shape the future of technology.*
> *And we all have an enormous responsibility to make sure that*
> *technology enables the future we aspire to.*

—KLAUS SCHWAB, FOUNDER AND EXECUTIVE CHAIRMAN,
WORLD ECONOMIC FORUM

As you join the growing ranks of those who "get" this space, you have an opportunity to influence its use in making our world better. I hope you do. Ask questions. They may be just as valuable as someone else's answers.

ACKNOWLEDGMENTS

While careening down a Tahoe mountainside on my snowboard, a challenge popped into my head. Could I break the complex, still-evolving world of block-chains into an aerial view so straightforward that any exec could understand it? I started sketching with the plan to write a series of articles. With some alarm, I realized after a few months that this required long form—much longer. Once I saw that, I couldn't unsee it (I tried!), and I battened down the hatches to write this book.

My first thank you is to those pioneers who are working in this challenging space because of their sheer desire for an alternate, better digital future for our world—you have renewed my hope.

Thank you to my dear Wyatt and Eleanor, who not only understand my intensity but also throw out so much love and encouragement that keep me going when I tire.

I am deeply grateful to all the business leaders, entrepreneurs, and visiona-ries who took the time to share their perspective, tell their stories, and provide their thoughts as I worked on this book. Most especially to Maja Vujinovic, Sheila Warren, Diana Biggs, and Lydia Krefta not only for sharing their personal stories with me so that my readers could learn, but also for the work they do to advocate for responsible and meaningful use of this technology. To Meltem Demirors for her suggestions, as well as her tireless work to advance this space.

To my clients who have helped me form my perspectives and given me the incredible experience of working with executives I not only respect, but also just plain love being around.

Thank you to the extraordinary Catherine Knepper, who started as my editor but ended up becoming a lifelong friend. To the talented and wise Stephen Swin-tek, who created the cover image.

And, finally, to my dear friends Roderick, Alex, and Rosalind: without your encouragement and support, this book would never have broken free of my com-puter and out into the world.

Notes

1. CNN Money, "The $1.7 Trillion dot.com Lesson," November 9, 2000, *https://money.cnn.com/2000/11/09/technology/overview*.
2. Vujinovic, Maja. Discussion with the author. June 2018.
3. Warren, Sheila. Discussion with the author. October 2018.
4. Seiff, Ken. Discussion with the author. October 2018.
5. Tim Berners-Lee, "One Small Step for the Web" Medium, September 29, 2018, *https://medium.com/@timberners_lee/one-small-step-for-the-web-87f92217d085*.
6. Bridget van Kralingen, "Industry Impact: Trust and Transparency Through Enterprise-Ready Blockchain," filmed April 2018 at MIT Technology Review Business of Blockchain, video, *https://events.technologyreview.com/video/watch/bridget-van-kralingen-ibm-trust-transparency*.
7. International Data Corporation (IDC), "Worldwide Semiannual Blockchain Spending Guide," 2018, *https://www.idc.com/tracker/showproductinfo.jsp?prod_id=1842*.
8. Deloitte, "2018 Global Blockchain Survey,"2018, *https://www2.deloitte.com/content/dam/Deloitte/cz/Documents/financial-services/cz-2018-deloitte-global-blockchain-survey.pdf*.
9. Chris Dixon, "Chris Dixon on How Trust Is the Best Lego Block—Ep.70," interview by Laura Shin, *Unchained*, July 3, 2018, audio, *http://unchained-podcast.co/chris-dixon-on-how-trust-is-the-best-lego-block-ep70*.
10. Kaili, Eva. Discussion with the author. June 2018.
11. McKie, Steven. Discussion with the author. August 2018.
12 Vitalik Buterin, "Change the Incentives, Change the World", *Cato Unbound*, June 16, 2017, *https://www.cato-unbound.org/2017/06/16/vitalik-buterin/change-incentives-change-world*.

13. Biggs, Diana. Discussion with the author. June 2018.

14. Vujinovic, Maja. Discussion with the author. June 2018.

15. Clippinger, John Henry. Discussion with the author. August 2018.

16. Graham Rapier, "13 Times Bosses Mocked New Technology and Got It Wrong," *Business Insider*, November 10, 2017, *https://www.businessinsider.com/bosses-mocked-new-technologyand-got-it-wrong-2017-6#blockbuster-ceo-jim-keyes-on-streaming-video-1.*

17. *http://www.handelsblatt.com/unternehmen/industrie/produktentwicklung-nokia-uebt-sich-in-selbstkritik;2490362*, translated with Google Translate.

18. Tonya Garcia, "Foot Locker Shares Plunge 28% as Brands Like Nike and Adidas Go Direct-to-Consumer," MarketWatch, August 18, 2017, *https://www.marketwatch.com/story/foot-locker-shares-plunge-26-as-brands-like-nike-and-adidas-go-direct-to-consumer-2017-08-18.*

19. Jill Carlson, jill-carlson.com, accessed August 2018, *http://jill-carlson.com/read.*

20. Nathaniel Popper, "Confused About Blockchains? Here's What You Need to Know," *New York Times*, June 27, 2018, *https://www.nytimes.com/2018/06/27/business/dealbook/blockchains-guide-information.html.*

21. Adam Greenfield, *Radical Technologies: The Design of Everyday Life* (London, New York: Verso, 2017).

22. Stuart Haber and W. Scott Stornetta, "How to Time-Stamp a Digital Document," *Journal of Cryptology* 3, no. 2 (1991): 99-111.

23. Julie Bort, "Retiring Cisco CEO Delivers Dire Prediction: 40% of Companies Will Be Dead in 10 Years," *Business Insider*, June 8, 2015, *https://www.businessinsider.com/chambers-40-of-companies-are-dying-2015-6.*

24. Center for the Digital Future, "Surveying the Digital Future, 2017," *Digital Future Project, http://www.digitalcenter.org/wp-content/uploads/2013/10/2017-Digital-Future-Report.pdf.*

25. eMarketer, "Among Affluents, Millennials Spend the Most Time Online," October 19, 2016, *https://www.emarketer.com/Article/Among-Affluents-Millennials-Spend-Most-Time-Online/1014618.*

26. Tim Berners-Lee, "Three Challenges for the Web, According to Its Inventor," *World Wide Web Foundation*, March 12, 2017, *https://webfoundation.org/2017/03/web-turns-28-letter.*

27. Tim Berners-Lee, "One Small Step for the Web..." September 29, 2018, Medium, *https://medium.com/@timberners_lee/one-small-step-for-the-web-87f92217d085.*

28. "Happy Birthday World Wide Web," *The Economist*, March 12, 2014, https://www.economist.com/graphic-detail/2014/03/12/happy-birthday-world-wide-web.

29. David Brooks, "A Generation Emerging from the Wreckage," *New York Times*, February 26, 2018, https://www.nytimes.com/2018/02/26/opinion/millennials-college-hopeful.html.

30. Gardner, Jeremy. Discussion with the author. August 2018.

31. Pew Research Center, "Millennials in Adulthood," March 7, 2014, http://www.pewsocialtrends.org/2014/03/07/millennials-in-adulthood.

32. Kaili, Eva. Discussion with the author. June 2018

33. Tim Wu, *The Master Switch: The Rise and Fall of Information Empires* (New York: Alfred A. Knopf/Borzoi Books, 2010).

34. Amber Baldet, "The Currency of the Future Is Personal Data," Quartz, September 25, 2018, https://qz.com/1381355/the-currency-of-the-future-is-personal-data.

35. Nathaniel Popper, "Confused About Blockchains? Here's What You Need to Know," *New York Times*, June 27, 2018, https://www.nytimes.com/2018/06/27/business/dealbook/blockchains-guide-information.html.

36. Bianchini, Gina. Discussion with the author. July 2018.

37. Juniper Research, "Blockchain Enterprise Survey," July 2017, https://www.juniperresearch.com/press/press-releases/6-in-10-large-corporations-considering-blockhain.

38. CB Insights, "8 Trends Shaping the Future of Blockchain Technology," May 2018, http://www.cbinsights.com/research/blockchain-future-trends.

39. European Parliament News, "Blockchain Technology: 'We Aspire to Make the EU the Leading Player,'" May 2018, http://www.europarl.europa.eu/news/en/headlines/economy/20180514STO03406/blockchain-technology-we-aspire-to-make-eu-leading-player.

40. Demirors, Meltem. Discussion with the author. May 2018.

41. Henok Mengistu et al., "The Evolutionary Origins of Hierarchy," *PLoS Computational Biology* 12, 6 (2016): e1004829.

42. Demirors, Meltem. Discussion with the author. May 2018.

43. Warren, Sheila. Discussion with the author. October 2018.

44. Soman, Nick. Discussion with the author. August 2018.

45. Biggs, Diana. Discussion with the author. June 2018.

46. Demirors, Meltem. Discussion with the author. May 2018.

47. Ibid.

48. Geoffrey Moore, *Crossing the Chasm* (New York: Harper Business, 2014).

49. Ly, Eric. Discussion with the author. May 2018.

50. Kerner, Lou. Discussion with the author. May 2018.

51. Groopman, Jessica. Discussion with the author. June 2018.

52. Chris Anderson, "TED Curator Chris Anderson on Crowd Accelerated Innovation," *Wired*, December 27, 2010, *http://www.wired.com/2010/12/ ff_tedvideos*.

53. Henry William Chesbrough, *Open Innovation: The New Imperative for Creating and Profiting from Technology* (Brighton, MA: Harvard Business Review Press, 2005).

54. Eric Von Hippel, *Democratizing Innovation* (Cambridge, MA: The MIT Press, 2005).

55. Laura Shin, "Here's the Man Who Created ICOs and This Is the New Token He's Backing," *Forbes*, September 2017, *https://www.forbes.com/sites/ laurashin/2017/09/21/heres-the-man-who-created-icos-and-this-is-the-new-token-hes-backing/d934c9211839*.

56. Matt Levine, Twitter, August 29, 2017, *https://twitter.com/matt_levine/ status/902617398620168196*.

57. Smith + Crown ICO Tracker, *http://www.smithandcrown.com/ico-tracker*.

58. Jobanputra, Jalak. Discussion with the author. July 2018.

59. CB Insights, "Venture Capital Funnel Shows Odds of Becoming a Unicorn Are Less than 1%, "March 2017, *http://www.cbinsights.com/research/venture-capital-funnel-2*.

60. Joseph Young, "Vitalik Buterin: 90% of ICOs Will Fail," *Coin Journal*, October 2017, *https://coinjournal.net/vitalik-buterin-90-icos-will-fail*.

61. Chwierut, Matt. Discussion with the author. May 2018.

62. Heather Whipps, "How Ancient Trade Changed the World," Live Science, February 17, 2018, *https://www.livescience.com/4823-ancient-trade-changed-world.html*.

63. Niam Yaraghi and Shamika Ravi, "The Current and Future State of the Sharing Economy," Brookings, December 29, 2016, *http://www.brookings.edu/research/the-current-and-future-state-of-the-sharing-economy*.

64. Simpson, Arianna. Discussion with the author. May 2018.

65. Rachel Wolfson, "Tim Draper on the Future of Cryptocurrency, His New Book and Why Bitcoin Will Hit \$250,000 by 2022," *Forbes*, May 2, 2018, *https://www.forbes.com/sites/rachelwolfson/2018/05/02/tim-draper-on-the-*

future-of-cryptocurrency-his-new-book-and-why-bitcoin-will-hit-250000-by-2022/
#627c390e2d71.

66. Bill Gates, *The Road Ahead* (New York: Viking Press, 1995).

67. The World Bank, "Remittance Prices Worldwide," March 2018, *https://remittanceprices.worldbank.org/sites/default/files/rpw_report_march2018.pdf.*

68. Vitalik Buterin, Twitter, April 16, 2018, *https://twitter.com/vitalikbuterin/status/986107008892846080.*

69. Juniper Research, "Ad Fraud to Cost Advertisers $19 Billion in 2018, Representing 9% of Total Digital Advertising Spend," September 26, 2017, *http://www.juniperresearch.com/press/press-releases/ad-fraud-to-cost-advertisers-$19-billion-in-2018.*

70. Soman, Nick. Discussion with the author. August 2018.

71. Kairos Future, "The Land Registry in the Blockchain Testbed," March 2017, *https://chromaway.com/papers/Blockchain_Landregistry_Report_2017.pdf.*

72. Hartman Group, "Sustainability 2017," September 2017, *http://store.hartman-group.com/content/Sustainability-2017-Overview.pdf.*

73. Nielsen, "Consumer-Goods' Brands That Demonstrate Commitment to Sustainability Outperform Those That Don't," October 12, 2015, *https://www.nielsen.com/us/en/press-room/2015/consumer-goods-brands-that-demonstrate-commitment-to-sustainability-outperform.html.*

74. FoodLogiQ, "What Consumers Care About in the Age of Transparency," 2017, *https://www.foodlogiq.com/resources/consumers-in-the-age-of-food-transparency.*

75. Susan McPherson, "8 Corporate Social Responsibility (CSR) Trends to Look for in 2018," *Forbes*, January 12, 2018, *https://www.forbes.com/sites/susanmcpherson/2018/01/12/8-corporate-social-responsibility-csr-trends-to-look-for-in-2018.*

76. KPMG, "The Road Ahead: The KPMG Survey of Corporate Responsibility Reporting 2017," 2017, *https://home.kpmg.com/content/dam/kpmg/campaigns/csr/pdf/CSR_Reporting_2017.pdf.*

77. Sustainability Academy, "Global Trends in Corporate Sustainability for 2017," January 18, 2017, *https://www.sustainability-academy.org/trends-sustainability-2017.*

78. Global Reporting Initiative, "Sustainability and Reporting Trends 2025—Preparing for the Future," May 2015, *http://www.globalreporting.org/resourcelibrary/Sustainability-and-Reporting-Trends-in-2025-1.pdf.*

79. Martha Filipic, "High Cost of Foodborne Illness: New Study Provides State-by-State Breakdown," Ohio State University, College of Food, Agricultural, and Environmental Sciences, June 3, 2015, *https://cfaes.osu.edu/ news/articles/high-cost-foodborne-illness-new-study-provides-state-by-state-breakdown*.

80. Beth Kowitt, "Why Our Food Keeps Making Us Sick," *Fortune*, May 6, 2016, *http://fortune.com/food-contamination*.

81. Tyco Integrated Security, "Recall: The Food Industry's Biggest Threat to Profitability," *Food Safety Magazine*, October 2012, *https://www.foodsafety-magazine.com/signature-series/recall-the-food-industrys-biggest-threat-to-profitability*.

82. The Association of Food, Beverage, and Consumer Products Companies, "Capturing Recall Costs: Measuring and Recovering the Losses," October 2011, *https://www.gmaonline.org/file-manager/images/gmapublications/ Capturing_Recall_Costs_GMA_Whitepaper_FINAL.pdf*.

83. World Health Organization, "Substandard and Falsified Medical Products," January 31, 2018, *http://www.who.int/en/news-room/fact-sheets/detail/ substandard-and-falsified-medical-products*.

84. Ben Hirschler, "Tens of Thousands Dying from $30 Billion Fake Drugs Trade, WHO Says," Reuters, November 28, 2017, *https://www.reuters.com/ article/us-pharmaceuticals-fakes/tens-of-thousands-dying-from-30-billion-fake-drugs-trade-who-says-idUSKBN1DS1XJ*.

85. Giselle A. Auger, "Trust Me, Trust Me Not: An Experimental Analysis of the Effect of Transparency on Organizations," *Journal of Public Relations Research*, August 2014, 26, no. 4 (2014): 325–43.

86. Charlie Arnot, "Transparency Is No Longer Optional: How Food Companies Can Restore Trust," *Forbes* November 30, 2015, *https://www.forbes.com/ sites/gmoanswers/2015/11/30/transparency-no-longer-optional*.

87. Chip Reid and Jennifer Janisch, "Wounded Warrior Project Accused of Wasting Donation Money," *CBS News*, January 26, 2016, *https:// www.cbsnews.com/news/wounded-warrior-project-accused-of-wasting-donation-money*.

88. Edelman, "2018 Edelman Trust Barometer Global Report," 2018, *https:// www.edelman.com/sites/g/files/aatuss191/files/ 2018-10/2018_Edelman_Trust_Barometer_Global_Report_FEB.pdf*.

89. Ibid.

90. Soroush Vosoughi, Deb Roy, and Sinan Aral, "The Spread of True and False News Online," *Science*, March 9, 2018, *https://science.sciencemag.org/content/359/6380/1146*.

91. David M. J. Lazer, et al., "The Science of Fake News," *Science*, March 9, 2018, *https://science.sciencemag.org/content/359/6380/1094.full*.

92. Lion Gu, Vladimir Kropotov, and Fyodor Yarochkin, "The Fake News Machine: How Propagandists Abuse the Internet and Manipulate the Public," Trend Micro, *https://documents.trendmicro.com/assets/white_papers/wp-fake-news-machine-how-propagandists-abuse-the-internet.pdf*.

93. Supasorn Suwajanakorn, Steven M. Seitz, and Ira Kemelmacher-Shlizerman, "Synthesizing Obama: Learning Lip Sync from Audio," *ACM Transactions on Graphics* 36, no. 4 (2017), *http://grail.cs.washington.edu/projects/AudioToObama/siggraph17_obama.pdf*.

94. Warren, Sheila. Discussion with the author. October 2018.

95. Shana Lynch, "What Matters Most to Top Business and Political Leaders," December 26, 2016, *https://stanford.io/2uCtkTi*.

96. Baker, Jessi. Discussion with the author. July 2018.

97. Smolenski, Natalie. Discussion with the author. July 2018.

98. Accredited Online Colleges, "Fake Schools, Fake Degrees: Avoiding Diploma Mills," *http://www.accredited-online-college.org/avoiding-diploma-mills*.

99. Smolenski, Natalie. Discussion with the author. July 2018.

100. World Bank Group, "Identification for Development, Strategic Framework," January 25, 2016, *http://pubdocs.worldbank.org/en/21571460567481655/April-2016-ID4D-Strategic-RoadmapID4D.pdf*.

101. Laura Shin, "The First Government to Secure Land Titles on the Bitcoin Blockchain Expands Project," February, 2017, *Forbes*, *https://www.forbes.com/sites/laurashin/2017/02/07/the-first-government-to-secure-land-titles-on-the-bitcoin-blockchain-expands-project*.

102. Alexis C. Madrigal, "Reading the Privacy Policies You Encounter in a Year Would Take 76 Work Days," *The Atlantic*, March 1, 2012, *https://www.theatlantic.com/technology/archive/2012/03/reading-the-privacy-policies-youencounter-in-a-year-would-take-76-work-days/253851*.

103. Claire Wolfe, "Little Brother Is Watching You: The Menace of Corporate America," 1999, *https://web.archive.org/web/20000823041233/http://www.loompanics.com/Articles/LittleBrother.html*.

104. Gartner, "Gartner Says 8.4 Billion Connected 'Things' Will Be in Use in 2017, Up 31 Percent from 2016," February 7, 2017, *https://www.gartner.com/newsroom/id/3598917*.

105. Paul Lewis, "'Our Minds Can Be Hijacked': The Tech Insiders Who Fear a Smartphone Dystopia," *The Guardian*, October 6, 2017, *http://www.theguardian.com/technology/2017/oct/05/smartphone-addiction-silicon-valley-dystopia*.

106. Brian Fung, "Move Deliberately, Fix Things: How Coinbase Is Building a Cryptocurrency Empire," *Washington Post*, May 17, 2018, *https://www.washingtonpost.com/business/economy/move-deliberately-fix-things-how-coinbase-is-building-a-cryptocurrency-empire/2018/05/17/623d950c-587c-11e8-858f-12becb4d6067_story.html?utm_term=.ab563e234455*.

107. Evans, Tavonia. Discussion with the author. July 2018.

108. Magid Media, "Magid Media Futures," 2017, *http://www.entmerch.org/digitalema/ema-annual-digital-forum-/magid-media-futures-present.pdf*.

109. *https://www.smithandcrown.com*.

110. Magid Media, "Magid Media Futures Study."

111. Timothy Moreym, Theodore Forbath, and Allison Schoop, "Customer Data: Designing for Transparency and Trust," *Harvard Business Review*, May 2015, *https://hbr.org/2015/05/customer-data-designing-for-transparency-and-trust*.

112 Teixeira, Thales S. Discussion with the author. May 2018.

113. Scott, Ned. Discussion with the author. August 2018.

114. Ibid.

115. Brendan Eich, "How to Fix the Web," filmed November 2016 at TEDxVienna, video, *http://www.youtube.com/watch?v=zlcnOr81lPc*.

116. Lisa Gevelber, "Micro-Moments Now: 3 New Consumer Behaviors Playing Out in Google Search Data," *Think with Google*, July 2017, *https://www.thinkwithgoogle.com/consumer-insights/micro-moments-consumer-behavior-expectations*.

117. David Court, et al., "The New Battleground for Marketing-Led Growth," *McKinsey Quarterly*, February 2017, *https://www.mckinsey.com/business-functions/marketing-and-sales/our-insights/the-new-battleground-for-marketing-led-growth*.

118. Teixeira, Thales S. Discussion with the author. May 2018.

119. Thales Teixeira, "The Rising Price of Attention," Economics of Attention, *http://www.economicsofattention.com*.

120. Sunil Gupta, "For Mobile Devices, Think Apps, Not Ads," *Harvard Business Review*, March 2013, *https://hbr.org/2013/03/for-mobile-devices-think-apps-not-ads*.

121. Sarah Perez, "Majority of U.S. Consumers Still Download Zero Apps per Month, Says comScore," TechCrunch, August 25, 2017, *https://techcrunch.com/2017/08/25/majority-of-u-s-consumers-still-download-zero-apps-per-month-says-comscore*.

122. ANA and White Ops, "Bot Baseline Report 2016–2017," May 2017, *https://www.whiteops.com/bot-baseline-report-2016-2017*.

123. Juniper Research, "Ad Fraud to Cost Advertisers \$19 Billion in 2018, Representing 9% of Total Digital Advertising Spend", September 26th, 2017, *https://www.juniperresearch.com/press/press-releases/ad-fraud-to-cost-advertisers-\$19-billion-in-2018*.

124. Colloquy, "The 2017 Colloquy Loyalty Census," June 29, 2017, *https://www.loyalty.com/home/insights/article-details/2017-colloquy-loyalty-census-report*.

125. Colloquy, "The 2015 Colloquy Loyalty Census," February 10, 2015, *https://www.loyalty.com/home/insights/article-details/the-2015-colloquy-loyalty-census-big-numbers-big-hurdles*.

126. David Court, et al., "The New Battleground for Marketing-Led Growth," *McKinsey Quarterly*, February 2017, *http://www.mckinsey.com/business-functions/marketing-and-sales/our-insights/the-new-battleground-for-marketing-led-growth*.

127. Bond Brand Loyalty, "The 2016 Bond Loyalty Report," *https://info.bondbrandloyalty.com/hubfs/Resources/2016_Bond_Loyalty_Report_Executive_Summary_US_Launch_Edition.pdf*.

128. Verbin, Elad. Discussion with the author. July 2018.

129. Trent McConaghy, "Can Blockchains Go Rogue?" *Medium*, February 27, 2018, *https://blog.oceanprotocol.com/can-blockchains-go-rogue-5134300ce790*.

130. Mary Meeker, "Internet Trends 2017," *Code Conference*, May 31, 2017, *https://www.kleinerperkins.com/perspectives/internet-trends-report-2017*.

131. Erickson, KJ. Discussion with the author. August 2018.

132. James Glasscock, "Here Come the Tiny Gorillas," *Medium*, May 30, 2018, *https://medium.com/thisisdna/here-come-the-tiny-gorillas-d15378889bf2*.

133. Ipsos Connect, "The YouTube Generation Study," November 2015, commissioned by Google.

134. Susan Sorenson and Amy Adkins, "Why Customer Engagement Matters So Much Now," *Gallup Business Journal,* July 22, 2014, *http:// news.gallup.com/businessjournal/172637/why-customer-engagement- matters.aspx.*

135. Clippinger, John Henry. Discussion with the author. August 2018.

136. Pamela Vagata and Kevin Wilfong, "Scaling the Facebook Data Warehouse to 300 PB," April 10, 2014, *https://code.fb.com/core-data/scaling-the-facebook- data-warehouse-to-300-pb.*

137. Michael Lesk, "How Much Information Is There in the World?" *https:// courses.cs.washington.edu/courses/cse590s/03au/lesk.pdf.*

138. Brian Barrett, "What Would Regulating Facebook Look Like," *Wired,* March 21, 2018, *https://www.wired.com/story/what-would-regulating-facebook- look-like.*

139. Coravos, Andy. Discussion with the author. May 2018.

140. Gartner, "Gartner Says 8.4 Billion Connected 'Things' Will Be in Use in 2017, Up 31 Percent from 2016," February 7, 2017, *https://www.gartner.com/ newsroom/id/3598917.*

141. Daniel Greenwood et al., "The New Deal on Data: A Framework for Insti- tutional Controls," in *Privacy, Big Data, and the Public Good: Frameworks for Engagement,* ed. Julia Lane et al. (Cambridge, UK: Cambridge University Press, 2014).

142. Ibid.

143. Ibid.

144. Demirors, Meltem (@Melt_Dem), "while this headline is cringe-worthy, this use case is a fascinating one with so much surface area for attack. self- sovereign identity *sounds* good but the implementation will likely be the battle of our lifetime." August 27, 2018, 8:43 AM. Tweet.

145. Peter Norvig, Google Zeitgeist, 2011.

146. KPMG, "Building Trust in Analytics," 2016, *https://assets.kpmg.com/ content/dam/kpmg/xx/pdf/2016/10/building-trust-in-analytics.pdf.*

147. Harvard Business Review Staff, "With Big Data Comes Big Responsibil- ity," *Harvard Business Review,* November 2014, *https://hbr.org/2014/11/with- big-data-comes-big-responsibility.*

148. Ibid.

149. Patil, DJ. Discussion with the author. July 2018.

150. Gartner, "Gartner Survey Finds Chief Data Officers Are Delivering Busi- ness Impact and Enabling Digital Transformation," December 6, 2017,

https://www.gartner.com/en/newsroom/press-releases/2017-12-06-gartner-survey-finds-chief-data-officers-are-delivering-business-impact-and-enabling-digital-transformation.

151. Timothy Moreym, Theodore Forbath, and Allison Schoop, "Customer Data: Designing for Transparency and Trust," *Harvard Business Review*, May 2015, *https://hbr.org/2015/05/customer-data-designing-for-transparency-and-trust.*

152. Rani Molla, "Mary Meeker's 2018 Internet Trends Report: All the Slides, Plus Analysis," May 30, 2018, *http://www.recode.net/2018/5/30/17385116/mary-meeker-slides-internet-trends-code-conference-2018.*

153. Tim Berners-Lee, "One Small Step for the Web," *Medium*, September 29, 2018, *https://medium.com/@timberners_lee/one-small-step-for-the-web-87f92217d085.*

154. Heck, Rouven. Discussion with the author. July 2018.

155. McConaghy, Trent. Discussion with the author. July 2018.

156. Ibid.

157. Kaili, Eva. Discussion with the author. June 2018.

158. Tyson O'Ham, "OpenBazaar in Depth: Interview with COO Sam Patterson," *Bitcoinist*, January 28, 2016, *https://bitcoinist.com/openbazaar-in-depth-interview-with-coo-sam-patterson.*

159. Lazooz.org, August 2018.

160. James Glasscock, "Here Come the Tiny Gorillas," *Medium*, May 30, 2018, *https://medium.com/thisisdna/here-come-the-tiny-gorillas-d15378889bf2.*

161. Joel Monégro, "Fat Protocols," Union Square Ventures Blog, August 8, 2016, *http://www.usv.com/blog/fat-protocols.*

162. Smolenski, Natalie. Discussion with the author. July 2018.

163. Rangan, Gopi. Discussion with the author. May 2018.

164. Chwierut, Matt. Discussion with the author. May 2018.

165. Bogart, Spencer. Discussion with the author. December 2018.

166. Owyang, Jeremiah. Discussion with the author. June 2018.

167. Lopardo, Joe. Discussion with the author. July 2018.

168. Owyang, Jeremiah. Discussion with the author. June 2018.

169. Peter Senge, *The Fifth Discipline: The Art and Practice of the Learning Organization* (New York: Doubleday, 2016).

170. CB Insights, "State of Innovation," 2018, *http://www.cbinsights.com/reports/CB-Insights_State-of-Innovation-2018.pdf.*

171. Owyang, Jeremiah. Discussion with the author. June 2018.

172. Fabiano, Amanda. Discussion with the author. July 2018.

173. Josh Bersin, "Agile Organization Models Are Going Mainstream," January 18, 2018, *https://joshbersin.com/2018/01/agile-organization-models-are-going-mainstream*.

174. Amy Edmondson and Susan Slater Reynolds, *Building the Future: Big Teaming for Audacious Innovation* (Oakland, CA: Berrett-Koehler Publishers, 2016).

175. Edmondson, Amy. Discussion with the author. June 2018.

176. *Last Week Tonight with John Oliver*, episode 123, aired March 11, 2018, on HBO, *https://www.youtube.com/watch?v=g6iDZspbRMg*.

177. Groopman, Jessica. Discussion with the author. June 2018.

178. Le Merle, Matthew and Davis, Alison. Discussion with the author. December 2018.

179. CB Insights, "Blockchain Investment Trends in Review," *https://www.cbinsights.com/research/report/blockchain-trends-opportunities*.

180. Jon Victor, "Harvard, Stanford, MIT Endowments Invest in Crypto Funds," The Information, October 10, 2018, *https://www.theinformation.com/articles/harvard-stanford-mit-endowments-invest-in-cryptofunds*.

181. Ibid.

182. Bogart, Spencer. Discussion with the author. December 2018.

183. Borda, Mason. Discussion with the author. December 2018.

184. CB Insights, "What's Next in Blockchain," 2019, *https://www.cbinsights.com/research/report/blockchain-trends-opportunities*.

185. Fred Ehrsam, "Blockchain Governance: Programming Our Future," *Medium*, November 27, 2017, *https://medium.com/%40FEhrsam/blockchain-governance-programming-our-future-c3bfe30f2d74*.

186. Ian Bogost, "Cryptocurrency Might Be a Path to Authoritarianism," *The Atlantic*, May 30, 2017, *https://www.theatlantic.com/technology/archive/2017/05/blockchain-of-command/528543*.

Index

About the Author

Alison McCauley is a best-selling author, speaker, and CEO and founder of Unblocked Future (*https://www.unblockedfuture.com*), a boutique consultancy that helps executives to establish and communicate their leadership at the digital frontier. She writes for several publications about the impact of emerging technology on our world, and her book, *Unblocked, How Blockchains Will Change Your Business (https://www.alisonmccauley.io)*, is an international best-seller. A social scientist by training, Alison has spent her career studying the intersection of human behavior and technology, with 20 years of consulting to technology-first startups and Fortune 500 companies. She helps businesses shape their role in our digitally driven future, communicate vision, and activate communities for change. You can follow Alison on Twitter @unblockedfuture or learn more at AlisonMcCauley.io.

Colophon

Cover image by Stephen Swintek; cover design by Randy Comer. The cover fonts are Gilroy Semibold and Guardian Sans. The text font is Adobe Minion Pro and the heading font is Adobe Myriad Condensed.

CPSIA information can be obtained
at www.ICGtesting.com
Printed in the USA
BVHW040919200619
551529BV00006B/34/P

9 781492 057970